Mentoring in Action: Guiding, Sharing, and Reflecting With Novice Teachers

A Month-by-Month Curriculum for Teacher Effectiveness

Second Edition

Carol Pelletier Radford

Foreword by Ellen Moir

CORWIN

A SAGE Publishing Company

FOR INFORMATION:

Corwin

A SAGE Company

2455 Teller Road

Thousand Oaks, California 91320

(800) 233-9936

www.corwin.com

SAGE Publications Ltd.

1 Oliver's Yard

55 City Road

London, EC1Y 1SP

United Kingdom

SAGE Publications India Pvt. Ltd.

B 1/I 1 Mohan Cooperative Industrial Area

Mathura Road, New Delhi 110 044

India

SAGE Publications Asia-Pacific Pte. Ltd.

3 Church Street

#10-04 Samsung Hub

Singapore 049483

Acquisitions Editor: Ariel Bartlett

Senior Associate Editor: Desirée A. Bartlett

Senior Editorial Assistant: Andrew Olson

Production Editor: Veronica Stapleton Hooper

Copy Editor: Beth Hammond

Typesetter: C&M Digitals (P) Ltd.

Proofreader: Alison Syring

Indexer: Jeanne R. Busemeyer

Cover Designer: Gail Buschman

Marketing Manager: Jill Margulies

Copyright © 2017 by Corwin

The Interstate Teacher Assessment and Support Consortium (INTASC) standards were developed by the Council of Chief State School Officers and member states. Copies may be downloaded from the Council's website at http://www.ccsso.org/.

Council of Chief State School Officers. (2011, April). Interstate Teacher Assessment and Support Consortium (InTASC) Model Core Teaching Standards: A Resource for State Dialogue. Washington, DC: Author. Copyright © 2011 by the Council of Chief State School Officers, Washington, DC.

This book was previously published by: Pearson Education, Inc.

Printed in the United States of America

Library of Congress Cataloging-in-Publication Data

Names: Radford, Carol Pelletier, author.

Title: Mentoring in action : guiding, sharing, and reflecting with notice teachers : a month-by-month curriculum for teacher effectiveness / Carol Pelletier Radford.

Description: Second edition. | Thousand Oaks, Calif. : Corwin, 2017. | Includes index.

Identifiers: LCCN 2016007886 | ISBN 9781506345116 (pbk. : alk. paper)

Subjects: LCSH: Mentoring in education. | First year teachers—Supervision. | First year teachers—In-service training. | Teacher effectiveness.

Classification: LCC LB1731.4 .R335 2017 | DDC 371.102—dc23

LC record available at https://lccn.loc.gov/2016007886

This book is printed on acid-free paper.

16 17 18 19 20 10 9 8 7 6 5 4 3 2 1

Praise for Mentoring in Action: Guiding, Sharing, and Reflecting With Novice Teachers

"This is a terrific resource for mentors and coaches at all levels. It strategically helps mentors reflect on what novice teachers might be thinking and needing, and what they as mentors could be doing to support them. Step by step, Radford guides us through the year. The book is chock full of ideas and questions to use with novice teachers. It's a really useful tool to have on hand."

—Jennifer Abrams, Author of *Hard Conversations Unpacked* and *The Multigenerational Workplace*

"In a profession that loses 50% of its entering teachers by Year Five, Carol Radford's Mentoring in Action *is a beautiful, wise, month-by-month guide to powerful, mindful mentoring of the novice instructor. Filled with decades of her own teaching, research and mentoring wisdom, Radford offers a move-by-move guide to building the mentoring relationship, examples of mentoring in action, and instructions and modeling of purposeful mentoring conversations. This book is a must-buy for any teacher leader, instructional coach, curriculum director . . . or even the brand-new teacher. We are lucky to have* Mentoring in Action *back fully revised and more complete than ever, to access Carol Radford's wisdom and guidance."*

—Dr. Kirsten Olson, Author of *Wounded By School* and *The Mindful School Leader*

"The 2nd edition of Mentoring in Action: Guiding, Sharing, and Reflecting with Novice Teachers *by Carol Pelletier Radford offers a very well-organized and practical roadmap that includes reflections, activities, tips, and forms to support mentors who work with beginning teachers. In addition, the companion website for this book offers extensive resources for mentors including many videos. This book offers support for those who lead by mentoring others whether they are new to mentoring or want to increase their knowledge and skill as a mentor. The best mentorship programs include support for the mentors, not just for new teachers. This book provides a roadmap for that support, whether it is followed by individual teacher-mentors or by those in charge of mentoring programs. In fact, everyone in a position of leadership should read and use the contents of this book."*

—Barbara Levin, Professor and Author of *Every Teacher a Leader*
University of North Carolina at Greensboro

"Carol Radford is the consummate professional educator. From the outset of my association with her, she has been a conscientious and dedicated administrator, a mentor, and a generous and supportive colleague. Readily able to foster constructive connections between course material and her own exemplary classroom experience, she has consistently provided innovative direction and support to classroom teachers by way of the books she has authored. Generations of educators have and will continue to use them.

Dr. Radford's commitment to teaching in urban populations has distinguished her contribution to the education profession. I continue to be impressed by her command of relevant research and effective instructional techniques. Her skill is facilitating communication. She effectively addresses the interface between practice and education with the primary objective of identifying the relevant issues in support of human well-being. Dr. Radford is truly a reflective practitioner, and I always appreciate opportunities to learn from her as she continues to clarify the relevant issues in educational practice by way of her latest publications."

—Cameron Marzelli, Adjunct Faculty, Graduate School of Arts and Social Sciences
Lesley University

"What amazes me about the Mentoring in Action *and* The First Years Matter *books is that every aspect of the teaching field is addressed."*

—Kerri Schoonover, History Teacher
Atlantis Charter High School

"I love the idea of having mentors and mentees work alongside each other with Mentoring in Action *and* The First Years Matter, *sharing their thoughts about challenges and successes each month and opening up a reflective dialogue."*

—Karen Mayotte, Grade 2 Classroom Teacher / Co-coordinator Mentor Program
Nashoba Regional School District

"The two texts, Mentoring in Action *and* The First Years Matter, *are companion texts that give both participants a guide for discussions, suggestions for activities, and a place to track reflections. They also allow for targeted differentiation."*

—Maureen Perkins, Reading Specialist
William A. Berkowitz School

"Integrating teacher evaluation standards fits naturally into the reflection prompts and activities in The First Years Matter *and* Mentoring in Action *texts."*

—Caitlin Corrieri, Mentor Coordinator
Belmont Public Schools

"I will most definitely use the Mentoring in Action *text paired with* The First Years Matter *text as a month-by-month curriculum to focus mentoring conversations."*

—Kristen Daly, Grade 1 Teacher
Kenneth Coombs School

"With the Mentoring in Action *and* The First Years Matter *books, training of mentors is consistent and comprehensive.* The First Years Matter *is structured enough to provide a clear path toward helping a new hire to achieve independence."*

—John Radosta, Mentoring Coordinator
Milton High School

*"*Mentoring in Action *and* The First Years Matter *are so important to guide discussions between mentor and mentee and are also helpful when differentiating for a new teacher's needs."*

—Elyse Hager, Kindergarten Teacher
Nathaniel Morton Elementary School

"Our district will use the Mentoring in Action *and* The First Years Matter *texts to directly align with teacher evaluation standards and create a common language among our mentors and novice teachers."*

—Bethany Botelho, Mentor Teacher Facilitator
Old Colony Regional HS

"This year we were trained to use the Mentoring in Action *book. This has provided a common language and framework for mentors, which has been most helpful to maintain a consistent program."*

—Marguerite Rancourt, Lead Mentor
Greenfield Public Schools

"The Mentoring in Action *and* The First Years Matter *books are critical resources that each mentor will need to provide support for becoming a qualified mentor."*

—Angela Downing, Grade 1 Teacher
Franklin Elementary School

"The Mentoring in Action *curriculum will guide mentors as they work with their mentees, providing some commonality while at the same time allowing for differentiation."*

—Joyce English, Grade 1 Teacher
Winthrop Public Schools

"The Mentoring in Action *and* The First Years Matter *books have given me so much knowledge and understanding of the mentoring process that I feel more than confident in my ability to direct a mentoring program."*

—Adam Crawford Crombie, Co-Director of Mentoring
Winthrop Middle School

CONTENTS

SEPTEMBER

OCTOBER

NOVEMBER

DECEMBER

JANUARY

FEBRUARY

MARCH

APRIL

MAY

JUNE

JULY

APPENDICES

Note from the Publisher: The author has provided video and web content throughout the book which is available to you through QR Codes. To read a QR Code, you must have a smartphone or tablet with a camera. We recommend that you download a QR Code reader app that is made specifically for your phone or tablet brand.

FOREWORD

Mentoring isn't just about teaching—really, it's all about learning. To go from being a great teacher of kids to a great teacher of other teachers doesn't happen overnight. The learning curve for new mentors is steep. It's critical for mentors to have intentional, guided curriculum that helps them grow from novices to excellent mentors. What makes mentoring such a thrilling part of a teacher's career ladder or lattice is precisely that challenge of a new learning curve, the new, broader opportunity for impact, and the opportunity for mentors, through the process of mentoring their new teachers, to strengthen their own teaching practice even more. I've made my life's work about developing amazing mentors who can, in turn, move teachers from novice to good to excellent. While there are countless lessons that my colleagues and I have learned about how to do so woven throughout this book, three stand out to me: (1) the right pacing can maximize learning, (2) this is active work, and (3) learning in communities is more powerful than learning alone.

One thing we know from research on adult learning is the importance of pacing to allow for just-in-time, ongoing learning, practice, and reflection. At New Teacher Center (NTC), this kind of time and pacing are embedded in all levels of our work. The structure of this book as a yearlong "calendar" for mentors supports mentors' ongoing learning and practice. It builds their habits of mind as practitioners for perseverance, reflection, and continuous improvement. A key role of the mentor is to help new teachers become more patient with themselves—to forgive themselves for not being experts on day one and to focus on their own development in two to three areas at a time. A spaced-out, year-long curriculum like Carol Pelletier Radford's in this book does something similar for new mentors: it gives them the time to slow down, focus, and engage in deeper learning. On a higher level, it sets the expectation that being a mentor comes with its own, multi-year learning curve. Just like being a great teacher—and even being a great student—it's about learning to learn for years to come.

My colleagues and I have also learned that this work is active, not passive. It's intentional, thoughtful, and requires practice (along with assessment and reflection) in order to grow. The kind of just-in-time learning that is embedded in our work at NTC, and the kind embedded in this book, works because it's built around action—actively implementing a practice, actively reflecting on it, and actively, continuously improving. Just like students learn through doing, and just like teachers improve through practice, mentors ultimately grow by taking action.

Perhaps the most powerful lesson from our work at NTC is the importance of learning with peers. It's so important that we build communities of practice into our work with all of our partner districts and, each year, host multiple national gatherings and network to deepen our learning with one another. *Mentoring in Action* points to the power of a group learning setting for new teachers. It's no different with mentors. While the curriculum, opportunities for practice and reflection, and framework presented in this book can be powerful for a mentor navigating his or her new role on their own, this book also provides an excellent foundation for a mentor community of practice. Whether in person, virtual, or even asynchronous, the structure of *Mentoring in Action*'s curriculum lends itself perfectly to the kind of inquiry, observation, and feedback that a community of practice can provide. In turn, those exact same practices and habits of mind—inquiry, reflection, and feedback—are what we want mentors to model for and develop in their new teachers (and they in their students!).

Just like teachers, great mentors are developed, not born. It's critical for mentors to engage in intentional, guided professional learning to put them on their own paths to excellence as teacher leaders. *Mentoring in Action* provides an important foundation for any mentor or community of mentors to launch, grow, or deepen their own practice. We are all doing such important work together, and I'm thrilled to continue driving with Dr. Radford and all of you to ensure that every new teacher gets differentiated, just-in-time support from a mentor so that, ultimately, every child in America is taught by an excellent teacher.

—*Ellen Moir*
Founder and CEO, New Teacher Center

PREFACE

This 2nd edition of *Mentoring in Action* is evidence of my evolving journey to support mentors and their novice teachers. I experienced teaching my first mentor course when I was a classroom teacher, and I have never stopped teaching mentors. Mentors shared with me that they found many of their novice teachers unprepared for the challenges of the classroom. To support the mentors, I wrote a companion book for the novice teacher. The *First Years Matter* aligns with the *Mentoring in Action* book and offers you both a common language for your mentoring conversations. By having their own book, novice teachers share that they feel empowered to bring their own questions to mentoring meetings.

The 2nd edition of *Mentoring in Action* introduces new tools and topics to expand your strategies for mentoring. The new cover image of the tree branches growing and stretching illustrates your role of guiding, sharing, and reflecting with your novice teacher. The book is refreshed and updated to provide you with a variety of activities and information to support you. A Mindful Mentoring Affirmation on every month's chapter title page will place an emphasis on mindfulness and intentional mentoring. The companion website, at https://resources.corwin.com/mentoringinaction with digital copies of selected forms, informative videos to support your mentoring skills, additional resources, and a Mentor Planning Guide and Journal, are provided to support you. This edition also encourages you to align your mentoring conversations with your own state or district teacher evaluation standards. Listening to students is integrated throughout this book to emphasize the importance of their voices in the development of an effective teacher. I hope you will find these new features useful and inspiring.

2nd edition features include the following:

- Twelve month curriculum with the addition of July for reflecting and planning
- Part I of the book includes an overview of ideas for sustainable mentoring and teacher leadership
- Part I also introduces group mentoring and updated roles for mentors
- Chapter overviews include updated InTASC standards and video introductions
- PLAN pages now include strategies for observing your novice teacher each month
- Revised CONNECT pages include Hot Topics, Student Voices, and Additional Resources
- ACT pages are revised with key questions, and a First ACT page is aligned to evaluation standards
- The REFLECT section includes new Mindful Mentoring Dilemmas
- A Mentor Planning Guide and Journal is provided to record thoughts and ideas throughout the year
- SET GOALS pages include a focus on social and emotional development of the novice
- A QR Code within book chapters is included to access videos on mobile devices
- The companion website includes the videos and digital forms indicated in the chapters. The companion website can be found at http://resources.corwin.com/mentoringinaction.

I hope you find this 2nd edition useful and inspiring as you mentor in action!

ACKNOWLEDGMENTS

Writing the second edition of *Mentoring in Action: Guiding, Sharing, and Reflecting With Novice Teachers* has been a labor of love. It reminds me of all that is possible as we work together to support the next generation of teachers.

It is also an opportunity for me to share my gratitude to all who made this possible.

Thank you to my *Mentoring in Action* team: Adam Pelletier, Alice Carey, Donna McDonald, Janet Arndt, Joanne Mendes, Joanne Koch, Kathi Rogers, Karen Gannon, Karen DeRusha, and Shonna Ryan. Each one of you has made a valuable contribution to sustaining the *Mentoring in Action* vision and sharing it with others.

To the teacher leaders who use this curriculum in the online courses: Adam Ingano, Alyssa Gurney, Amy McLaughlin-Hatch, Ginny Turner, Jill Pelletier, Janet Fitzgerald, Jenna Monahan, Julie MacDonald, Liz Talbot, Lori Harper, Maryanne Margiotta, and Scott Connery, I am truly grateful for your expertise and passion for supporting mentors.

Thank you, Kat Johnston, for always believing in me. Your willingness to attend my mentoring workshops and share this curriculum with the Massachusetts Department of Elementary and Secondary Education will never be forgotten.

I am forever grateful to my personal board of mentors. These inspiring women have influenced my thinking and encouraged me to reach for the stars. Cameron Marzelli, Deborah Donahue-Keegan, Diane Kovanda, Kristen Lee Costa, Kristina Lamour-Sansone, and Maria Clark bring their wisdom to the world with grace and kindness. Find them on MentoringinAction.com and learn how they can support your dreams.

Thank you, Corwin. A more professional publishing experience does not exist. Thanks to Gail for your design sense and to Veronica for your attention to detail and your patience. This book is so much better because of you and your team. Ariel, you have been an amazing partner on this journey. Thank you for your sincere collaboration, your editorial skills, and your true commitment to this book.

ABOUT THE AUTHOR

Carol Pelletier Radford is an education consultant recently transitioning from the position of Project SUCCESS Program Director, a Massachusetts statewide hybrid mentor "train the trainer" leadership program. She received her EdD from Harvard University where she focused her studies on teacher leadership, preparing cooperating teachers, and professional development. She has served in higher education for 20 years working as an administrator, a licensing officer, and alternative certification program director.

In more than 20 years as a public school teacher, she has received numerous teacher leadership awards, among them the prestigious Christa McAuliffe Fellowship sponsored by the U.S. Department of Education.

She is the author of *Mentoring in Action: Guiding, Sharing, and Reflecting With Novice Teachers*; *The First Years Matter: Becoming an Effective Teacher*; *Strategies for Successful Student Teaching 3rd edition*; *The First Year Matters: Being Mentored in Action*; *Mentoring in Action: A Month-By-Month Curriculum*; *Touch the Future TEACH!*; and *Techniques and Strategies for Coaching Student Teachers 2nd edition*.

Carol is actively engaged in using video to teach and communicate with mentors and novice teachers. Her online graduate courses include Becoming a Qualified Mentor, Maintaining Your Balance—Novice Teacher Development After Year 1, and Mindful Leadership in Action— Supporting Principals to Lead Induction Programs. She is a passionate advocate for teacher leadership and the inclusion of student voices in classroom practice. Her current focus is integrating mindfulness practices into her courses and presentations. You can find her resources and books on MentoringinAction.com.

This book is dedicated to my mother and first mentor.

Marian V. Marra

INTRODUCTION

WELCOME TO MENTORING IN ACTION!

If you are reading this, you are preparing to mentor a novice teacher. Let me begin by saying, "Thank you."

You have made a commitment to support a beginner in the journey to become an effective teacher. This role takes time away from your own classroom and your personal life. I know your dedication to be a mentor is a choice you made after careful thought.

Your willingness to help others learn the art and craft of teaching demonstrates your choice to serve.

serv·ice ˈsərvəs/ *noun* 1. the action of helping or doing work for someone. "Millions are involved in voluntary service" *synonyms:* favor, kindness, good turn, helping hand.

By being of service to others, you influence a cycle of support for novice teachers. You create a system where everyone is helping everyone else. Your participation as a mentor in your school acknowledges your heart is open to help others. It also demonstrates the hope and love you have for the teaching profession. You become a role model for your novice teacher as well as all teachers in your school who see you stepping up to share and help another teacher. A mentor is a leader who becomes an important part of a "ripple effect."

Lao Tzu says it this way . . .

> *Do you want to be a positive influence in the world?*
>
> *First get your own life in order.*
>
> *Ground yourself in the single principle so your behavior is wholesome and effective.*
>
> *If you do that you will earn respect and be a powerful influence.*
>
> *Remember that your influence begins with you and ripples outward.*
>
> *So be sure your influence is both potent and wholesome.*
>
> *How do I know this works? All growth spreads outward from a fertile and potent nucleus.*
>
> *You are a nucleus.*
>
> Excerpt from "The Ripple Effect," *The Tao of Leadership* by John Heider

To me, to "get your own life in order" means that you need to learn *how* to mentor. Dedicate yourself to being the best mentor you can be. Take your role seriously and recognize the important influence and role model you are for the teachers you are serving. Take courses related to mentor skills, attend workshops on mentoring, and register for conferences where mentors share ideas. This will ensure that your influence is wholesome and positive for teachers and the education profession.

This generation of novice teachers brings vitality, idealism, and some excellent social networking skills with them. Your role is to empower these novices to share, integrate into the school community, and emerge as leaders who will take your place in the future. We all agree that systematically supporting novice teachers into the profession works. Research has been done to prove it, and common sense tells us that mentoring is the right thing to do. We all have our own stories of "being mentored" that first year. The "sink or swim" method of mentoring doesn't provide any support to novice teachers. So what is the problem? Why aren't we systematically supporting our novices?

As I meet mentors from all over the United States, I have discovered that many districts are facing similar issues. No funds for the training of mentors, no ongoing support for mentors who have been prepared, and some districts don't have funding for one-on-one mentoring. If mentors are available, they are often volunteers and more time is spent "matching" the mentor and mentee than actually engaging in discussions about teaching and learning. Sometimes after mentors are assigned, they don't know what they should do or talk about with a novice each week. These challenges of funding, training, and support influence the quality of the mentoring program and may be impacting the retention rate for novice teachers.

This Book Is a Practical Resource for Mentors

We want to retain the teachers we are bringing into the profession. To do that, mentors need to focus on what is important to keep them teaching! Some teachers enter through traditional pathways in teacher preparation programs and others by alternative fast track routes. Mentors may have to differentiate their mentoring based on the needs of the novice teachers with whom they will be working. This guide will help a mentor review topics for novice teachers who come well prepared by colleges of education. It will also provide content for other teachers who have entered teaching through alternative routes who need more in-depth mentoring.

This book serves as a curriculum guide for you while you are "in the act of" mentoring. If all the mentors in your district used this curriculum, there would be a common language you could refer to together. Formalizing the mentoring program and what mentors are doing demonstrates the value of mentoring. It says mentoring is important, and we will provide resources and support to our mentors!

I have a passion for this work. I have been a teacher and a teacher educator for more than 40 years. During my visits to schools, my talks with mentors led me to create this 2nd edition. My intention is to offer you an updated resource that supports you in being a powerful influence on a novice teacher.

Use the practical ideas to inspire you as you share your wisdom. Use the positive energy and vitality from your mentee to sustain you and remind you of the joys of teaching. Remember, you are mentoring the next generation of teachers into this noble profession.

Sincerely,
Carol Pelletier Radford EdD
MentoringinAction.com

PART I

INDUCTING A NOVICE TEACHER INTO THE TEACHING PROFESSION

Induction Programs Must Prepare and Support Mentors

The intent of a teacher induction program is to provide systematic support for beginning teachers. Because researchers and policy makers still lack a clear definition of what "teacher induction" consists of, the programs that are offered are often inconsistent. What some schools call induction may include an orientation to the district and an informal mentor, while other districts have formally trained mentors who receive a stipend. Most states mandate some kind of induction for teachers, but because the process varies, mentor training is not always a required component of the process.

Ellen Moir, CEO and Founder of the New Teacher Center, is a passionate advocate for the implementation of quality induction programs and well-trained mentors. In her public appearances, she consistently states that mentor training is critical to the role of supporting novice teachers. Being an effective classroom teacher does not transfer to being a qualified mentor. Mentors need to be reflective practitioners, know how to facilitate adult learning, as well as observe and provide feedback. Foundational courses and ongoing professional development are required to prepare and support mentors. I have attended many New Teacher Center

Symposiums, and their work inspired me to write *Mentoring in Action* and the *First Years Matter*, and I offer them to you as a resource.

Successful induction programs have a vision with a plan that supports the development of the mentor who is guiding the novice teacher. Click on the Sample District Induction Program Plans link on the companion website (https://resources.corwin.com/mentoringinaction) to compare your district's induction program plan to the samples online. These sample plans use the *Mentoring in Action* and *First Years Matter* curriculum to provide their mentors and novice teachers with a guide that assists them in their day-to-day conversations. Review the PDF titled *Interactive District Action Plan* on the companion website to learn how to write a plan for induction and mentoring or enhance your existing plan. Review the "Prepare" step in the sample plans to see specific components of a mentor preparation program.

Mentors Are Teacher Leaders

Your leadership is demonstrated by your commitment to publicly support another teacher entering the teaching profession. As you review Figure 1, notice that teacher leadership is the foundation of a mentoring program. The roots of the tree sustain the growth of the program and illustrate the important role of mentors. You are a teacher leader in your role as a mentor.

Figure 1 Mentoring Program Sustainability Tree

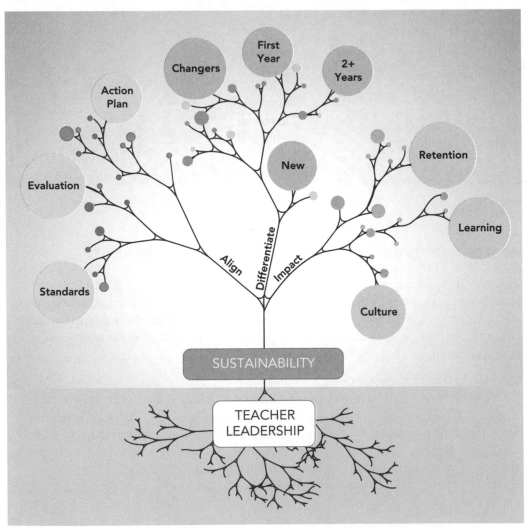

Your actions and words are powerful influences on other mentors and novice teachers in your school and the district. Your leadership is demonstrated in a variety of ways as you facilitate the growth of another teacher and reflect on your own skills as a practicing teacher. How far will you ripple the effect of your positive support and leadership?

Leadership begins in the classroom. An effective teacher leads her students to be engaged and motivated learners. How will you model effective teaching for your novice teacher? By demonstrating your teaching strategies, sharing your philosophy of teaching, and providing support, you influence the novice teacher's beliefs and skills. Your actions with your students model classroom teacher leadership.

Your leadership emerges as you share ideas beyond your classroom. Do you share with other teachers and mentors in your school? By sharing freely with other teachers, you model generosity and a willingness to support the success of a school team. Novice teachers who observe their mentor as someone who shares with others will be more likely to share with others. Lead mentors can support the development of their mentor colleagues and provide support using the *Mentoring in Action* curriculum in monthly mentor support meetings.

You can help your novice teacher become a leader too. Encouraging novice teachers to lead their own sharing best practices groups is one way you can support emerging leadership. Video 1.1 on the companion website titled *Sharing Best Practices: Novice Teachers as Leaders* will provide you with an example of how these group mentoring meetings can be organized.

Sustainable Mentoring

All the mentors working together with a district action plan can create a powerful influence on the induction of novice teachers and their integration into your school and this profession. As a teacher leader, you not only model leadership as mentioned in the previous section, you implement the components of a sustainable program. The three branches of Figure 1 illustrate topics that are important to sustain any mentoring program. Review these ideas and see how they can be integrated into your current mentoring and induction program.

Align Mentoring to Standards

The first branch of the sustainability tree is to align mentoring to standards, teacher evaluation, and the district action plan if you have one. The state standards for curriculum and instruction are important regulations that need to be included in mentoring conversations. The Interstate New Teacher Assessment and Support Consortium (InTASC) has published Model Core Teaching Standards to ensure that beginning teachers integrate knowledge into student learning. Refer to Figure 2 to review these 10 standards. Each chapter will review the standards that relate to the topic featured that month. If you are not guided by InTASC standards in your school, find out which state standards you should be using.

Novice teachers will be assessed through observation by their principal or department chair. The school evaluation rubric needs to be reviewed so your novice understands how she will be assessed. This is a high-stakes observation because it may influence the decision to rehire this teacher. Some novice teachers have shared with me, "I don't have time for mentoring because I have to focus on my teacher evaluation!" Mentoring for successful performance on the teacher evaluation is an important motivation for a novice to meet with you regularly. Integrating the evaluation standards and indicators into mentoring conversations will demonstrate the importance of successful performance on evaluation. See Figure 3 for a sample of how you can align this book to your state evaluation standards.

The author has provided video and web content throughout the book which is available to you through QR Codes. To read a QR Code, you must have a smartphone or tablet with a camera. We recommend that you download a QR Code reader app that is made specifically for your phone or tablet brand.

VIDEO 1.1

Sharing Best Practices: Novice Teachers as Leaders

Figure 2 InTASC Model Core Teaching Standards

Standard	Description
1	**Learner Development** The teacher understands how learners grow and develop, recognizing that patterns of learning and development vary individually within and across the cognitive, linguistic, social, emotional, and physical areas, and designs and implements developmentally appropriate and challenging learning experiences.
2	**Learning Differences** The teacher uses understanding of individual differences and diverse cultures and communities to ensure inclusive learning environments that enable each learner to meet high standards.
3	**Learning Environments** The teacher works with others to create environments that support individual and collaborative learning, and that encourage positive social interaction, active engagement in learning, and self motivation.
4	**Content Knowledge** The teacher understands the central concepts, tools of inquiry, and structures of the discipline(s) he or she teaches and creates learning experiences that make these aspects of the discipline accessible and meaningful for learners to ensure mastery of the content.
5	**Application of Content** The teacher understands how to connect concepts and use differing perspectives to engage learners in critical thinking, creativity, and collaborative problem solving related to authentic local and global issues.
6	**Assessment** The teacher understands and uses multiple methods of assessment to engage learners in their own growth, to monitor learner progress, and to guide the teacher's and learner's decision making.
7	**Planning for Instruction** The teacher plans instruction that supports every student in meeting rigorous learning goals by drawing upon knowledge of content areas, curriculum, cross-disciplinary skills, and pedagogy, as well as knowledge of learners and the community context.
8	**Instructional Strategies** The teacher understands and uses a variety of instructional strategies to encourage learners to develop deep understanding of content areas and their connections, and to build skills to apply knowledge in meaningful ways.
9	**Professional Learning and Ethical Practice** The teacher engages in ongoing professional learning and uses evidence to continually evaluate his/her practice, particularly the effects of his/her choices and actions on others (learners, families, other professionals, and the community), and adapts practice to meet the needs of each learner.
10	**Leadership and Collaboration** The teacher seeks appropriate leadership roles and opportunities to take responsibility for student learning, to collaborate with learners, families, colleagues, other school professionals, and community members to ensure learner growth, and to advance the profession.

Developed by CCSSO's Interstate Teacher Assessment and Support Consortium (InTASC) April 2011

Figure 3   Evaluation Alignment Tool

Directions: Each state or district has criteria for teacher evaluation. Align this book with your district evaluation process by comparing your evaluation criteria with the ACTs listed each month.

Step 1. Find the rubric or district evaluation criteria headings that will be used to assess your novice teacher in your school. For example: Here are four standards used in one state that are used in district teacher evaluations.

1. Curriculum Planning and Assessment—This standard includes indicators such as subject matter knowledge; standards-based lessons and units; using a variety of assessments, modifications and adjustments to lessons as needed; analysis and conclusions; as well as sharing assessment results with parents and students.

2. Teaching All Students—This standard includes student engagement, quality of effort and work, diverse needs of students being met, collaborative and safe learning environment, respect for differences, as well as clear, high expectations for all students.

3. Family and Community Engagement—This standard includes a process for communicating with families, as well as culturally proficient communication options for parents and guardians.

4. Professional Culture—This standard includes reflective practice, professional learning and growth, professional collaboration with colleagues, and reliability and responsibility as a teacher.

As you read the indicators, you get a sense of what that standard means. As you read the ACTs in the Table of Contents, you can actually match each ACT topic to a standard.

Step 2: Select a color for each standard your district uses. In this sample, we use four colors, one for each standard. Pink for Curriculum, blue for Teaching all Students, green for Family and Community Engagement, and yellow for Professional Culture. You need to be familiar with the indicators listed under each standard. For example, "reflection" is listed under Professional Culture in this state so anything with "reflection" would be color-coded yellow. These colors are often included as a package for highlighters. You can also use colored dots to place on the pages instead of the highlighter.

Step 3: Review the topics listed for each chapter and scan the ACTs for each month to make a decision about which standard relates most closely to this topic. Highlight the ACT on the page in the book so you can see which standard it relates to when you are having a mentoring conversation. A sample using these four standards, titled *Aligning Standards to Mentoring in Action,* is available on the companion website. This will give you an idea of how easy this is to do! It proves to be a very important alignment for the novice teacher!

Aligning the mentor program goals with your own district induction plan will ensure there is a common language in the district so mentors are not inventing their own curriculum with each novice teacher. If you don't have a district or school plan, refer to the Sample District Induction Program Plans link on the companion website (https://resources.corwin.com/mentoringinaction) for examples.

Companion Website

Career changers, new to district hires, and first time in the classroom teachers will have different needs. Many induction and mentoring programs provide a one-size-fits-all model to their novice teachers. As a mentor, you need to know when to modify your mentoring conversation to meet the needs of your mentee. Novice teachers usually know what is stressing them out and how you can help. By being proactive and offering a variety of topics, you will be able to offer more meaningful support. This book encourages you to select the ACTs that will be most helpful to you and your mentee(s). If your district plan includes mentoring beyond year 1, you can revisit the ACT pages each year and acknowledge the continued growth over time. If the novices are using the *First Years Matter* book, they can refer to their notes, date the pages, and see how much they have learned in their beginning years of teaching.

Measure the Impact of Induction

The third branch of the tree highlights three areas that illustrate the possible impact of mentoring. School culture can be impacted when a community of learners is created that shares and supports one another. This culture of respect extends to students and families as well as sharing ideas with our colleagues. How you model your interaction with students, families, and community leaders makes an impression on your mentee. The success of a school culture is measured in the retention rate of the novice teachers. How many novice teachers stay at your school? If teachers are choosing not to come back the next year or are leaving before the end of the school year, there is a problem. Ultimately, the greatest impact of mentoring is that the students in these novice teachers' classrooms are successful. You, in your role as a mentor, are a powerful influence on the novice teacher's ability to navigate school culture, the decision your mentee may make to stay teaching at your school, and the increased success of student learning in your novice teacher's classroom.

What Is Mentoring in Action?

This guide is titled *Mentoring in Action* because as a mentor you will be "in action" when you are doing this work. You most likely will be teaching full time or on a reduced teaching load if you have the resources in your district to do that. The mentoring you are doing can be done with one novice teacher who is engaged in her first year of teaching, or it can also be used with small groups of novice teachers in years 1 or in 2+ years of teaching. Mentoring does not have to stop after the first year. In fact, successful programs continue their mentoring support beyond year 1!

This book provides you with resources such as videos, agendas for meetings, and teaching skills organized by topics. It is a road map for planning your mentoring conversations as well as reflecting on your mentoring skills. *Mentoring in Action* means meeting the needs of the novice teachers and creating a common language among mentors and novices so you can communicate clearly, and the ultimate goal is more effective teaching in all classrooms. Novice teachers who are mentored are more competent and confident. Mentors who have used *Mentoring in Action* say they are also better teachers because they had to focus on their own teaching skills before they could model for their mentee. Video 1.2 on the companion website titled *Mentoring in Action Testimonials* provides you with specific ways mentors have used this resource to meet their needs.

VIDEO 1.2

To get to know this book quickly, skim the table of contents to find the topics that stand out for you as being the most useful right now. Tag key pages, align the book to your district standards, and make it a hands-on resource to guide you as you begin the mentoring experience. As shown in Figure 4, the goal is to create a common language with these resources so together you can help students succeed in the classroom.

Figure 4 Mentoring in Action

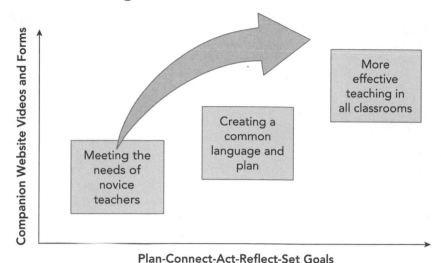

The *First Years Matter* is a companion book for the novice teacher. The book includes the Part II month-by-month topics you have in this book so he can read and reflect before meeting with you. Novice teachers have shared that having their own book is empowering because it provides them with a common language. They like to read ahead and also look back on topics that you have discussed with them. If you encourage your novice teacher to write in the book and maintain it like a journal, the notes will be useful to document conversations and reflection. This could even be used as evidence for teacher evaluation. To learn more about how novice teachers have used this book, watch Video 1.3, *The First Year Matters: Being Mentored in Action* on the companion website, or scan the QR code on a mobile device.

VIDEO 1.3

The First Year Matters: Being Mentored in Action

Principles for Effective Mentoring

Most of what I have learned about mentoring relates to five guiding principles. These principles shown in Figure 5 still seem to capture all the big ideas that mentors have shared with me, but there is a new context for this work that I would like to introduce. The context for mentoring that will enhance each of these principles is mindfulness. Being intentional and purposeful with each principle will enhance your mentoring experiences and focus you on what matters most at that given moment in time. Slowing down and paying attention will minimize your rational mind's urgency to do it all and to do it all at once.

So many teachers and mentors are stressed out because everyone is trying to multitask. Mindfulness doesn't mean you and your mentee won't get stressed! You will! Mindfulness is learning how to manage stress.

Approach each of these principles from a mindfulness attitude as opposed to a "list" of things you need to accomplish. Being mindful means being conscious and aware of what you are doing and saying. You are focusing on the present moment without judgment. As a mentor, your ability to make your conversation with your mentee the most important thing that is happening will model the value of your relationship. Mindfulness takes practice. The Mindful Mentoring Affirmations at the beginning of each monthly chapter will remind you to be mindful. Remember why you chose to be a teacher? Integrate more of that feeling and bring your positive memories into these guiding principles.

Figure 5 Principles for Effective Mentoring

Principles	Principles in Action
Acknowledging Who You Are and What You Bring to the Mentoring Experience	Who you are as a person, a teacher, and a colleague impacts the ways in which you mentor. Have your experiences of mentoring been positive? What do you do well? How will you filter your judgments and opinions so your mentee can make his own decisions?
Building a Relationship With Your Mentee	Building a relationship requires trust. Confidentiality is required in all conversations and observations. The Relationship Profile in Figure 7 provides you with a tool for comparing and sharing your experiences and perspectives. Your goal is to assist your mentee in uncovering her own strengths and teaching styles. In the process, you will also learn a lot about yourself.
Creating Opportunities for Mentoring Conversations	Mentoring does not mean the mentor does all the talking. The key is to balance your talking and your listening so the novice teacher has an entry point into the conversation. How will you ensure your mentee has time to talk? Video Collection 1.6, *Mentoring Conversations*, is available on the companion website. Sample templates are in Appendices.
Participating in Ongoing Reflection	Planning meetings, thinking about what should be discussed, asking questions, and documenting the novice teacher's progress are all forms of reflection. Reflection is not an optional activity. With reflection comes competence and confidence.
Maintaining a Professional Community of Learners	As a mentor, you can collaborate with other mentors to share ideas. Using group mentoring, you can also bring your novices together so they can collaborate. Your professional community also includes professional organizations, the Teachers' Union, and other education groups. Bring your mentee along to these professional meetings. Create your own community!

Qualities and Skills of Effective Mentors

If your district has developed a written job description that includes your roles and responsibilities for mentoring, review it now and make sure you clearly understand your role. If you don't have a job description, write one and share your ideas with the person who assigned you to a mentee. This will ensure everyone is on the same page. Consider integrating the ideas in this book into your roles and responsibilities.

Mentoring is complex, and if it is your first time supporting a mentee, the task can be daunting. If you have mentored before, you may be aware of paradigm shift that relates to mentoring. Review the Changes in Approaches to Mentoring table to compare how mentoring is evolving. Mentees who can engage and have their own *First Years Matter* book are participating in mentoring rather than just attending mentoring meetings. These novice teachers will be more willing to accept leadership roles in schools and feel more confident in sharing because you are giving them information up front.

The Changes in Approaches to Mentoring shown in Figure 6 coincides with some of the changes in education that embrace collaboration, reflection, and inquiry. Empowering your mentee to be

Figure 6 Changes in Approaches to Mentoring

	Used to . . .	Now . . .
Mentoring Programs	Be informal	Are required by most states and districts
Mentor	Tell novice what to do	Supports novice teacher growth
Novice Teacher	Respond to mentor direction	Participates as a reflective practitioner
Meetings and Mentoring Conversations	Be scheduled during school days	Use technology
Purpose of Mentoring	Be to orient the novice teacher to school	Is to help the novice learn to be an effective teacher

more actively engaged in the mentoring process means you have to be more of a facilitator and less directive. By inviting your mentee to ask questions, you shift to that role easily. This book supports a reflective approach to mentoring and offers you forms and topics to share with the mentee prior to any mentoring conversation. Everyone is so busy, and it is difficult to meet in person all the time. How will you shift your mentoring paradigm to include technology so you can stay connected to your mentee?

There are three ways to think about your roles and responsibilities. The first is to review the qualities and skills of effective mentors who have come before you. How you embrace these qualities will influence your approach to mentoring. A second role you may consider is how to use group mentoring to facilitate the sharing of successful teaching practices and solve common classroom problems. Building communities of mentors and novice teachers is a way to enhance your one-on-one mentoring role. A third role to consider is supporting the social and emotional well-being of your mentee and other novice teachers in your school. Teaching is stressful, and the life of a novice can include many social and emotional issues. Getting married, having children, moving, having aging parents, and other life issues may influence the novice teacher's time and ability to handle classroom challenges. As you review these three roles and responsibilities, assess your skill set and the qualities you bring to mentoring. What do you already bring? What will you add?

What Are the Qualities of Effective Mentors? We have all experienced or observed effective mentors. Remember those people who listened to us and guided us to be our best selves. Who were your mentors? What qualities or skills did they exhibit? Review the list in the *Qualities of Effective Mentors* to see if you recognize any. These 10 qualities have been mentioned by novice teachers and mentors as important. This is by no means all-inclusive, and you may add your own qualities to the list.

1. *An Effective Mentor Is a Competent Teacher.* A mentor needs to be proficient in all teaching practices as evaluated by the district. This means you are comfortable demonstrating and discussing effective teaching practices. This includes the district teacher evaluation standards, state curriculum frameworks, and the national InTASC principles in this book. All mentors may not be assigned to a novice in the same content area. It is okay to be a mentor of "teaching practices" because good teaching

is what is important in the classroom. However, content is crucial, and if your content areas don't match, you need to have someone in the school or district respond to the novice's content questions.

2. *An Effective Mentor Is Prepared to Be a Mentor.* A mentor needs to know basic mentoring strategies and have a plan to support a novice teacher in a proactive, positive, and systematic way throughout the school year. This book is a training guide for mentors who have not been formally trained and also a tool for mentors who have been trained and are looking for a practical day-to-day resource. *Mentoring in Action* allows you to learn as you mentor, applying the ideas as you learn them. It doesn't exclude taking mentoring courses, reading books, or attending formal trainings in your district. It is designed to enhance those experiences.

3. *An Effective Mentor Shares the Joys of Teaching.* Novice teachers embrace mentors who are passionate about teaching because it helps them to stay positive through the many challenges of the first year. A mentor who loves his content and daily interactions with students models a powerful image of teaching. Don't be afraid to share how much you love to teach and what gives you the most joy. Adding a sense of humor doesn't hurt either!

4. *An Effective Mentor Integrates Student Perspectives Into Mentoring Conversations.* In this age of standardized tests, outcomes, and value-added teaching, novice teachers need to know that relationships with students matter most. Students have so many learning needs, and when the novice just focuses on the tests without getting to know the students, teaching often fails. A PDF titled *An Interactive Guide to Using Student Perspectives* is available on the companion website. This resource includes sample student surveys, a protocol for the mentor, and videos of mentoring conversations that illustrate how to talk about student survey data with a novice teacher.

5. *An Effective Mentor Is a Good Listener.* How many times have you done three things at the same time? Correcting papers, while walking around the room, and giving a student "the look" to stop talking? Sometimes multitasking works. To be an effective listener, however, you need to pay attention, make eye contact, and be fully present. Don't answer your phone when you are in a scheduled meeting. Instead of don't text and drive, your motto is don't text when listening! Refer to Figure 8 to see how you rate as a listener.

6. *An Effective Mentor Provides Nonjudgmental Feedback.* Novice teachers want mentors who will help them improve. They need specific feedback with evidence that shows them where their strengths are and how they can engage their students. Mentor observations and postconferences also serve this purpose. In each chapter, you will be reminded about how you will provide feedback to your mentee. If you don't feel confident in observation and feedback strategies, watch two videos available on the companion website titled *Observation and Feedback Tools Parts 1 and 2* (Videos 1.7 and 1.8; see page 20) to hear an experienced observer share his ideas.

7. *An Effective Mentor Schedules Regular Meetings With the Mentee.* Novice teachers want to meet consistently and on a schedule so they can benefit from mentoring conversations. As noted in Figure 6, Changes in Approaches to Mentoring, meetings don't have to be in person all of the time. You can use e-mail, phone, and Skype to stay connected. Use the PLAN calendar in the book or the digital copy on the companion website to schedule your meetings or online dialogues.

8. *An Effective Mentor Brings a Positive Disposition to the Relationship.* Novice teachers want to collaborate with mentors who bring hope and optimism to their mentoring. We know there are challenges, but sharing complaints about school problems and administrators can be confusing to a novice. Mindful Mentoring Affirmations are reminders of the importance of a caring and supportive disposition for a mentor.

9. *An Effective Mentor Is a Confidential Colleague.* Even though you are helping a novice be successful on the teacher evaluation, you are not an evaluator. Your role as a confidential colleague ensures you maintain a trusting relationship. Novice teachers need to know the mentor will not repeat what is said or seen. Trust is key to mentoring. Clarify your role with district evaluators so there is no misunderstanding.

10. *An Effective Mentor Is Committed to Mentoring!* When you sign on as a mentor, it means you will accept the novice teacher wherever she is in her development. Making a commitment to serve and help another teacher improve is a serious commitment. The *Mentoring in Action* book is offered to you as a resource as you complete this commitment for an entire school year.

Facilitating Novice Teacher Groups. A second role you should consider learning is how to facilitate a small group of novice teachers. Sharing ideas and solving common teaching problems is more effective in a small group. Consider bringing other mentors together with their novice teachers. Novice teachers in their first year like to be connected to other novice teachers, even when they are not at their grade level or in their content area, they enjoy talking about their common needs. They can relate to each other, socialize a bit, and share survival stories. Keeping novice teachers isolated with separate mentors may not be in their best interest, nor is it effective in integrating them into the school culture.

Mentors can lead these groups and use topics from this book to guide a purposeful discussion. The Group Mentoring Agenda in Figure 9 is one way to organize these meetings. If you are mentoring beginning teachers in their 2+ years of teaching, you may consider co-leading the meetings and letting a novice facilitate. You may even consider letting the novices in their 2+ years meet on their own to share best practices. The mentor doesn't always have to be there at every meeting. A PDF titled *Group Mentoring Interactive Guide* is available on the companion website. This resource shares three videos and examples of agendas for two types of groups.

VIDEO 1.4

Managing Your Stress to Promote Well-Being

Supporting the Social and Emotional Well-Being of Novice Teachers. A third role and responsibility that will emerge in your relationship with your mentee is how you will provide emotional support. Because teaching is emotionally draining at times and because we are all humans with lives outside of school, novices may bring other issues to you. Certainly you will have feelings for this novice and you may feel compelled to provide advice and share your own personal stories. You certainly want to be empathetic and provide some support, but your role is not psychologist or parent, and your advice on personal issues may not be appropriate. This might be the time to watch Video 1.4, *Managing Your Stress to Promote Well-Being* and Video 1.5, *Managing Your Stress: Take a Break* available on the companion website. You may consider watching these videos together and having a mentoring conversation about this topic.

VIDEO 1.5

Managing Your Stress: Take a Break

The Board of Mentors process can also assist you in encouraging your mentee to reflect on who can help her with social and emotional issues. Your role is to connect the novice to others who can help. Use the Board of Mentors process in Figure 10 to guide your conversation. A digital version is available on the companion website.

Figure 7 The Relationship Profile: A Process for the Mentor and Novice Teacher

Directions: Use this template as a guide to learn about each other. Feel free to add your own columns to the table. What would you like to know about each other? If you are mentoring more than one teacher, complete a form for each person. A digital copy of this form is on the companion website.

Topics	Philosophy of Teaching	Career Stage and Age	Teaching and Learning Styles	Personality and Life Goals
Questions	*Why did we choose teaching?*	*How do our ages and teaching experience compare?*	*How would we describe our teaching styles? How do we learn?*	*How do we interact with others?*
Novice Teacher				
Mentor				
Similarities and Differences— What Shows Up?				

Acknowledging diverse perspectives and respecting these differences publicly promotes a trusting relationship. This is one way to build a relationship with the novice teachers. Confidentiality is critical to trust.

Figure 8 Are You Listening?

Directions: Ask yourself, "Am I really listening, or am I thinking about what I want to say next?" Mentors need to be active listeners who don't judge, preach, or lecture to mentees. These statements reflect some barriers to actively listening. Read each statement and rate yourself.

What do you do?	Always Sometimes Never!
Do you assume what the speaker is going to say before she finishes her statement?	
Do you finish other people's sentences?	
Are you easily distracted (by phone, e-mail, someone walking by) when in a conversation?	
Do you argue or try to strongly persuade someone to do it your way?	
Would you say you like to control the conversation?	
Do you encourage people to ask questions?	
Do you ask people questions?	
Do you multitask in meetings?	
Do you put your phone on silent when you are in a meeting?	
Are you writing your shopping list in your head (or for real on paper) while listening?	

Companion Website

Figure 9   The Group Mentoring Agenda

Directions: As a mentor you may be working with more than one novice teacher in your school or district. Watch the video, *Group Mentoring: Problems to Possibilities*, available on the companion website to see a mentor leading a group of novice teachers in a discussion about classroom management.

Tips for a successful group mentoring session! Find a comfortable space and put a sign on the door that says "Group Mentoring Meeting in session; do not disturb!" Invite the novices to bring snacks and drinks to share. Host the first meeting in your classroom to model how a meeting should be organized. Rotate meetings to other teachers' classrooms each month. Include a show and tell as part of the agenda in the host teacher's classroom, so he can show off parts of his room. Ask the novices to bring their *The First Years Matter* books to the meeting. Some novice teachers like to meet before school and call the meeting the breakfast club, or after school for coffee.

Sample Agenda—30 Minutes

Welcome and introductions: Host teacher shares her classroom then invites others to share something that is going well in their classrooms. Review *The First Years Matter* book and see if they have any questions from the PLAN section that need to be addressed this month.

Take some time to be quiet: Select a prompt from the REFLECT page this month and ask everyone to write a response. Report out the responses and discuss the issues that came up.

Share a problem with the group: Ask everyone to share a challenge they are facing in their classroom that is based on a topic you are focusing on.

Select one problem: As the mentor, you will facilitate and lead the group to discuss ONE of the problems that the group would like to talk about. Each person in the group will have an opportunity to share some "possible ideas" that could help this teacher. The teacher does not talk. She just listens and takes notes.

Wrap up the discussion: When the time limit for discussion is over (10–15 minutes), the teacher who had the issue may speak and thank the group for the ideas and share what her next steps will be.

Closing and acknowledgment: Recognize the development of each teacher in the group and focus on what they are doing well. Remind them to complete REFLECT and SET GOALS pages in their books. End the meeting on time.

Figure 10 Board of Mentors Process

Directions: Use this tool to support your novice teacher in discovering who is in her support system. You are only one person, and you cannot meet all the social and emotional needs of your mentee. If you are using *The First Years Matter* book with your novice, have her bring it to a meeting so she can write in her book. A digital version of this form is available on the companion website.

Invite your mentee to print her name in one of the chairs at the table. Discuss how she is her own leader and that she guides her practice by reflecting. There is a line near every chair and the line is the "role" this mentor plays on the Board of Mentors. For example, the mentee's line would say "reflective practitioner." Your name will be in one of the chairs, and on the line it will say "district mentor." Through conversation, help the mentee find other people in her life who support her in different ways.

These mentors help the novice in life. For example, if she is moving to a new apartment, her best friend might be her mentor. We all have mentors who help us with finances, social networking, spiritual support, and educational decisions. Your role in this process is to help her acknowledge that she does have other people to help her. Consider doing the Board of Mentors for yourself and sharing your support system with her so she understands we all need support from time to time.

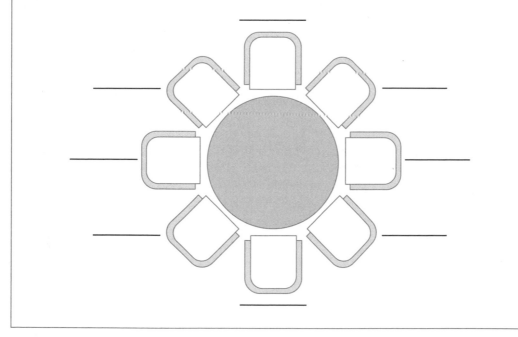

Companion Website

Purposeful Mentoring Conversations

If you have already been a mentor, you may have noticed that most of mentoring is talking with your novice teacher. Many mentors have asked me, "What are we supposed to talk about?" This book can be used as conversation starters with your mentee. If your mentee is using the *First Years Matter* book, he can read the chapters ahead of time and come prepared to a mentoring meeting to discuss a topic that is of particular interest to him. The ACTs in each chapter provide you with many options for conversations. Use the book as a resource from which you can pick and choose the topics and pages that would be the meaningful conversations based on your mentee's needs. The questions in the PLAN section of each chapter also offer you options for conversations based on a question the novice brings to you.

Purposeful mentoring conversations are those that are planned and that forward teaching skills and strategies for the classroom. By reflecting on what is important and what the next step is for a novice, you can provide focus and a road map of sorts to minimize the overwhelming details of day-to-day teaching. To lead these kinds of conversations, you need tools and structure.

Templates to Promote Mindful Mentoring. Being mindful means that you are attentive to the needs of your mentee and aware of how you can be supportive. By paying attention and focusing on the present moment without judgment, you can provide a context for support that is meaningful to forward teaching practices. Skim the templates in the Appendices to become familiar with each topic and how you can use these agendas in the future.

I developed these templates because mentors shared with me that they felt overwhelmed with the responsibility of designing mentoring conversation agendas. They also said that they often only had a few minutes to meet and wanted to focus their time. You will find meeting agendas for 5, 10, and 15 minute meetings as well as 20, 30, and 60 minute meetings. Do what effective teachers do, adapt these, modify them, and make them your own! The idea here is to purposefully schedule meetings. To know what the purpose of the meeting is and why you are conducting it makes the meeting a good use of your time. My favorite meeting is the 5 Minute Meeting!

Mindful mentoring conversations can be short. It is more effective to meet each week for 10 minutes than it is to meet once a month for an hour. The consistent contact creates a pattern of support and positive interaction. Watch the collection of 11 videos titled *Mentoring Conversations* available on the companion website (Video Collection 1.6 code in margin) to see mentors and mentees in action discussing pages from this book. The conversations not only demonstrate an ACT topic they show you what can be done in 5 minutes. Select the topic that is most meaningful to you or watch all 11 videos to learn how conversations can be led.

Documenting Conversations and Collecting Evidence for Teacher Evaluation. School districts assess and evaluate the success of a teacher in a variety of ways. All districts will have standards and expectations for proficiency, and these must be discussed in your mentoring conversations. Sometimes we assume the novice understands evaluation and standards. Novice teachers need to understand that your role is to help them be successful and to pass their evaluation observations.

This book can be aligned to your state or district standards so you and your mentee can discuss how the ACT topics relate to the required standards. Simply by color-coding the book to your standards, you will create a visual connection that can easily be individualized to your state or district. Review again the sample Evaluation Alignment Tool in Figure 3 on page 7 to get started.

Some districts require a professional portfolio as evidence of completed evaluation standards, and others require a log that documents the novice has met with a mentor for a number of hours during the year. All districts usually require a performance assessment that includes an observation of the novice teacher in her classroom. As a mentor, you can be mindful of what is needed in your district to retain teachers and support your mentee in meeting these requirements.

If developing a portfolio is a requirement for your district or state, refer to Portfolio Development ideas in Figure 11 to guide the process of development. If a portfolio is not required, it is a good idea to encourage the novice teacher to consider creating one to remember the first year of teaching. The first year is unlike any other year of teaching, and having a memory book with student photos and highlights of special activities is an activity you can do together.

You can use the *Mentoring in Action* book as evidence of conversations by simply dating the corner of the page when you use that page in a mentoring conversation. You may find that you revisit an ACT page more than once, and this will remind you of when you talked about this topic. This can serve as your log, or you can use the Mentoring Conversation Log in Figure 12, also available in digital form on the companion website. If your mentee is using the *First Years Matter* book, he can date his pages and keep track of his own personal reflections as well as conversations with you. If you watch videos, be sure to note the date watched in your book(s)! Your books become a living

Figure 11 Developing a Portfolio

Directions: Set a time to discuss the purposes of a professional portfolio. If your district or state requires a beginning teacher to create one as evidence for state licensing, you need to follow the format required. If this is not required, you may still encourage the novice to collect artifacts as a memory of the first years of teaching. Portfolios can be shared with parents at open house night or with district administrators who are evaluating the novice.

Follow these steps and discuss these ideas with your novice teacher. A digital version of this form is available on the companion website.

1. Review the purpose of a professional portfolio. Why is it an important tool?

2. Assist the novice in writing a three-paragraph philosophy statement. Use this as a format.

   a. List three words to describe yourself as a teacher and why these are important.

   b. Write three beliefs you have about teaching and learning.

   c. List three ways you demonstrate your words and beliefs in the classroom.

3. Encourage her to collect artifact samples in a box or online folder to be reviewed later.

   a. Student work, lesson plans, photographs, evaluation comments, professional development, and courses of students working in the classroom. Remember to get permissions for any photos you put into your portfolio.

4. Discuss the best way to present a portfolio. Should it be digital or hard copy?

5. If this is for the state, when is it due? Assist the novice in doing this in parts so it is not being done all at once at the end of the year.

6. Help the novice put the portfolio together following these tips.

   a. Select the most meaningful samples from the artifact box or online folder. The examples the novice selects should either relate to a standard or illustrate an area that is documenting proficiency. Your mentee should not keep samples that do not relate to required evidence needed unless you can make a connection to a teaching skill.

   b. Reflect on why this evidence is important and help the novice write a short caption or description for each artifact. The reflection is the explanation as to why this photo or sample of student work relates to teacher development. Help the novice connect the dots so she can see how what she does in the classroom relates to standards.

   c. Assist your mentee in creating a layout that uses samples of the artifacts collected throughout the year. Organize a table of contents, place the philosophy statement up front, and place the reflections near the evidence.

7. Review the completed portfolio and compliment your novice on all she has learned this year!

Companion Website

Figure 12 Mentoring Conversation Log

Directions: If you are a formal mentor and are being compensated for your services, you may be required to maintain a log. Use this form as a guide, or download a digital version from the companion website.

Date	ACTivity in Book (page #), Video You Watched, Observation, etc.	Notes

log of your reflections and development over time. By writing in the books or downloading the forms from the companion website, you are documenting the process of mentoring.

Observation and feedback are important components of a mentoring program. Mentors have shared with me that they don't have release time to observe the mentee in action and their preparation times do not match. If this is the case for you, I encourage you to use video technology to observe and provide feedback to your novice teacher. Explore the options in your district for scheduling a high school student to go to the novice teacher's classroom to tape a lesson she would like you to observe. She can even get the students involved to create the video and introduce themselves to you. Use a mobile device if video equipment is not available. You don't need a long video. Ask for a 10–20 minute clip that includes highlights of the beginning of a lesson, some activity in the middle, and the closing of the lesson. That will be plenty to talk about! It is surprising how long one class period is for an observation. Less is more in this case. Focus on specific skills that relate to evaluation requirements so you can stay aligned to your goal of helping the novice achieve success on her evaluation.

VIDEO 1.7

Observation and Feedback Tools, Part 1

If you have never observed a teacher or you would like to refresh your observation and feedback skills, watch Videos 1.7 and 1.8, *Observation and Feedback Tools Parts 1 and 2*. These videos are available on the companion website or by scanning the QR code in the margin using a mobile device. An observation tip will be provided in each chapter to remind you to observe and provide feedback as much as possible.

VIDEO 1.8

Observation and Feedback Tools, Part 2

Documenting your mentoring practices validates the importance of your role. Keep an accurate record of your meetings in your book or use the Mentor Planning Guide and Journal. Don't skip this important aspect of mentoring. By keeping track of the ongoing reflections, conversations, and observations, you maintain tangible evidence of what a mentor does. Many mentors have shared that documenting what they do shows them how much work mentoring is and how important the role of the mentor is to a novice teacher's development. They realized how good they were as teachers and how they took for granted their ability to manage a classroom and just stand up and teach a lesson. You will rediscover your teaching strengths as you participate as a mentor. Enjoy the process and acknowledge what you do well.

PART II

MONTH-BY-MONTH MENTORING

Why Do We Need a Mentoring Curriculum?

Many mentoring programs simply assign mentors to novice teachers and say, "Go mentor." Even if you feel competent as a teacher, you might not feel the same competence in the role of mentor. In an informal program, most mentors introduce themselves and say something like, "Let me know if you need any help." Then they wait for their mentee to come to them. In these informal programs, if the mentees come at all, it is often when they are in crisis mode and the mentor ends up putting out fires.

So what do you do? You use this book to guide you to become a formal proactive mentor. You use the content to empower you to take the lead in scheduling consistent short meetings to avoid a "crisis problem-solving" mentoring approach. You review all the materials and videos and become aware of the resources available to you so you differentiate and be the best mentor possible for this novice teacher.

The *Mentoring in Action* book can support you in learning how to mentor while you are in the act of mentoring. It can prepare you for your role, provide you with background information each month, offer you suggestions to reflect on your own mentoring skills, and provide you with lots of ideas for mentoring conversations. This book will provide you with videos, forms, and practical strategies for deepening your mentoring conversations and staying focused on the novice teacher's proficiency. The month-by-month topics offer you an organized approach to talking about teaching and learning. Each month you are encouraged to touch base weekly, even if it is just for a short meeting or a phone or e-mail connection.

This book works best when your novice is using the *First Years Matter* companion book because she can come to meetings prepared to talk with you and also reflect on her teaching practices when she is not with you. Novice teachers like to see the entire year because they can see what is coming and how to plan. Using their own book to document their thinking, record notes, review topics for future months, and see what possible questions they might have encourages the mentees to engage and not just come to mentoring conversations as passive participants.

The butterfly image in Figure 15 shows the novice emerging from the egg through the chrysalis stages to the butterfly. This process illustrates the transformation that will take place in the beginning years of teaching. The best way to differentiate and use this book is to begin with your mentee's strengths. Encourage your school to mentor novices for a minimum of 3 years to ensure the best teaching practices are established. Beyond year 1 in 2+ years, group mentoring options provide a model that builds a learning community.

A Month-by-Month Cycle for Mentoring

Part II of the book is organized by months because that is how a school year operates. School districts often give novice teachers all the information they need for the entire year in a two or three day orientation. Mentors often do the same. Novice teachers tell me that this is just too overwhelming and not only does it create anxiety for them, but it is also confusing. This guide is organized to review and/or introduce topics throughout the school year in an organized way. Even with your best intentions, you may forget to review important teaching topics with your mentee. With a curriculum, you are guaranteed to touch on the important topics as you review each month. You don't need to wait for the novice teacher to bring up a topic when she has a crisis. Be proactive!

This book is organized around the following strategies: PLAN, CONNECT, ACT, REFLECT, and SET GOALS. This structure will provide focus as you move through the mentoring process each month.

Figure 13   Cycle of Monthly Mentoring

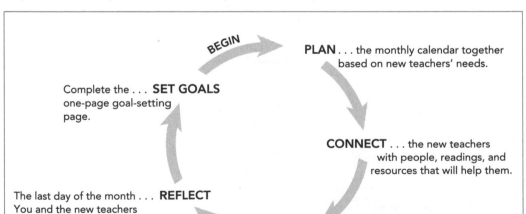

Figure 14 Organization of the Book

Mentoring Focus	Resources in the Book
PLAN to meet with your mentee weekly.	Read the chapter overview to get a sense of the content for this month.
CONNECT your novice teacher to resources.	This page provides an overview of topics and what is available on the companion website.
ACT through mentoring conversations.	Select the pages that are most meaningful to discuss with your mentee.
REFLECT on your experience.	Take the time to think about what is working and how you can improve.
SET GOALS to move ahead.	Support your mentee by setting measurable goals that lead to success in the classroom.

Each month begins with a chapter overview that includes guiding questions for the chapter as well as the national InTASC Standard that is featured. The overview also includes a novice teacher phase, a Mindful Mentoring Affirmation, as well as a quote from a student or novice teacher.

The Transformation of a Teacher

The words on the triangle image in Figure 16 guide us to think about mentoring as a transformational experience. Our ultimate goal is to transform the novice teacher into that emerging butterfly. Transformation is a process that takes time and you may not see that ultimate change in your novice teacher's development in year 1. We have to trust that the work we are doing will influence his development over time and the students will benefit from the strategies and effective teaching practices you have discussed.

As I mentioned in the Introduction: Welcome to Mentoring in Action, your heart will guide you to serve and support this beginner. That is why the heart is at the center of the triangle logo I use on my MentoringinAction.com website. Your heart will keep you centered as you PLAN,

Figure 15 Developmental Continuum

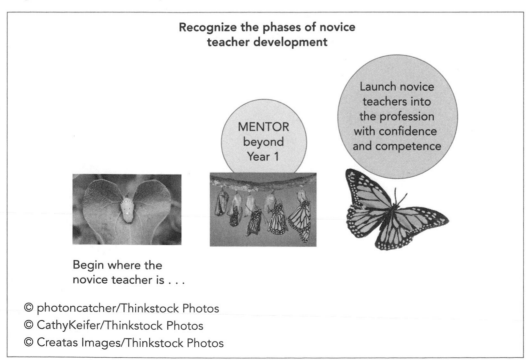

Recognize the phases of novice teacher development

Launch novice teachers into the profession with confidence and competence

MENTOR beyond Year 1

Begin where the novice teacher is . . .

© photoncatcher/Thinkstock Photos
© CathyKeifer/Thinkstock Photos
© Creatas Images/Thinkstock Photos

CONNECT, ACT, REFLECT, and SET GOALS with your mentee. It is the place of compassion and service that will guide you to know what to do next. To hear this mentor talk about her experience of her mentees' development over a year, watch Video 2.1, *The Transformation of a Teacher*, available on the companion website or by scanning the QR code in the margin..

Balance Is Key to Teacher Development. Help your mentee take her learning one step at a time. She will in turn share this message of balance with the students in her classroom. A teacher can't be at her best with students if she is stressed and burned out. You create a positive ripple effect when you manage your stress in healthy ways to promote health and well-being. A mindful mentor models balance.

Inspire Novice Teachers to Be the Best Teachers They Can Be. He may share his problems and challenges he faces in his classroom with you. Your role is to acknowledge those hurdles and to support him in finding ways to overcome them. Your optimism, joy of teaching, and hope will inspire your mentee to love this craft. Then he will feel he can help his students find joy in school and overcome their challenges. How you inspire your novice teacher is key to his success, and this may influence his decision to continue teaching.

Lead by Example. Your words and actions will be so important. Think carefully about your comments and ask yourself, "How will my comment or response assist this novice to be more effective in the classroom? Your professionalism using a mindfulness approach will influence her development. This is not the time to agree with the complaints raised by the novice teacher. This is the time to be a positive influence.

Everything you do has a ripple effect. Be intentional with your influence.

Figure 16   Transformation of a Teacher

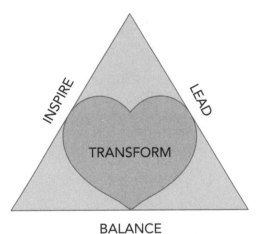

"

Good teachers care about their students, know
who they are, and would go to any length to help
them get the education they deserve."

—HIGH SCHOOL STUDENT

NEW TEACHER PHASE: ANTICIPATION

"I'm so excited to have my own classroom!"

MINDFUL MENTORING AFFIRMATION

I will listen to my novice teacher's needs
and be a compassionate mentor.

AUGUST

ORIENTATION TO THE SCHOOL AND COMMUNITY

Resources and Values

GUIDING QUESTIONS

1. What do you bring to mentoring? The *Reflect ACTivities* will provide ways to think about what your skills and qualities for mentoring a novice teacher should be.

2. How will you introduce your mentee to learn about important school information? The *Introduce ACTivities* provide you with topics you may want to share.

3. How can you help your mentee prepare for the first weeks of school? The *Prepare ACTivities* provide you with information and conversation starters to focus your time with your novice teacher.

Interstate Teacher Assessment and Support Consortium—InTASC Standards

Review all 10 of the InTASC Standards on page 6 in Part I. On the front page of each month, you will find the standards that relate to that chapter's focus. Support your novice teacher in understanding how your mentoring conversations align with teacher evaluation requirements. A sample Evaluation Alignment Tool is available on page 7 in Part I.

Chapter Overview

As a mentor, you have an opportunity to impact beginning teachers by providing support, successful ideas, resources, and insight into the culture of your school and its surrounding community. Many of us did not have mentors when we began our work in schools, and we know how painful it was to be isolated and alone in the classroom. This chapter will guide your conversations to ensure you discuss these important topics with your mentee and minimize any anxiety and uncertainty this novice is facing. You are a lifeline for this beginner, and this book is going to support you so you have a proactive plan for engaging your mentee in meaningful and timely conversations.

Most novice teachers are so excited to enter their first classroom, and then some are confused when they see their space with few materials. Make sure your mentee has the classroom resources required to set up an organized and efficient classroom that will engage learners. Many beginners don't even know what they are supposed to have for supplies and books at the beginning of the year. Go to the mentee's classroom and make sure the materials are there. We have all heard the horror stories of novice teachers trying to start their first year in empty classrooms with no materials. Your role is to make sure this does not happen.

The community and what it values will influence the way the school operates and supports its teachers. If your mentee did not grow up in this town, you need to share the town's history and cultural makeup to provide a context for the educational system. Be aware of your own judgments and mindfully share only the information that will forward your novice's understanding of students and families.

Your Mindful Mentoring Affirmation for this month is, "I will listen to my novice teacher's needs and be a compassionate mentor." We all had a first year. We all have stories of setting up that very first classroom and learning how to navigate the school culture as well as the students and families. This is not an easy task, but a worthwhile profession. As the student says in the quote at the beginning of this chapter, good teachers help students get the education they deserve. Your role as a mentor is to remember this and guide, share, and reflect with your mentee so she will understand how important she is.

Follow the PLAN, CONNECT, ACT, REFLECT, and SET GOALS sections in this chapter to guide your mentoring conversations and reflections.

Watch and listen to a mentor share her insights in the August Chapter Introduction (Video 2.2), available on the companion website or by scanning the QR code on a mobile device.

A Mentor Planning Guide and Journal is available on the companion website. This tool provides a place for you to record notes and write your reflections for each chapter. At the end of the year, it can be shared with district leaders to serve as documentation of your mentoring experience. You may also write in this book to note ideas and plans for mentoring conversations.

VIDEO 2.2

**August Chapter
Introduction**

Use Questions to Guide Mentoring Conversations

Sometimes beginning teachers don't know what to ask their mentors because they don't know what they don't know! If your novice teacher doesn't have any questions, share this list and invite the mentee to choose some questions. What is your PLAN for responding to your mentee's questions? How will you listen to your mentee's needs?

Anticipate Beginning Teachers' Possible Questions

1. Who are my students and their families?
2. What do I need to know about the community?
3. What do I need to know about this school and its procedures?
4. What values, expectations, or cultural norms are in operation in this school and the community?
5. Is there a written mission statement for the school that you can review with me?
6. Do you have any suggestions for me as I organize my first classroom?
7. How do I get materials for my classroom and my students?
8. Are there any restrictions or expectations for my classroom space?

Note the other questions your novice teacher asked you so you will have them for the future.

Questions for Your Novice Teacher

1. What do you already know about this community and school?
2. What is your experience in organizing a classroom?
3. What are your first steps to setting up the classroom?
4. How can I support you right now?

Meetings and Observations

Plan brief weekly meetings with your mentee. The ACTs in this chapter serve as mentoring conversation starters and can also be used to assess or review what your mentee may already know about a given topic. Use the Appendices to guide you in scheduling short meetings as well as longer conversations.

Plan to meet at times that allow you to have quality time together in a place without interruptions. Knowing when you will meet each week reduces anxiety for both of you. Novice teachers look forward to regularly scheduled meetings even if they are short. Use a calendar to plan your meetings and classroom visits to ensure they will happen! Include watching videos and reading pages in the *Mentoring in Action* book as part of your *PLAN* for mentoring. A digital version of this calendar (August Calendar.pdf) is available on the companion website.

Are you willing to have the novice teacher observe you? Use the form in the Appendices "A Novice Observes a Mentor" to guide this process. It is an opportunity for you to share your skills in action. Schedule an observation this month. Are you required to observe your novice teacher this year? Discuss this with your mentee and plan ahead to ensure this happens.

August Calendar

MONDAY	TUESDAY	WEDNESDAY	THURSDAY	FRIDAY

Use this calendar to PLAN the month as well as to document meetings and mentor planning.

CONNECT to Additional Resources

CONNECT to School and District Resources

What resources exist in your school and community that could assist novice teachers in setting up their classrooms? What did your mentee say he "needed" this month? How can you help?

CONNECT With Colleagues, Parents, and Families

Who in the school building (e.g., experienced teachers, other beginning teachers, custodians, secretaries) may be able to help your mentee?

How does your mentee introduce himself to the parents and families?

CONNECT to Student Voices

What does "respect" look like in a classroom, and how can you ensure your mentee includes this important quality as he creates a community of learners? Review the ideas on the form "What Does Respect Look Like in the Classroom" available on the companion website for specific ways to integrate respect.

CONNECT to Education Hot Topics

Use portable devices for learning! Back to school means school supplies. Portable devices are now part of the student's backpack. How can you talk with your novice teacher about using these devices appropriately? What is the role of social media and its proper use in school? Review Hot Topics on the We Are Teachers website (http://www.weareteachers.com/) to identify the strategies that work best.

CONNECT With the Companion Website

Video links, forms for this chapter, a featured book, and other resources are located at http://resources.corwin.com/mentoringinaction.

Companion Website

The First ACT!

Differentiating Mentoring Conversations

Teaching is complex work, and novice teachers can easily become overwhelmed. It is appropriate to customize your mentoring conversations to respond to the varied needs and skills of the mentee.

Directions: Interview your mentee at the beginning of the month to document her areas of strength and needs. Skim the ACTs for this month and decide together which topics are most relevant. Use your state or district teaching standards to focus the mentee's responses to each prompt so you are also teaching her the "common language" of the standards.

Mentee _____ Date _____

Monthly Needs Assessment

1. What is going well in your classroom? (i.e., What is working?) As a teacher, what do you feel you are doing well right now? *Refer to the teaching standards to guide your response.*	3. What would you like to improve or enhance in your practice this month? *Refer to the teaching standards to guide your response.*
2. How do you know your practice is working? (i.e., What is your evidence of success? or Why do you feel confident or competent in an aspect of your teaching?)	4. Review the ACT mentoring conversations for this month with your mentee. Ask which of the ACTs will support you in enhancing your teaching practice? (i.e., What would you like us to focus on this month?)

Companion Website

A digital version of this template (Monthly Needs Assessment Sample With Standards.pdf) is available on the companion website. Keep a copy of this assessment for your files and make a copy for the mentee.

Overview of the ACTs for August Conversations

Directions: Skim the ACTivities listed here and complete the pages that will forward your novice teacher's learning. Your mentee also has complementary ACTs in *The First Years Matter.* Digital copies of any of the reproducible ACTs are available on the companion website.

Key Question Topic	ACTivities	PAGE
Reflect	ACT 1 **Preparing to Mentor a Novice Teacher**	34
Reflect	ACT 2 **Before You Meet Your Novice Teacher**	35
Introduce	ACT 3 **How Does a Novice Teacher Contribute to Your School?**	36
Introduce	ACT 4 **Introducing the School and District**	37
Introduce	ACT 5 **Getting to Know the Students and Their Families**	38
Introduce	ACT 6 **Creating a Survival Packet**	39
Prepare	ACT 7 **Building a Mentoring Relationship**	40
Prepare	ACT 8 **The Importance of Lesson Planning**	41
Prepare	ACT 9 **Daily Lesson Plans for Student Success**	42
Prepare	ACT 10 **The First Days and Weeks of School**	43

Preparing to Mentor a Novice Teacher

Key Question: What experiences and skills do you bring to mentoring?

Directions: Reflect on your previous mentoring experiences and complete the prompts. Record your reflections on this page or use the Mentor Planning Guide and Journal provided on the companion website to type your responses. Share your answers with your district mentoring coordinator or with other mentors.

1. Name three mentors in your life (they do not have to relate to education).

2. Why were these mentors important to you? List any specific positive qualities that stand out for you.

3. How will you use your mentors' qualities with this novice teacher?

4. How have your mentors prepared you for your role as a mentor?

5. Have you been a mentor before? If yes, what will you do differently this time?

6. What is your mentoring philosophy? Complete this sentence. *I believe mentoring is . . .*

7. What is your job description for being a mentor? Share this with your mentee.

8. Why did you say yes to being a mentor for a novice teacher?

9. What are your strengths as a teacher?

10. What are your strengths as a mentor?

11. Where can you grow as a teacher?

12. Where can you grow as a mentor?

Before You Meet Your Novice Teacher

Key Question: How does an effective mentor prepare for mentoring?

Directions: Read the questions below and reflect on your role. If you are unclear about any of your required duties, ask your district or school coordinator to clarify. Share your answers with your district mentoring coordinator or with other mentors. Record your reflections on this page or use the Mentor Planning Guide and Journal provided on the companion website to type your responses. A digital version of this page is also available on the companion website.

1. How did you officially become a mentor? Did you complete an application? Why is it important to apply for a mentoring position?

2. Are you trained to be a mentor? How were you trained? Do you feel confident in your skills?

3. Review your job description. Do you understand all of the duties listed? Do you need to complete a log to document mentoring duties? Are you receiving a stipend? If you need clarification, meet with district coordinators to define your roles and responsibilities. Plan to share your description with your mentee so she understands what you are expected to do for her.

4. Set goals for this experience. What would you like to learn? What are your expectations?

5. Consider hosting a coffee hour or social in your classroom and invite members of the school community to stop by to meet your novice teacher. Be sure to include other novice teachers at the school so they can network with each other.

6. How will you be supported during this experience? Will there be a mentor support group for you?

7. At the end of the experience, how will you know you have been successful as a mentor?

Companion
Website

How Does a Novice Teacher Contribute to Your School?

Key Question: What does your mentee bring to teaching?

Directions: Many mentors share that beginning teachers bring energy, passion, and new ideas into the classroom and the school. We often dive into teaching and miss important information and strengths novice teachers bring to teaching. Effective mentors acknowledge the strengths of their novice teachers and use these strengths to enhance teacher leadership roles in the school.

Your novice teacher will have this Novice Teacher Profile in their book, *The First Years Matter*. At a meeting, be prepared to discuss his/her answers to the questions in the profile.

Novice Teacher Profile

Directions for Novice Teacher: Respond to the prompts in a narrative and e-mail your completed profile to your mentor.

1. Teacher Preparation

    A. Describe your preparation for teaching. What path did you take to become certified? Describe one course that you took in your preparation at the college that stands out for you as being a useful preparation for teaching and why.

    B. List your previous experiences in schools as a student teacher or previous teaching experiences.

2. Skills and Experiences

    A. Do you speak a world language? Explain.

    B. Do you or have you played or coached sports? Explain.

    C. Where have you traveled? Why did you visit these places?

    D. Do you have musical, drama, or any arts ability? Explain.

    E. What is your level of proficiency with computers and other technology?

    F. Other hobbies?

3. Life and Professional Goals

    A. Where do you see yourself in 5 years? 10 years? 20 years?

    B. Why did you choose teaching at this time?

4. Personal Joys and Strengths

    A. What do you most enjoy in your life?

    B. What are you really good at?

5. What would you like me to know about you?

6. What would you like to know about me?

Introducing the School and District

Key Question: Who and what does your mentee need to know to be successful?

Directions: Knowing the important facts about the school, the district, and who is important to a novice teacher's success is crucial information.

Your novice teacher will have the School Scavenger Hunt in their book, *The First Years Matter.* At a meeting, be prepared to discuss his answers to the questions. A digital version can be found on the companion website. Don't forget to introduce your mentee to the important people on this list.

School Scavenger Hunt

Directions for Novice Teacher: Find the responses to these questions by using the school website, talking with teachers, or reviewing school materials.

1. What is the name of the school and why does it have this name? How old is the school? Also list the phone, e-mail, and website address.

2. How many students are enrolled in this school? What is the diversity of students by ethnicity? What are the languages spoken?

3. What are the official school hours? Are there recess times for students? What is the schedule for classes? When do teachers arrive at school and leave at the end of the day? What is the lunch period for teachers? Do you have lesson planning time? Will you have duties?

4. Is public transportation available to the school? If so, what is the schedule?

5. Is there a school theme or mission of the school? How is it displayed?

6. How is the school organized? What is the number of teachers at each grade level and content areas?

7. How many experienced teachers are working at this school? How many teachers in their first 3 years of teaching?

8. Who is the principal and assistant principal? Who is the superintendent? (Spelling counts!)

9. How many specialist teachers are at the school? Will your students participate in these classes?

10. How will special education influence your teaching schedule? Are there paraprofessional aides?

11. Who are the secretaries and custodians you should get to know?

12. Is there a parent volunteer program? Will it relate to you?

13. Are there any special programs or activities at this school or in this district?

14. What are teachers most proud of in this school? (You may ask several teachers and compare.)

15. How does this school's image and reputation relate to other schools in the district and the state?

Is there anything else you would like to know about the school or district? Ask your mentor!

Companion Website

AUGUST

Getting to Know the Students and Their Families

Key Question: How can you introduce the students and families to your novice teacher?

Directions: Getting to know the students and the local community is important for any novice teacher, especially if the novice teacher has moved in from another town or state. Ask your mentee to find the answers to the questions in ACT 5 and either bring them to a future meeting or e-mail them to you. This form is located in the *First Years Matter* book and a digital version is on the companion website.

Ways to Introduce Yourself and Learn About Students and Families

Directions for Novice Teacher: Review the ideas listed here and be prepared to discuss your responses with your mentor. Feel free to add your own ideas to this list.

1. Interviewing students: One way to find out about the school is to talk with students. They are usually hanging around the school in August waiting for it to start! Ask students what they like about this school, what they find challenging, and how teachers can help them learn. Create other interview questions to find out what you would like to learn about this school. The students tell it like it is! Don't be surprised by their responses!

2. Interviewing parents: Where there are students there may be parents. Take this opportunity to introduce yourself and ask the parents about the school and the district. This simple informal research will give you lots of insight into the perspective of the parents and what they think about the school.

3. Observe the community: If you don't live in the town, you need to learn about it. Some orientation programs provide a tour of the town and all the schools in the district. If that is not available, take a drive or a bus and see what the community looks like. Note where the schools are located within the town. Where is the downtown area? Is there a public library? What do the neighborhoods look like, and how does that impact the schools? Are there other resources you can use in the town? Museums? Recycle Centers?

4. Review the school website: This will help you find the answers for the Scavenger Hunt in ACT 4. You need to know how the website is used in this district and if it is important to you.

5. Write a letter to the students: Introduce yourself before the school year begins or during the first week of school. Share your background, your interests, and what you are looking forward to!

6. Write a letter to the parents and/or guardians sharing what you will be doing this year and how they can reach you if they have any questions. Be sure to include how excited you are to be teaching.

Are there other ways you can learn about students and families? Discuss with your mentor!

Companion
Website

Creating a Survival Packet

Key Question: What do novice teachers need to know now?

Directions: Surviving the first year of teaching is a goal for most novice teachers. A way to help your novice teacher survive is to help her with the information on this page. Watch Video 2.3 to see a mentor and novice talking about the survival packet.

Creating a Survival Packet

Survival Packet Important Information

1. *School and District Materials and Where to Find Them*

   - Schedules (daily, weekly, block, holiday) and student and school handbooks with policies

   - Mission statements, vision statements, curriculum guides

   - Class lists (how to get them and who creates them) and list of faculty and e-mails

   - Report cards, parent communication, discipline policies, and policy for reporting abuse or neglect

   - Professional development schedule and school closing policies (emergency and snow closings)

2. *Buzz Words (here is a sample of education jargon)*

   - BBST, ESL, ELL, IEP, AYP, KWL, AFT, and NEA, Title I, InTASC

   - Words or initials you have heard that you don't know

   _____

3. *Procedures and School Culture Protocols*

   - Fire drill and other building exiting procedures

   - Protocols and expectations that are not written (how teachers get lunch and where they eat)

   - Sending students to the nurse (from colds to crisis—how to know the difference)

   - Getting support for students in crisis (home problems that students bring to school)

   - Guidelines for referring students for misbehavior (Where do they go? What do you write?)

   - Supervisory duties and expectations for new teachers (hall duty, cafeteria, recess duty, bus duty)

   - How and where to make copies for lessons and take out library books

4. *Building Floor Plan and School Organization*

   - Map of school with room numbers and exits clearly labeled (also nurse, office, workrooms, bathrooms, staff lounges) and map of schoolyard, where buses drop off, and entrances

5. *Teacher Union Information and State Licensing Information*

   - Reviewing the teacher contract and state requirements

   - Reviewing union benefits

Companion Website

Building a Mentoring Relationship

Key Question: How can you help a novice teacher get the most out of being mentored?

Directions: Review the ideas and use any that relate to you and your mentee. Discuss the Self-Assessment to find out how your mentee feels about each area listed. Ask your mentee to rate himself using a scale of 1–5 (with 1 being low) for each of the following areas:

1. **Self-Assessment**

	Competence I have experience . . .	Confidence I feel . . .
Setting up a classroom		
Introducing myself to students and parents		
Lesson and unit planning		
Creating and implementing classroom routines		
Managing disruptive behavior students		
Working with students from other cultures		
Learning how to navigate school culture		
Other topics:		

VIDEO 2.4

Design Alliance

2. Watch Video 2.4, *Design Alliance*, together and discuss the ideas that are presented that support a mentoring relationship.

3. Invite your mentee to ask you questions. Create boundaries for your time to avoid too many questions. You can create a time during the week or suggest e-mail.

4. Start a dialogue journal on e-mail. Write back and forth with questions and ideas.

5. Invite the novice teacher to observe you in your classroom! This will help her see how you organize your space and prepare for the students at the beginning of the year.

6. Find out if the university provides any support for novice teachers and encourage the novice to make connections to support systems.

The Importance of Lesson Planning

Key Question: What does your mentee need to know about planning effective lessons?

Directions: Review the key ideas on this page and discuss the most relevant topics with your mentee.

Lesson Planning Overview

1. Review lesson and unit planning requirements.

2. Discuss specific ways lesson planning can minimize student distraction and engage learners.

3. Illustrate how school and state standards are supposed to be reflected in lesson plans.

4. Share daily plans in short form as well as long form plans that are used at your school.

5. Review curriculum and expectations for the novice teacher to design unit plans.

6. Share specific plans for the first days of school and review why you include certain components.

7. Ask the novice teacher to share his experience of daily planning and show you some plans.

8. Co-plan with the novice to ensure the first days of school include necessary introduction activities.

9. Skim the October chapter in the *Mentoring in Action* book to see more lesson and unit planning.

10. Listen to the novice teacher's questions about plans and share any pages that are helpful.

Daily Lesson Plans for Student Success

Key Question: What does your mentee need to know about daily lesson planning?

Directions: Review the key ideas on this page in a mentoring conversation with your novice teacher. Explain that an effective teacher knows that the lesson plan is a way of organizing information the students are learning. What a teacher wants her students to know and be able to do is the purpose of the plan. Use these ideas to review the important questions a teacher needs to think about when developing a plan. Take a sample lesson plan and see if you can answer these questions.

Lesson Planning Questions

1. Why am I teaching this lesson?

2. Which standards am I addressing? Where are they noted on the plan?

3. Am I presenting the content in a way that is relevant to students?

4. Am I including higher order thinking in my activities?

5. What do I want all students to learn?

6. How will I modify for special students?

7. What assessment tools will I use to measure success?

8. What is the motivation for students to stay engaged?

9. How much teacher talking time is in this plan? (i.e., lecture)

10. Do students have an opportunity to practice and share? How long?

11. Is there an opportunity for students to reflect on their learning and set goals?

12. What routines and systems are in place to minimize student distractions?

The First Days and Weeks of School

Key Question: How can you prepare your mentee for the first days and weeks of school?

Directions: Review the four ideas on this page with your mentee. Add any resources that are needed to have your mentee be successful.

1. *Design Classroom Space*

Share your classroom floor plan and discuss why you have arranged the room that way. Ask the novice to draw a floor plan of her room. Include teacher's desk and students' seats. Include traffic flow and make sure all students can see the teacher with this plan.

2. *Establish Effective Routines*

Discuss the importance of routines and why they need to be established on the first days of school. Ask the mentee which routines he plans to use. Share your routines. Discuss how the novice teacher will share these routines with the students? Offer suggestions as needed and allow the novice teachers to modify your suggestions.

3. *First Day Lesson Plans*

What should a mentee teach in the beginning days of school? Share the agendas you have used on the first days of classes. Learning students' names, perhaps taking a photo of each student, and sharing the course content are all important.

4. *Materials and Supplies*

How and where does the novice teacher get books, supplies, and materials for the first weeks of school? Assist in this process and help design the beginning of the year lesson plans together.

Novice teachers will gain confidence if you help them present themselves competently in the first weeks of school. Your support is integral to helping that novice maintain balance.

August Mentor Reflections

Directions: Complete any of these prompts that stand out for you. Write your responses here or use your Mentor Planning Guide and Journal on the companion website. Share your reflections with your mentor coordinator or with other mentors at a mentor support meeting.

What has stood out for me as I have prepared to mentor novice teachers is . . .

One thing I found difficult during this orientation process is . . .

Something I will do differently next time is . . .

I am enjoying . . .

I remember feeling supported during my first year when . . .

Something I need to share is . . .

Using Mindfulness to Explore Mentoring Dilemmas

Teaching is complex, and often there are not clear answers to situations that arise while you are mentoring a novice teacher. The mentoring dilemmas introduced at the end of each month in the REFLECT section may not apply to your mentee in this situation; however, the process of reflecting on this dilemma will help you think about what you might do if this did happen to you. Sometimes when a situation arises that we didn't anticipate, we react and say things before we think. This reflection process will allow you to "pause" and think about what you would like to say next.

Dilemma 1: Choosing to Be a Teacher

You have been assigned a mentee and have had your first meeting at the orientation. You are an experienced dedicated teacher who absolutely loves teaching. You are ready to share ideas and support a beginner. He is a personable young man, and you shared the Relationship Profile (page 14 Part 1) with him to begin the conversation. During the conversation, you discover that he isn't really sure he wants to be a teacher. His parents and other friends have questioned his decision and said, "You are so smart, why are you going to be a teacher?" His advisor at college says he is a natural, but now he is unsure as he prepares for his first classroom. *What do you say at a future meeting?*

Respond to these prompts in your Mentor Planning Guide and Journal available on the companion website.

1. State the mentor dilemma as clearly as possible in one sentence if you can.

2. What decision do you need to make in regard to this situation?

3. Write about the emotions that come up for you that relate to this situation. If you have two choices, write how the emotions might be different.

4. Stop and reread what you have written. Underline any key words or phrases that stand out for you.

5. Soften your eyes or close them and take three deep breaths. Ask yourself, what am I missing that I have not noticed? Write that down in your journal.

6. What will you say to your mentee? Write your reflection in your journal.

7. If you are truly stuck, bring your dilemma to your lead mentor, a mentor support group, or another experienced mentor. Ask him or her to listen to what you have written and to ask you questions to clarify your dilemma. *Your lead mentor's role is not to tell you what to do! No advice!* Just questions to help you clarify what you want to do.

8. After you have spoken to your mentee, write his reaction and how you feel about this dilemma now. All dilemmas are not resolved! This is a process of clarifying and understanding how you feel and how you could respond.

Directions: Complete all three goal-setting processes and write your responses on this page or in your Mentor Planning Guide and Journal available on the companion website.

1. *Goal for Improving Your Mentee's Teaching Practices*

   - Review the PLAN–CONNECT–ACT–REFLECT pages you completed in this chapter with your mentee. Look ahead to September ACTs to see what you may focus on to continue development.

   - Acknowledge what your mentee is learning. Be specific and consider using the 5 Minute Meeting *Giving an Authentic Compliment* in the Appendices to guide you.

   - Agree on ONE goal to focus on and reinforce for next month.

   - Goal:

2. *Goal to Support the Social and Emotional Well-Being of Your Mentee*

   - Discuss any challenges your mentee may be facing right now. Challenges often bring stress.

   - Don't ignore any signs of stress in your mentee. Pay attention and teach her ways to manage her stress. Using mindfulness practices can help reduce stress. To learn more about mindfulness and managing stress, watch the *Mindfulness* video and read the "Benefits of Mindfulness" article and discuss it together. Both are available on the companion website.

   - Goal:

3. *Goal for Enhancing Your Mentoring Skills*

   - Reflect on your own mentoring experience this month. How did you use your strengths and interests to mentor? What will you do differently next month? Write a reflection in your Mentor Planning Guide and Journal.

   - Goal:

"

A good teacher is someone who is helpful, thoughtful, smart, knows how to teach, and loves kids."

—THIRD-GRADE STUDENT

NEW TEACHER PHASE: NERVOUS AND READY

"I feel prepared to teach, but I don't know what to do the first day."

MINDFUL MENTORING AFFIRMATION

I am an advocate for my novice teacher.

SEPTEMBER

BEGINNING THE SCHOOL YEAR SUCCESSFULLY

Creating a Community of Learners in the Classroom

GUIDING QUESTIONS

1. How do you help your novice teacher create a community of learners? The **Relationship ACTivities** will provide ways to approach this task.

2. How will you help your novice teacher in implementing routines? The **Routines ACTivities** offer you ideas to discuss.

3. How will you reinforce classroom and behavior management and introduce looking at student work? Use the **Student ACTivities** as a way to begin the focus on student products. There will be a page on this topic each month.

4. Why is it important to encourage your mentee to reach out to parents? Use the **Communication ACTivity** as a way to focus on ways to connect with parents and families.

Interstate Teacher Assessment and Support Consortium—InTASC Standards

This month will focus on introducing InTASC Standards 1 and 2.

For the complete list of standards, go to page 6 in Part I of this book.

- **Standard 1 Learner Development**

The teacher understands how learners grow and develop, recognizing that patterns of learning and development vary individually within and across the cognitive, linguistic, social, emotional, and physical areas, and designs and implements developmentally appropriate and challenging learning experiences.

- **Standard 2 Learning Differences**

The teacher uses understanding of individual differences and diverse cultures and communities to ensure inclusive learning environments that enable each learner to meet high standards.

Chapter Overview

A wise person once said, "Wisdom is not knowing what to do ultimately, it is knowing what to do next." As a mentor, you must be willing to have conversations that relate to building student learning communities in the classroom. Relationships with students are crucial to a novice teacher's success in the classroom. Students are disruptive if they are bored or if they feel the teacher doesn't know them. By helping your mentee relate to students, you can help maximize student learning in your novice teacher's classroom.

Mentoring is not about "telling" but more about "creating" opportunities where your mentee can discover what to do next. As a mentor, you will have lots of advice about survival and creating a community of learners. Your challenge will be holding back a bit and allowing the novice teacher to experience the process while you guide, question, and assist. Hold back. Become a listener. This may not be as easy as it sounds, especially in September when there is so much to do.

If you are working with more than one novice, consider bringing them together in a group and have them share what they are doing to create community in their classrooms. Facilitate the discussion and minimize your talking. Share the student's quote from the beginning of this chapter with the group and see how they react. Students still want to be liked by their teacher. Invite the novice teachers to share what they think this student means.

Your Mindful Mentoring Affirmation this month is, "I am an advocate for my novice teacher." Take the time to learn what your novice teacher needs right now. You will be the closest person to this beginner, and your guidance is essential to his growth.

Follow the PLAN, CONNECT, ACT, REFLECT, and SET GOALS sections in this chapter to guide your mentoring conversations and reflections.

Watch and listen to a mentor share her insights in the September Chapter Introduction (Video 2.5), available on the companion website or by scanning the QR code on a mobile device.

Use the Mentor Planning Guide and Journal to plan your meetings and record your reflections for this month.

VIDEO 2.5

September Chapter Introduction

Use Questions to Guide Mentoring Conversations

Sometimes beginning teachers don't know what to ask their mentors because they don't know what they don't know! If your novice teacher doesn't have any questions, share this list and invite the mentee to choose some questions. What is your PLAN for responding to your mentee's questions? How will you listen to your mentee's needs?

Anticipate Beginning Teachers' Possible Questions

1. How do I create a community of learners? What does that mean?

2. Can you review how children learn at this age level?

3. How many of my students need support in English language learning, and what should I do to help them integrate socially and academically?

4. I need some help setting up routines in my classroom that will avoid misbehavior. Can you share some successful ways for setting up a classroom in September?

5. What are self-motivating strategies for students?

6. What do I do if a student misbehaves?

Note the other questions your novice teacher asked you so you will have them for the future.

Questions for Your Novice Teacher

Try to ask more questions to learn about your novice teacher, rather than telling.

1. What is your understanding of child/adolescent development?

2. At which level did you complete your student teaching?

3. How confident are you in starting the year?

4. What can I do to assist you right now that will reduce your anxiety?

Meetings and Observations

Plan brief weekly meetings with your mentee. The ACTs in this chapter serve as mentoring conversation starters and can also be used to assess or review what your mentee may already know about a given topic. Use the Appendices to guide you in scheduling short meetings as well as longer conversations.

Plan to meet at times that allow you to have quality time together in a place without interruptions. Knowing when you will meet each week reduces anxiety for both of you. Novice teachers look forward to regularly scheduled meetings even if they are short. Use a calendar to plan your meetings and classroom visits to ensure they will happen! Include watching videos and reading pages in the *Mentoring in Action* book as part of your *PLAN* for mentoring. A digital version of this calendar (September Calendar.pdf) is available on the companion website.

You don't have to observe the teacher "teaching" right now, but it is important to at least visit her classroom. A before school or after school visit is an opportunity for you to observe how the room is organized as well as to have her show and tell you what she has done so far. Plan a classroom visit now to ensure you fit it into your schedule.

September Calendar

MONDAY	TUESDAY	WEDNESDAY	THURSDAY	FRIDAY

Use this calendar to PLAN the month as well as to document meetings and mentor planning.

CONNECT to Additional Resources

CONNECT to School and District Resources

What resources exist in your school and community that could assist novice teachers in beginning the school year successfully?

CONNECT With Colleagues and Parents

1. Who are the teachers you want your mentee to know?

2. Who or what agency in the community could provide resources or support for no or low cost?

3. How will you share the nontraditional family models that may exist within your school and district? (e.g., Grandparents, single mothers or fathers, legal guardians, same gender parents, etc.)

CONNECT to Student Voices

When you walk into a classroom, you should see positive evidence of students. Whether their names are on the walls, photos are posted, or student work is on the wall of fame. Seeing students "in the room" when they are not physically in the room demonstrates the visible mark that students have in the classroom. Discuss this important topic, using the form titled "How Do Students *Show Up* in the Classroom?" available on the companion website.

CONNECT to Education Hot Topics

Organize your space! As you assist your mentee in organizing her first classroom, discuss the ways the space can be most effectively. Search for online tips such as "Easy ways to make your space work for you and your students." Explore articles online to find out how wall color, lighting, and eliminating clutter influence the classroom environment.

CONNECT With the Companion Website

Video links, forms for this chapter, a featured book, and other resources are located at http://resources.corwin.com/mentoringinaction.

The First ACT!

Differentiating Mentoring Conversations

Teaching is complex work, and novice teachers can easily become overwhelmed. It is appropriate to customize your mentoring conversations to respond to the varied needs and skills of the mentee.

Directions: Interview your mentee at the beginning of the month to document her areas of strength and needs. Skim the ACTs for this month and decide together which topics are most relevant. Use your state or district teaching standards to focus the mentee's responses to each prompt so you are also teaching her the "common language" of the standards.

Mentee _____ Date _____

Monthly Needs Assessment

1. What is going well in your classroom? (i.e., What is working?) As a teacher, what do you feel you are doing well right now? *Refer to the teaching standards to guide your response.*	3. What would you like to improve or enhance in your practice this month? *Refer to the teaching standards to guide your response.*
2. How do you know your practice is working? (i.e., What is your evidence of success? or Why do you feel confident or competent in an aspect of your teaching?)	4. Review the ACT mentoring conversations for this month with your mentee. Ask which of the ACTs will support you in enhancing your teaching practice? (i.e., What would you like us to focus on this month?)

Companion Website

A digital version of this template (Monthly Needs Assessment Sample With Standards.pdf) is available on the companion website. Keep a copy of this assessment for your files and make a copy for the mentee.

Overview of the ACTs for September Conversations

Directions: Skim the ACTivities listed here and complete the pages that will forward your novice teacher's learning. Your mentee also has complementary ACTs in *The First Years Matter*. Digital copies of any of the reproducible ACTs are available on the companion website.

Key Question Topic	ACTivities	PAGE
Relationship	ACT 1 **Creating a Community of Learners in the Classroom**	56
Relationship	ACT 2 **Getting to Know the Students**	57
Relationship	ACT 3 **Creating a Classroom Profile**	58
Relationship	ACT 4 **Learning How Students Learn**	59
Routines	ACT 5 **Establishing and Implementing Routines**	60
Routines	ACT 6 **Rules, Rewards, and Consequences**	61
Routines	ACT 7 **Learning School Procedures**	62
Students	ACT 8 **Classroom and Behavior Management Issues**	63
Students	ACT 9 **Looking at Student Work Together**	64
Communicate	ACT 10 **Communicating With Parents**	65

SEPTEMBER

Creating a Community of Learners in the Classroom

Key Question: What should you review about building a learning community?

Directions: Review the list of ideas on this page and choose the topics that are most relevant to your novice teacher.

1. How does an effective teacher include students of other cultures in the community?

2. What does "respect" look like in the classroom, and how does a novice teacher create a respectful classroom?

3. Invite your mentee to share what she knows about team building and student communities.

4. How can student sharing create a safe and respectful classroom? Discuss this idea. Start the day or class with 5 minutes of student sharing time. Rationale: Students come to school with lots of issues related to their personal lives. Getting to know each other, learning how to listen, and respecting the lives of others can enhance a classroom community.

5. How can student partners help to build a spirit of teamwork? Discuss this idea. Allow students to work together, sit together, and support each other in learning. Rationale: Students want to talk to each other. By trying to keep them quiet all day, we attempt an impossible task. Letting students talk to a partner allows them to release energy and stay on task. By organizing sharing partners, novice teachers can structure student talking time and use it to create a sharing classroom. For example, when a student is absent, his or her partner can collect all the work and share.

6. How can learning teams and small groups make school more engaging for students who want to interact? Teams can work on projects, create team slogans, and challenge each other in academic contests. Why is it important to rotate teams periodically? Rationale: Teamwork is more fun for some students and teaches students how to work together to achieve learning goals.

7. How can student compliments encourage kindness? Students who give each other compliments at the end of the day as part of the teacher's routine feel good when they leave school and want to come back the next day. Rationale for this activity: Everyone likes to hear that his classmates notice what he is doing to build a community in the classroom. Discuss how the teacher has to model the compliment process by giving compliments to students. Positive words create caring communities.

What ideas does your mentee have for creating positive learning environments?

.udents?

: needs, and responding to their
. Many first-year teachers make the
ifficulty being a teacher later in the year.
ə assist your mentee. Your novice teacher
he First Years Matter. At a meeting,
A digital version can be found on the

ı complete a short-answer survey.

- What do you like most about school?

- What do you think your strengths are in the classroom?

- How do you learn best?

- What is your favorite subject? Why?

- What language do you speak at home?

- Have you ever traveled to another country?

- What could I help you learn this year?

- What do you wish you could do in school?

- What is your favorite sport or hobby?

- Do you play a musical instrument?

- Adapt questions to meet the needs and ages of students. Novice teachers may have to read the questions to younger children and write their answers on the board, or students can circle a smiley or frown faces to express their opinion.

    1. *Option:* Select a question and have students write the answers on an index card. Make sure students write their names on the cards!

    2. *Take photographs of each student.* Students love it, and it will help you learn their names and faces. This may be more appropriate for younger students. A whole-class photograph is fun for all age groups.

    3. *Interview a few students.* Ask them to talk about their experiences in school and share how they best learn. You can assist your novice teacher in documenting the responses using audio features on phones or tablets. Be sure to get permission from students and parents.

    4. *What are your ideas for getting to know your students?*

Companion
Website

Creating a Classroom Profile

Key Question: Why is it important for a novice to see the entire classroom in one document?

Directions: Assist your novice teacher in charting the students in the classroom. You may want to do this in your classroom first to model the process and illustrate the value of seeing the big picture of who the students are in your room. These data are important to defining the community of learners. The novice teacher and you can find the information about the students through observing, reviewing class records, distributing a written survey, conducting interviews, and talking with other teachers. The more the novice knows about the students the easier it is to create and maintain a positive learning environment. Your novice teacher will have the Student Profiles form in their book, *The First Years Matter*. At a meeting, be prepared to discuss his answers to the questions. A digital version can be found on the companion website.

Directions to the Novice Teacher: Modify the categories with those you would find more useful.

STUDENT Name	Gender	Ethnicity	Age	First Language	Musical Talent	Artistic Interests	Athletic Ability	Learning Style	Special Need

Learning How Students Learn

Key Question: How does a novice teacher find out his students' learning preferences?

Directions: Being able to recognize the variety of learning styles will assist your mentee in designing effective lessons and engaging students in the learning process. Your novice teacher will have the Class Overview of Learning Preferences in their book, *The First Years Matter*. At a meeting, be prepared to discuss his answers to the questions. A digital version can be found on the companion website.

Discuss with the mentee how to be mindful of her preferred teaching style so she can meet the preferred learning needs of her students.

Class Overview of Learning Preferences

Directions for the Novice Teacher: Create a survey or interview your students to find out their learning preferences. Integrate these options into your lesson plans to engage more students.

I learn best by . . .	List the names of the students in your class who prefer each learning method.
Listening to the teacher, an audio book, etc.	
Seeing a visual diagram, map, or agenda, etc.	
Using manipulatives, blocks, building models, etc.	
Writing essays, paper pencil, or computer typing	
Writing poetry, songs, or raps	
Singing songs and performing	
Debating, interviewing, and presenting information	
Producing videos	
Reading text in books or on the computer	
Drawing, painting making diagrams, or charts	
Using the web to research and find answers	
Acting, dramatization, role playing	
Ask your students to respond to these two prompts.	Names of students
1. I prefer to work in groups with other students.	
2. I prefer to learn alone.	

Companion Website

Establishing and Implementing Routines

Key Question: Why is it important to discuss routines with your mentee?

Directions: Routines are important for maintaining consistency and moving through a teaching day in a predictable manner so students know what to expect. Establishing routines can save valuable time and energy that can be put into academic areas. Discuss these sample routines listed here and review the questions at the end of the page. Assist your mentee in creating appropriate routines for his classroom.

1. *Routines at the beginning of the day or beginning of a class*
   - Attendance and how to handle students who are absent so they get make-up work
   - Lunch count
   - Collecting homework and recording it

2. *Procedures for students' moving*
   - Walking to classes or in the classroom
   - Leaving during class time to go to the restroom or locker
   - Fire drills and emergency exits

3. *Routines and procedures for academic work*
   - Rewarding good behavior and/or consequences for misbehavior
   - How to listen to others during a discussion
   - What to do when students forget books, pencils, or materials
   - What students do who finish early

4. *Closing of the school day or a class*
   - Collecting work at the end of the day or class
   - Cleaning up materials and supplies
   - Exiting the class or building

Review these questions with your mentee.

1. What is the purpose of routines, and why are they important to classroom management?

2. How will you know when students understand a routine?

3. How does an effective teacher reinforce a routine that is already established?

4. How does an effective teacher introduce a new routine to the class?

5. How do routines save time that can be used for teaching and learning?

Rules, Rewards, and Consequences

Key Question: How do the rules, rewards, and consequences a teacher creates and implements contribute to establishing a positive community of learners?

Directions: Discuss the ways rules are created in this school and the types of rules you have in your classroom. Novice teachers who have difficulty managing a classroom often tend to create harsh rules like "no talking!" or "no getting out of your seat," and these "no rules" are problematic for many students who have difficulty if their preferred style of learning is more social. How will you support a novice teacher in creating appropriate rules? Your novice teacher will have the form below in their book, *The First Years Matter*. At a meeting, be prepared to discuss his answers to the questions. A digital version can be found on the companion website.

Creating Rules, Rewards, and Consequences
That Promote a Positive Learning Environment

Directions for the novice teacher: Reflect and respond to these questions. E-mail your responses to your mentor and discuss them at your next meeting. Bring a copy of your rules, a sample of rewards, and what consequences you are using.

1. What rules, rewards, or consequences systems are working for you so far?

2. How do you let students know what the consequences are *prior* to their breaking a rule?

3. What are some problems, issues, or concerns you have about this topic?

4. How is "respect" demonstrated in your classroom? How do you model respect?

5. What does being a "culturally sensitive teacher" mean to you? How do you demonstrate that?

Companion
Website

Learning School Procedures

Key Question: What does your mentee need to know about the following procedures?

Directions: Getting oriented to the systems and procedures in a school and district can be frustrating and confusing for a novice teacher. One way you can help is to be proactive and discuss the procedures early on and share any specific issues that would be helpful. We all have had experiences of touching a book in the library and finding out there is a "procedure" that this librarian uses. Save your mentee from the distress of learning the hard way. Discuss the procedures below and add your own.

1. **How does a teacher . . .**

   - Sign out books from the resource center or library?
   - Use any computers or other equipment—where to get it and how to sign it out?
   - Reserve books for class lessons?
   - Order paper and school supplies?
   - Deal with medical emergencies?
   - Access student records and special education files?
   - Call for a substitute and leave work for the day?

2. What does a teacher do . . .

   - Before school; and how does she enter the building?
   - During homeroom or lunch room?
   - At recess, bus duty, or study hall?

3. How does a teacher use . . .

   - Faculty-only rooms?
   - The library or computer room?
   - An aide or paraprofessional in the classroom?

Classroom and Behavior Management Issues

Key Question: How do routines minimize disruptions and promote a positive learning environment?

Directions: We all have heard that a prepared and organized teacher has fewer discipline issues in the classroom. To ensure your mentee is prepared means you have to be proactive in reviewing routines and organizational structures that need to be in place. You can't assume he understands how to organize his time, classroom space, and materials even though you may have touched on it. By discussing these topics up front, you minimize the stress that can be created from a disorganized classroom. Review the following topics and select the topics that are most appropriate for you and your mentee right now.

1. *Classroom Routines and Organization*

   - Review what your novice teacher is doing in their classrooms to organize their space, time, and materials. Visit the classroom and have her show and tell what she is doing.

   - Share effective systems that work for you for correcting papers, organizing materials, and grading student work. Focus on routines that save time and that may have taken years for you to figure out. Let the mentee know that she doesn't need to reinvent the wheel. But be careful not to dictate ideas and expect them all to be followed. Allow the novice to select the systems that fit for her and have that be okay with you.

   - Organize a "sharing" meeting and invite other novice teachers to meet with your mentee to share successful ideas for organizing systems that save time in the classroom.

   - Share efficient ways to begin and end lessons so that housekeeping activities required (such as collecting lunch money or homework) take minimal time away from classroom instruction.

2. *Behavior Issues With Individual Students or the Whole Class*

   - Ask novice teachers if they are having any problems right now. If you are working with a small group of novice teachers, take one of the problems and work together to give the group some suggestions regarding possible solutions. Use the Problems to Possibilities template in the Appendices to guide your inquiry.

   - Schedule time for your mentee to interview teachers at the school who have creative ways to avoid behavior problems.

   - Discuss appropriate consequences for situations that arise in the classroom. Share the difference between students not completing homework and students who are seriously disrespectful to others and why the consequences have to be different.

Companion Website

SEPTEMBER

Looking at Student Work Together

Key Question: How can looking at student work samples help a novice improve her practice?

Directions: Reflect on your skill as a teacher and mentor in looking at student work and assessing progress. If you feel confident with your skill, invite your mentee to bring a stack of student assignments to a meeting with you. Have her select three students from the class randomly (without looking at names). If you are using a school-based rubric for assessing student work, use that to review the assignment and grade the student. If you are not confident at this time, learn how to do this together! A mentor does not have to be perfect at everything!

1. Decide on the criteria for assessment and then rate the three random papers separately using the school rubric or this one. You will be using the same three papers for this activity.

1	2	3	4	5
Does Not Meet Any Criteria	**Meets a Few Criteria**	**Meets Some Criteria**	**Meets Most Criteria**	**Meets All Criteria**

2. Compare and share how you rated the students with your mentee. Discuss any differences in ratings and explain why you rated a student that way.

3. What is difficult about rating student work?

4. Why is this important to review student work with each other each month?

Communicating With Parents

Key Question: Why is it important to communicate with parents regularly?

Directions: Discuss ways you and your mentee could communicate with parents this month. Review the examples here and add your own.

1. *Examples of communication may include the following:*

   - *A letter mailed to the home:* Share samples of letters that have been sent to parents from you or other teachers in the school. If the school sends a formal letter welcoming students, give the new teachers a copy. Some teachers also write a letter directly to the students too.

   - A *letter sent via the students:* It may be easier to write a letter and give it to the students to hand deliver to the parents sometime during the first week of school. Novice teachers may want to have a return receipt to ensure the parents or guardians received the communication.

   - *An e-mail to parents:* Some school systems have parent communication through e-mail. If this is an option at your school, discuss the appropriate ways to do this. The downside for e-mail is that the parents then have access to the novice teachers 24 hours a day, and this may be overwhelming.

   - *Letters or e-mails could include a brief biography of the novice teacher, some examples of what the curriculum will include, and ways the parents can keep in touch. Policies for homework and expectations for materials students should bring to class may also be included.*

2. **Organizing a Classroom Social**

If the school does not sponsor an official Open House, you may help your novice teacher organize a social to meet and greet the parents. It could be "coffee and conversation" early in the morning before students arrive or an early evening after parents leave work. The goal is to have parents meet the novice teacher and see the classroom. You could attend to ensure all goes smoothly.

3. *Why It Is Important to Connect With Parents Early?*

   - Builds a relationship with the teacher before there are any student behavior issues.

   - Demonstrates that the teacher is reaching out to share what is going on in the classroom.

   - Allows the teacher to share expectations for learning and homework and gain support.

   - Based on the response from parents, teachers get an indication of who is willing and able to connect (e.g., those parents who may not speak English or parents who work night shifts and can't attend meetings). This gives the novice teacher time to create alternative ways to communicate throughout the school year. It also lets the novice teacher know that parents who cannot attend scheduled conferences still care about their children's progress.

September Mentor Reflections

Directions: Complete any of these prompts that stand out for you and add your own prompts to the blank stems. Write your responses here or use your Mentor Planning Guide and Journal on the companion website. Share your reflections with your mentor coordinator or with other mentors at a mentor support meeting.

Something I learned from my mentee . . .

A goal we need to work on is . . .

Something I would like to work on together . . .

Questions I have . . .

Using Mindfulness to Explore Mentoring Dilemmas

Directions: Read the mentoring dilemma and think about how you would respond in this situation. Consider discussing this dilemma at a mentor support meeting or with another mentor. Share your perspectives about how you would proceed and why you think this would be the best way to forward your novice teacher's practice.

Dilemma 2: Including All Students in the Community of Learners

Your mentee is beginning the school year on a good note, and you have visited her classroom to see how she is organizing the space. You notice that she has several students separated from the class in their own corner. When you ask about this, she says that other teachers in her grade level have told her that these students cause trouble and it is best to keep them separate. When you look at the roster and at the student photos in the room, you notice that these three students are the only students of color in the classroom. *What do you say in your next mentoring conversation?*

Respond to these prompts in your Planning Guide and Journal available on the companion website.

1. State the mentor dilemma as clearly as possible in one sentence if you can.

2. What decision do you need to make in regard to this situation?

3. Write about the emotions that come up for you that relate to this situation. If you have two choices, write how the emotions might be different.

4. Stop and reread what you have written. Underline any key words or phrases that stand out for you.

5. Soften your eyes or close them and take three deep breaths. Ask yourself, what am I missing that I have not noticed? Write that down in your journal.

6. What will you say to your mentee? Write your reflection in your journal.

7. If you are truly stuck, bring your dilemma to your lead mentor, a mentor support group meeting, or another experienced mentor. Ask him or her to listen to what you have written and to ask you questions to clarify your dilemma. *Your lead mentor's role is not to tell you what to do! No advice!* Just questions to help you clarify what you want to do.

8. After you have spoken to your mentee, write his reaction and how you feel about this dilemma now. All dilemmas are not resolved! This is a process of clarifying and understanding how you feel and how you could respond.

Directions: Complete all three goal-setting processes and write your responses on this page or in your Mentor Planning Guide and Journal available on the companion website.

1. *Goal for Improving Your Mentee's Teaching Practices*

   - Review the PLAN–CONNECT–ACT–REFLECT pages you completed in this chapter with your mentee. Look ahead to October ACTs to see what you may focus on to continue development.

   - Acknowledge what your mentee is learning. Be specific about what you have seen that is working.

   - Agree on ONE goal to focus on and reinforce for next month.

   - Goal:

2. *Goal to Support the Social and Emotional Well-Being of Your Mentee*

   - Discuss any challenges your mentee may be facing right now. Challenges often bring stress.

   - Don't ignore any signs of stress in your mentee. Pay attention and teach her ways to manage her stress.

   - Continue to learn about mindfulness by reading *Five Simple Lessons for Social and Emotional Learning for Adults*, available on the companion website.

   - Goal:

3. *Goal for Enhancing Your Mentoring Skills*

   - Reflect on your own mentoring experience this month. How did you use your strengths and interests to mentor? What will you do differently next month? Write a reflection in your Mentor Planning Guide and Journal.

   - Goal:

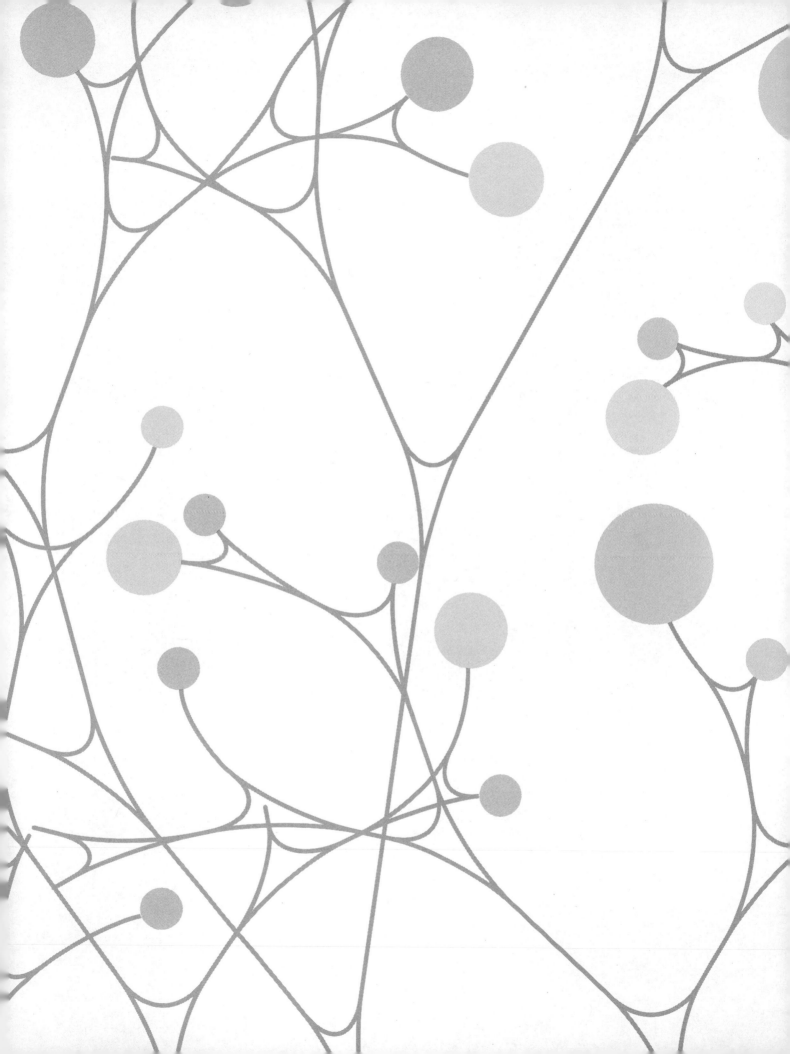

"

A good teacher walks around the classroom helping
everyone do things they don't understand."
—SEVENTH-GRADE STUDENT

NEW TEACHER PHASE: OVERWHELMED

"There is so much to do in one day!"

MINDFUL MENTORING AFFIRMATION

I inspire novice teachers to be their best selves.

OCTOBER

TEACHING FOR UNDERSTANDING
Planning and Delivering Effective Instruction

GUIDING QUESTIONS

1. How do you support your novice in designing effective lesson and unit plans? The *Planning ACTivities* will provide ways to approach this task.

2. How will you include students in your mentoring conversations? Use the *Student ACTivities* as a way to focus on student voices and work.

3. Why is it important to encourage your mentee to reach out to parents? Use the *Communication ACTivity* as a way to focus on ways to connect with parents and families.

Interstate Teacher Assessment and Support Consortium—InTASC Standards

Review InTASC Standards 4 and 7.

- **Standard 4 Content Knowledge**

The teacher understands the central concepts, tools of inquiry, and structures of the discipline(s) he or she teaches and creates learning experiences that make these aspects of the discipline accessible and meaningful for learners to ensure mastery of the content.

- **Standard 7 Planning for Instruction**

The teacher plans instruction that supports every student in meeting rigorous learning goals by drawing upon knowledge of content areas, curriculum, cross-disciplinary skills, and pedagogy, as well as knowledge of learners and the community context.

Chapter Overview

Getting through the first 2 months of school for any new teacher takes energy and lots of support. Every effective teacher will tell you that lesson planning is critical to success. The way a teacher plans influences her ability to organize and structure her time in the classroom. It also minimizes classroom disruption and lets the novice teacher have a clear outline for what will be done in a class or over a timeframe if it is a unit of study. As a mentor, you can provide a safe place for the novice teacher to talk and share her lesson plans. Planning has different formats, and it must be clear to the mentee what is expected by the district. Show her your lesson plans so she understands what the district uses as a format. Use this month to talk about teaching expectations and curriculum requirements too.

If you are working with more than one novice, consider bringing them together in a group and have them share what they are doing to create community in their classrooms. Facilitate the discussion and minimize your talking. Novice teachers feel less overwhelmed when they are talking with other beginners who are facing the same issues.

Your Mindful Mentoring Affirmation this month is, "I inspire novice teachers to be their best selves." This means you need to start where they are, not where you think they should be. Beginning teachers get overwhelmed when they see how easy it is for their mentor, and that it is challenging for them. You can inspire your mentee and other novice teachers in the school to just do their best at this point in time. Tell them it does get easier and that you are there to help. They need to focus on the quote from the student this month and help their students. That is the goal.

Follow the PLAN, CONNECT, ACT, REFLECT, and SET GOALS sections in this chapter to guide your mentoring conversations and reflections.

Watch and listen to a mentor share her insights in the October Chapter Introduction (Video 2.6), available on the companion website or by scanning the QR code on a mobile device.

VIDEO 2.6

October Chapter Introduction

Use Questions to Guide Mentoring Conversations

Invite your mentee to write down a short list of questions and bring them to your first meeting in October. Use the questions below as a guide for your discussions throughout the month.

Anticipate Beginning Teachers' Possible Questions

1   What does the district expect of me as a first-year teacher?

2   How can I learn the district curriculum and goals?

3   How do I make content meaningful when I have the test scores as outcomes of success?

4   How much planning do I have to do? Are my lesson plans reviewed by the principal?

5   Will I be observed this month?

6   How can I backward plan so I can get through the content in a timely way?

7   Can you give me some successful strategies for engaging learners in interactive ways that won't lead to misbehavior?

List the other questions your novice teacher brought to the meeting below so you will have them for your next mentoring cycle.

Questions for Your Novice Teacher

Try to ask more questions to learn about your new teachers, rather than telling.

1   What do you know about teaching for understanding? Have you taken a course that covers this topic?

2   What do you already know about our district goals and curriculum?

3   How did your favorite teachers make content meaningful for you as a student?

4   What can I do to assist you right now that would reduce your anxiety?

Meetings and Observations

Plan brief weekly meetings with your mentee. The ACTs in this chapter serve as mentoring conversation starters and can also be used to assess or review what your mentee may already know about a given topic. Use the Appendices to guide you in scheduling short meetings as well as longer conversations.

Plan to meet at times that allow you to have quality time together in a place without interruptions. Knowing when you will meet each week reduces anxiety for both of you. Novice teachers look forward to regularly scheduled meetings even if they are short. Use a calendar to plan your meetings and classroom visits to ensure they will happen! Include watching videos and reading pages in the *Mentoring in Action* book as part of your *PLAN* for mentoring. A digital version of this calendar (October Calendar.pdf) is available on the companion website.

If you haven't visited your mentee's classroom yet, do so this month. Ask the teacher to give you a tour of the classroom space and have her explain why things are in certain places. Also invite your mentee to visit your classroom and do a tour for her. Compare and share how you use space in each of your classrooms. Discuss how students' work and personalities will be integrated into the space.

October Calendar

MONDAY	TUESDAY	WEDNESDAY	THURSDAY	FRIDAY

Use this calendar to PLAN the month as well as to document meetings and mentor planning.

CONNECT to Additional Resources

CONNECT to School and District Resources

What resources exist in your school and community that could assist novice teachers in October?

CONNECT With Colleagues, Parents, and Families

What are the protocols for communicating with parents and families?

CONNECT to Student Voices

Watch the *Teachers Make a Difference* video available on the companion website with your mentee to hear a candid statement from a high school student. Respond to these prompts together. What surprised you in what Jennifer shared? How does Jennifer's perspective influence your thinking about teaching and learning?

CONNECT to Education Hot Topics

Include the arts! Creativity and the arts can get lost in the classroom when the focus is often on test scores and achievement. Review the articles on Teach HUB to find some ideas for integrating creativity into everyday school assignments. By giving students options for demonstrating their learning, she will be engaging more learners.

CONNECT With the Companion Website

Video links, forms for this chapter, a featured book, and other resources are located at http://resources.corwin.com/mentoringinaction.

The First ACT!

Differentiating Mentoring Conversations

Teaching is complex work, and novice teachers can easily become overwhelmed. It is appropriate to customize your mentoring conversations to respond to the varied needs and skills of the mentee.

Directions: Interview your mentee at the beginning of the month to document her areas of strength and needs. Skim the ACTs for this month and decide together which topics are most relevant. Use your state or district teaching standards to focus the mentee's responses to each prompt so you are also teaching her the "common language" of the standards.

Mentee _____ Date _____

Monthly Needs Assessment

1. What is going well in your classroom? (i.e., What is working?) As a teacher, what do you feel you are doing well right now? *Refer to the teaching standards to guide your response.*	3. What would you like to improve or enhance in your practice this month? *Refer to the teaching standards to guide your response.*
2. How do you know your practice is working? (i.e., What is your evidence of success? or Why do you feel confident or competent in an aspect of your teaching?)	4. Review the ACT mentoring conversations for this month with your mentee. Ask which of the ACTs will support you in enhancing your teaching practice? (i.e., What would you like us to focus on this month?)

A digital version of this template (Monthly Needs Assessment Sample With Standards.pdf) is available on the companion website. Keep a copy of this assessment for your files and make a copy for the mentee.

Overview of the ACTs for October Conversations

Directions: Skim the ACTivities listed here and complete the pages that will forward your novice teacher's learning. Your mentee has complementary ACTs in *The First Years Matter.* Digital copies of any of the reproducible ACTs are available on the companion website.

Key Question Topic	ACTivities	PAGE
Planning	ACT 1 **Organizing a Lesson Plan**	78
Planning	ACT 2 **Questions About Planning**	79
Planning	ACT 3 **Planning for Understanding**	80
Planning	ACT 4 **Engaging Learners**	81
Planning	ACT 5 **Pacing a Lesson**	82
Planning	ACT 6 **Unit Planning**	83
Students	ACT 7 **Student Perspectives**	84
Students	ACT 8 **Classroom and Behavior Management Issues**	85
Students	ACT 9 **Looking at Student Work Together**	86
Communicate	ACT 10 **Communicating With Parents**	87

Organizing a Lesson Plan

Key Question: How will you review lesson plan formats with your mentee?

Directions: Review this sample format for a lesson plan with your mentee and review the questions in each section. If your district requires a different format, share that now. Discuss ways to use a long form plan and a shorter version for the plan book. Share your planning process and why it is important.

Sample Planning Template

Lesson plan title: *Write the name of the topic or class here*   **Date:** *Day you teach lesson*

Time of class: *Period or time*   **Length of period:** *How much time to teach*

Subject: *Content*

Purpose of lesson: *Why are you teaching this lesson?*

State Standard: *What is the standard you are reaching?*

Objective: *Bloom's taxonomy verb—what the student will achieve or accomplish*

Theme or unit #___: *Is this an isolated lesson or part of a bigger curriculum unit?*

Key questions: *The questions you will introduce to the students to guide the discussion and activities of the lesson should be broadly designed to encourage discussion and critical thinking.*

Procedure: *Note that the class period includes other housekeeping activities, such as collecting papers, announcing future school activities, or collecting lunch money. These need to be incorporated into the lesson plan to avoid running out of teaching time.*

Closing the lesson: *How will you know students learned? Is there a summary? Will you use any informal assessments here?*

Homework: *Required or enrichment?*

Questions About Planning

Key Question: What does your mentee need to know about planning?

Directions: Co-plan a lesson with your mentee using the following questions to guide your discussion.

1. *Why am I teaching this lesson?* required curriculum? student interest? new teacher interest? other?

2. *What do I hope to accomplish?* skill development? concept to be discussed for understanding? product to be produced?

3. *Who are the students?* range of abilities? range of ages? ethnic diversity and varying cultures?

4. *What is the time frame for teaching this lesson?* part of a unit? one period or block schedule? isolated lesson?

5. *How will I begin the lesson to capture student attention?* story, anecdote? relevance to their lives? props or visual displays?

6. *Will I need other resources to teach this lesson?* audiovisual or technology? student handouts? manipulatives or visual displays?

7. *How will students spend their time during the lesson?* small-group discussion? individual? large group? hands-on activity or experiment? taking notes or observing?

8. *How will the learning in this lesson be assessed?* formal? quiz or test? informal? observation of learning? open-ended questions? written? verbal?

9. *How will I summarize the lesson and close the class period?* review and summary? collecting papers? giving next assignment? allowing time for homework or questions?

10. *Will there be homework or enrichment activities offered?* how will I collect later? is it required or extra? will it count? what is cooperating teacher's policy? how will I grade it?

11. *How will I know whether I succeeded in teaching the lesson?* self-assessment? response of students? cooperating teacher input?

12. *How will the next lesson relate to or build on this one?*

Planning for Understanding

Key Question: Why do novice teachers need to understand how planning relates to learning?

Directions: An effective lesson plan promotes student learning and skill development. Discuss with your mentee what her students should know, understand, and be able to do *as a result of teaching a lesson?*

Four Steps to Effective Lesson Planning

1. *Think about breadth or depth* as you design your lessons and units.

    Are you aiming for breadth in your lessons (e.g., being able to connect this concept to other concepts or relevant experiences)?

    - Students explain why or why not.
    - Students extend the concept to others.
    - Students think about and give examples of similar concepts.

    Are you aiming for depth in your lessons (i.e., looking more at the detail about this idea)?

    - Students question the information.
    - Students analyze the facts.
    - Students prove something.

2. *Set priorities* for assessing student growth in lessons and units.

    What do you expect all students to be familiar with?

    - To be able to do in this class?
    - To really understand for lasting learning?

3. *Select measurement tools* to determine student understanding.

    How will you know students understand what you are teaching?

    - What do *all* students have to know? How will you know?
    - What do *most* students have to know? How will you know?
    - What will *some* students have to know? How will you know?

4. *Create meaningful learning experiences* that engage and support learning (not just busywork).

    - Have you included a "hook" to gain attention and provide relevance?
    - Do you have key questions that promote discussion and thinking?
    - Do you have time for students to practice and engage in activity?
    - Do you allow students time to reflect on their work and set goals?

Engaging Learners

Key Question: What strategies will help your mentee engage learners throughout the class?

Directions: Engaging learners when they are transitioning from the hallway to a classroom can be challenging. Beginning the class with a reading, a prop, or a demonstration creates curiosity and a focus on the teacher. Higher order thinking also engages learners because their responses take more time and they need to think about them. Bloom's Taxonomy is one way to integrate language into the lesson plan. Review the chart with your mentee and discuss ways to engage through these activities.

Level of Understanding	Example Verbs
6 Evaluation	choose, conclude, evaluate, defend, rank, support, rate
5 Synthesis	construct, create, formulate, revise, write, plan, predict
4 Analysis	analyze, classify, compare, contrast, debate, categorize
3 Application	apply, demonstrate, draw, show, solve, illustrate
2 Comprehension	describe, explain, paraphrase, summarize, rewrite
1 Knowledge	define, identify, label, list, memorize, spell, name

Companion Website

Pacing a Lesson

Key Question: How will you support your mentee in structuring teaching time effectively?

Directions: One of the biggest concerns teachers have about teaching is that they don't have enough time in the day to do all there is to do. The majority of the time spent in class should be on teaching the curriculum, not on making announcements, collecting lunch money, passing out materials, getting students into groups, or cleaning up. However, these tasks do need to get done too.

A class period is your "allocated teaching time," but it also needs to include housekeeping activities. "Instructional time" is the time when students are actually engaged in learning activities. A lesson plan is the way to organize a teacher's time to ensure the focus is on teaching and learning.

Use the time chart below with one of your mentee's lesson plans and put in the number of minutes that should be allotted to complete each section of the plan.

Allocated Class Time: How Much Should You Spend?		
How much time? 5%	Starting Class Period Housekeeping Activities	• Required tasks • Collection of homework
10%	BEGINNING LESSON Introducing or connecting to previous day Introducing objectives, vocabulary, and key questions	• Motivation/relevance • Overview • Directions • Purpose of lesson
70%	MIDDLE Facilitating a variety of activities for student learning	• Objective • Key questions • Students engaged in learning • Activity • Knowledge • Student sharing • Informal assessment and checking for understanding
10%	CLOSING Summarizing and reviewing lesson Setting goals for next lesson	• Wrap up • Review of key points • Collection of materials/papers
5%	Ending Class Period Housekeeping Activities	• Required tasks • Collection of class work

Companion Website

Unit Planning

Key Question: How will you guide your mentee to develop effective unit plans?

A unit is an organized group of lesson plans with a beginning, various activities, and a culmination activity. The unit may be subject based, interdisciplinary, or thematic. It can last as long as a semester or as short as a week. It has overarching themes and concepts to be learned through daily lessons. A unit will have a general outline or plan for implementation and the daily lesson plans that demonstrate in detail how the plan is to be carried out in the classroom. Lesson plans are part of the unit and would follow the format required.

Directions: Teachers typically organize their teaching in units by skills for early childhood, by subjects or themes for elementary/middle, or by subject area topics at secondary levels. Units are organized around books students have read, historical events, science themes, topics, or anything teachers can think of that relates to knowledge. Discuss how your school organizes units of study with your mentee. Review these overarching questions.

Questions to Review With Your Mentee

- What is the purpose of the unit?

- How much time is allotted to complete the unit? How many lessons?

- What do students already know about this topic?

- What would students like to learn or know?

- How will the unit be introduced?

- What are the key questions that need to be answered?

- Is prior knowledge necessary?

- Will the unit have a theme?

- Will the unit cross disciplines? Is team teaching involved?

- Will any special activities be part of the unit?

- Will I need special materials or audiovisual for this unit?

- Will guest speakers or field trips be part of the unit?

- Other questions you may introduce . . .

Companion Website

OCTOBER

Student Perspectives

Key Question: Why do student perspectives matter?

Planning and delivering effective instruction requires the students be full participants in their learning. Novice teachers often struggle because they know their content but say the students just won't listen. Planning effective lessons certainly is important but clearly the students have a lot to say about how they learn best.

In Part I, Qualities of Effective Mentors, a PDF titled *An Interactive Guide to Using Student Perspectives* was highlighted as a way to talk about students with your mentee. This resource includes sample student surveys, a protocol for the mentor, and videos of mentoring conversations that illustrate how to talk about student survey data with a novice teacher.

Directions: Watch Video 2.7, *Reactions to the Student Survey*, with your novice teacher and discuss why it is important to ask the students what they think. Review the sample surveys available in the *Using Student Perspectives Interactive Guide* PDF located in Part I on the companion website. Review these questions to guide your discussion.

VIDEO 2.7

Reactions to the Student Survey

Creating an Anonymous Student Survey

1. What was your mentee's reaction to the video?

2. What does she want to know from the students to improve her teaching?

VIDEO 2.8

Using a Seven Step Protocol to Discuss Student Survey Data With Novice Teachers

3. Which questions on the sample survey can you use?

4. What new questions will you add?

VIDEO COLLECTION 2.9

Sample Mentoring Conversations

5. How will you help your mentee administer the survey?

6. When will you review the data?

Companion Website

Before meeting to discuss the data, watch Video 2.8, *Using a Seven Step Protocol to Discuss Student Survey Data With Novice Teachers*, to guide your conference and review the videos of sample mentoring conversations (Video Collection 2.9) on the companion website.

Classroom and Behavior Management Issues

Key Question: What does your mentee need to think about before disciplining a student?

Directions: Review these questions with your mentee so they become more familiar.

1. Who is the student?

   Does this student have a prearranged plan when disruptive?

   For example, send to guidance, principal, or resource or learning center classroom?

   Is this a first offense, or is this repeated misbehavior? Is this common misbehavior for others?

   Does this student have a special need that has not been addressed?

   Are there other adults who need to be notified when this student is disruptive?

2. What rule did the student break?

   Is it a major offense? For example, hitting someone or possessing a weapon.

   Is it a minor offense? For example, chewing gum or wearing a hat.

   Is it related to academic work? For example, not doing homework or cheating.

   Is it related to work habits? For example, not listening in class.

   What did the student specifically do or say?

   Is this misbehavior appropriate for the student's age?

3. Where did the misbehavior take place?

   In classroom?

   On playground, hallway, cafeteria, en route to class?

   Off school grounds but near school?

4. Do you have personal feelings about this student?

   Have you interacted positively or negatively before this?

   Do you know this student at all?

5. What are your legal rights when dealing with disruptive students?

   State and local guidelines for restraining students, searching lockers, etc.?

   School policies related to alcohol, drugs, weapons?

   Students with educational plans?

Companion
Website

Looking at Student Work Together

Key Question: How can looking at student work samples assist your mentee?

Directions: Invite your mentee to bring several samples from one lesson to a meeting. Review the samples following these lenses: Standards, Quality, and Expectations. Discuss the importance of looking at student work systematically.

Three Lenses for Looking at Work

1. **Standards**

   What was the objective of this assignment? Is that clear in the samples?

   What were the students supposed to accomplish? Did they?

2. **Quality**

   What did the work look like? Is it presented neatly?

   Can you tell if the students are proud of their work?

3. **Expectations**

   What did the novice teacher expect the student(s) to do on this assignment?

   Are those expectations limiting the student's achievement?

Communicating With Parents

Key Question: Why is it important for your mentee to tell parents what is going on in school?

Directions: Discuss possible ways your new teachers can let parents know about the curriculum and the routines of your classroom. Parents often ask their children, "What did you do in school today?" Students respond, "Nothing!" We all know that is not true. Often communication comes when there is a problem and then parents are on the defensive. Discuss these positive ways to connect with parents.

Newsletters

Why not put the students to work and have them write short articles about the lessons they are learning in school and turn it into a newsletter for parents? Novice teachers can use this as a learning experience for students while informing parents. *Education Matters!* could be the name of the newsletter, or students could vote on a name they like. Students can hand deliver the newsletter, or it could be mailed or e-mailed directly to the parents.

Classroom Open House

Another way novice teachers can connect with parents and share what is going in the classroom is to host an open house in the classroom. Invite the parents in for "coffee and conversation" early in the morning before students arrive or include students. Share the logistics of this type of event with your mentee. Brainstorm ways students can show off their work and how your mentee can let parents know how they can help their children learn.

Classroom Web Page

Many teachers entering the profession have technology skills and are able to create web pages. If your school and district have the capabilities for a web-based newsletter, encourage the novice teachers to do it. It is a fun and easy way to get the parents' attention!

Cable TV Show

Another option for sharing what is going on could be a classroom TV show. Let students produce and direct a show that lets parents know what they are learning. Novice teachers may not have time for one on their own, but perhaps several teachers could get together and put on short segments. It would also be a great way to introduce the novice teachers to the school district!

October Mentor Reflections

Directions: Complete any of these prompts that stand out for you and add your own prompts to the blank stems. Write your responses here or use your Mentor Planning Guide and Journal on the companion website. Share your reflections with your mentor coordinator or with other mentors at a mentor support meeting.

A compliment I have for my new teachers . . .

What I am learning about being a mentor . . .

Questions I need to ask my new teachers . . .

Something I would like to share is . . .

Using Mindfulness to Explore Mentoring Dilemmas

Directions: Read the mentoring dilemma and think about how you would respond in this situation. Consider discussing this dilemma at a mentor support meeting or with another mentor. Share your perspectives about how you would proceed and why you think this would be the best way to forward your novice teacher's practice.

Dilemma 3: So Many Teaching Practices Off Track

You decide to pop in for an unannounced short observation (which your mentee said is okay to do) and watch the opening of a lesson. You notice several teaching practices that she is not implementing, and you wonder if she has a formal lesson plan because it seems a bit disorganized. You made an assumption that she knew how to do lesson plans and had an understanding of engaging learners in relevant ways. What you are seeing is direct instruction with silent students doing worksheets. She took 10 minutes to give instructions, and students still had so many questions they didn't know what to do. She started to get frustrated and called for heads down! You left the room to go to your class. *What do you say in your postconference?*

Respond to these prompts in your Mentor Planning Guide and Journal available on the companion website.

1. State the mentor dilemma as clearly as possible in one sentence if you can.

2. What decision do you need to make in regard to this situation?

3. Write about the emotions that come up for you that relate to this situation. If you have two choices, write how the emotions might be different.

4. Stop and reread what you have written. Underline any key words or phrases that stand out for you.

5. Soften your eyes or close them and take three deep breaths. Ask yourself, what am I missing that I have not noticed? Write that down in your journal.

6. What will you say to your mentee? Write your reflection in your journal.

7. If you are truly stuck, bring your dilemma to your lead mentor, a mentor support group meeting, or another experienced mentor. Ask him or her to listen to what you have written and to ask you questions to clarify your dilemma. *Your lead mentor's role is not to tell you what to do! No advice!* Just questions to help you clarify what you want to do.

8. After you have spoken to your mentee, write his reaction and how you feel about this dilemma now. All dilemmas are not resolved! This is a process of clarifying and understanding how you feel and how you could respond.

Directions: Complete all three goal-setting processes and write your responses on this page or in your Mentor Planning Guide and Journal available on the companion website.

1. *Goal for Improving Your Mentee's Teaching Practices*

    - Review the PLAN–CONNECT–ACT–REFLECT pages you completed in this chapter with your mentee. Look ahead to November ACTs to see what you may focus on to continue development.

    - Acknowledge what your mentee is learning. Visit her classroom and point out something good.

    - Agree on ONE goal to focus on and reinforce for next month.

    - Goal:

2. *Goal to Support the Social and Emotional Well-Being of Your Mentee*

    - Discuss any challenges your mentee may be facing right now. Challenges often bring stress.

    - Don't ignore any signs of stress in your mentee. Pay attention and teach her ways to manage her stress. Using mindfulness practices can help reduce stress.

    - Continue to learn about mindfulness by watching Kelly McGonigle's Ted Talk "How to Make Stress Your Friend."

    - Goal:

3. *Goal for Enhancing Your Mentoring Skills*

    - Reflect on your own mentoring experience this month. How did you use your strengths and interests to mentor? What will you do differently next month? Write a reflection in your Mentor Planning Guide and Journal.

    - Goal:

"
I know I have learned something when I have the confidence to do it alone."

—FOURTH-GRADE STUDENT

NEW TEACHER PHASE: DISILLUSIONED

"I'm not sure if I made the right choice to teach. This is really hard."

MINDFUL MENTORING AFFIRMATION

My ability to assist my mentee in listening to student perspectives has the potential to transform her teaching practices.

NOVEMBER

ASSESSING DIVERSE LEARNERS

*How Do Teachers Know
Students Have Learned?*

GUIDING QUESTIONS

1. How do you help your novice teacher plan with assessment in mind? The *Planning ACTivities* will provide ways to think about integrating assessment into lesson plans.

2. How will you help your novice teacher understand assessment tools? The *Tools ACTivities* offer you ideas to discuss.

3. How will you reinforce the student perspective and voice? Use the *Student ACTivities* as a way to guide your conversations.

4. What is important to review regarding parents this month? Use the *Communication ACTivity* as a way to focus.

Interstate Teacher Assessment and Support Consortium—InTASC Standards

Review InTASC Standard 6.

- **Standard 6 Assessment**

The teacher understands and uses multiple methods of assessment to engage learners in their own growth, to monitor learner progress, and to guide the teacher's and learner's decision making.

Chapter Overview

Your mentee may have started teaching idealistically and be full of ideas, but by November she may be disillusioned and question whether she can do this at all. As a mentor, you can provide nurturing and support that reassures her that this is a common phase of teaching. In fact, some experienced teachers are disillusioned in November!

Like the fourth-grade student's quote on the first page of this chapter, "I know I have learned something when I have the confidence to do it alone." In some ways, this comment is similar to what beginning teachers feel. Most novice teachers will have questions, and you can help them with school details, but what they need most of all is confidence. Confidence leads to competence. Competence in teaching then leads to more confidence. Novice teachers are learners, just as their students are this year. Assessing how much students learn will be a parallel process to assessing how much your mentee is learning about how to be an effective teacher.

Your Mindful Mentoring Affirmation this month is, "My ability to assist my mentee in listening to student perspectives has the potential to transform her teaching practices." Refer back to the resources in October ACT 7 to review ways to survey students to keep them central to teaching and use the ideas in this chapter to focus your mentee on students. When students are engaged with their teacher, it does transform the classroom and the relationship with the teacher. Instead of being disinterested and unmotivated, students will know that the teacher cares. This matters to students. They want teachers who listen to them. Share the ways you connect with students and watch the video on the CONNECT page to get some ideas.

Follow the PLAN, CONNECT, ACT, REFLECT, and SET GOALS sections in this chapter to guide your mentoring conversations and reflections.

Watch and listen to a mentor share her insights in the November Chapter Introduction (Video 2.10), available on the companion website or by scanning the QR code on a mobile device.

VIDEO 2.10

November Chapter Introduction

Use Questions to Guide Mentoring Conversations

Invite your mentee to write down a short list of questions and bring them to your first November meeting. Use the questions below as a guide for your discussions throughout the month.

Anticipate Beginning Teachers' Possible Questions

1. Who are my students (languages, learning styles, special needs, learning modifications, family background, etc.)?
2. What do I need to know about their parents that will assist me?
3. How can I set up my lessons and learning to adapt for the needs of my diverse learners?
4. What high-stakes formal assessments are a part of district expectations?
5. What formal assessments should I be creating or using this year?
6. Can you review informal assessments with me?

List the other questions your novice teachers brought to the meeting so you will have them for your next mentoring cycle.

Questions for Your Novice Teacher

Try to ask more questions to learn about your novice teachers, rather than telling.

1. What do you already know about tests and assessments?
2. What do you already know about teaching diverse learners?
3. Share one strategy you have used that assisted a student who was struggling to learn new information.
4. What can I do to assist you right now that would reduce your anxiety?

Meetings and Observations

Plan brief weekly meetings with your mentee. The ACTs in this chapter serve as mentoring conversation starters and can also be used to assess or review what your mentee may already know about a given topic. Use the Appendices to guide you in scheduling short meetings as well as longer conversations.

Plan to meet at times that allow you to have quality time together in a place without interruptions. Knowing when you will meet each week reduces anxiety for both of you. Novice teachers look forward to regularly scheduled meetings even if they are short. Use a calendar to plan your meetings and classroom visits to ensure they will happen! Include watching videos and reading pages in the *Mentoring in Action* book as part of your *PLAN* for mentoring. A digital version of this calendar (November Calendar.pdf) is available on the companion website.

Review your observation policy, and if you are required to observe, schedule time now. Short observations are fine. You can learn a lot by just visiting for 10–15 minutes and having a postconference. For example, just schedule a time to see the "opening" of a lesson to observe how your mentee gives directions and gets students started on a lesson. Or perhaps if closing a lesson is a challenge for her, you may pop in for the last 15 minutes and see how she ends a lesson.

November Calendar

MONDAY	TUESDAY	WEDNESDAY	THURSDAY	FRIDAY

Use this calendar to PLAN the month as well as to document meetings and mentor planning.

CONNECT to Additional Resources

CONNECT to School and District Resources

What resources exist in your school and community that could assist novice teachers in November?

CONNECT With Colleagues, Parents, and Families

How can parents be helpful in having new teachers understand students' learning styles?

CONNECT to Student Voices

Watch the *Qualities of Effective Teachers Through Students Eyes* video available on the companion website with your mentee. Respond to these prompts together. What three things stood out for you in this video? How do these students influence your thinking? What will you change in your teaching as a result of this video?

CONNECT to Education Hot Topics

Grief counseling! Your novice may lose a family member or spouse while you are mentoring. Be prepared to support her in finding the resources to process her grief. She may also have students who need this support. Share the grief support school policies and search for articles online that may help.

CONNECT With the Companion Website

Video links, forms for this chapter, a featured book, and other resources are located at http://resources.corwin.com/mentoringinaction.

The First ACT!

Differentiating Mentoring Conversations

Teaching is complex work, and novice teachers can easily become overwhelmed. It is appropriate to customize your mentoring conversations to respond to the varied needs and skills of the mentee.

Directions: Interview your mentee at the beginning of the month to document her areas of strength and needs. Skim the ACTs for this month and decide together which topics are most relevant. Use your state or district teaching standards to focus the mentee's responses to each prompt so you are also teaching her the "common language" of the standards.

Mentee _____ Date _____

Monthly Needs Assessment

1. What is going well in your classroom? (i.e., What is working?) As a teacher, what do you feel you are doing well right now? *Refer to the teaching standards to guide your response.*	3. What would you like to improve or enhance in your practice this month? *Refer to the teaching standards to guide your response.*
2. How do you know your practice is working? (i.e., What is your evidence of success? or Why do you feel confident or competent in an aspect of your teaching?)	4. Review the ACT mentoring conversations for this month with your mentee. Ask which of the ACTs will support you in enhancing your teaching practice? (i.e., What would you like us to focus on this month?)

A digital version of this template (Monthly Needs Assessment Sample With Standards.pdf) is available on the companion website. Keep a copy of this assessment for your files and make a copy for the mentee.

Overview of the ACTs for November Conversations

Directions: Skim the ACTivities listed here and complete the pages that will forward your novice teacher's learning. Your mentee has complementary ACTs in *The First Years Matter.* Digital copies of any of the reproducible ACTs are available on the companion website.

Key Question Topic	ACTivities	PAGE
Planning	ACT 1 **How Are Students Assessed in the Classroom and District?**	100
Planning	ACT 2 **Linking Lesson Plans to Assessment**	101
Planning	ACT 3 **Product or Process?**	102
Tools	ACT 4 **Formative and Summative Assessments**	103
Tools	ACT 5 **Evidence and Documentation of Progress**	104
Students	ACT 6 **Communicating With Students**	105
Students	ACT 7 **Students Can Share Their Learning**	106
Students	ACT 8 **Classroom and Behavior Management Issues**	107
Students	ACT 9 **Looking at Student Work Together**	108
Communicate	ACT 10 **Communicating With Parents**	109

How Are Students Assessed in the Classroom and District?

Key Question: How will you provide an overview of assessment policies to your mentee?

Directions: Share samples of all the district tests the students will be required to take this year. Explain the reason for the tests and the impact of any testing on the teachers in the district. Then share classroom tests and quizzes you have made or used in the past and how these tests inform the district tests.

1. **State Testing Initiatives**

   Does the state have a statewide testing program? What is its purpose? Are there other state tests required? Which grade levels? Ask to review a copy of the tests if they are at your grade level.

   On what standards or frameworks are the tests based?

2. **District Testing Program**

   Are the students required to pass a high school exit exam? When is it given? What is the test?

   How will this state test affect the curriculum you teach in your classroom?

   What is the purpose of these tests?

   Are these tests similar to the state tests? How?

3. **Classroom Assessment and Procedures**

   Discuss informal assessments. Share all your strategies with your student teacher.

   Discuss formal assessments. Review teacher-made tests, publishing company tests, performance assessments, and portfolios. Share all assessment tools with the novice teachers.

Linking Lesson Plans to Assessment

Key Question: How does including assessment in a lesson plan improve teaching?

Lesson planning and assessment are linked. Remind your mentee that the lesson plan should include an assessment tool of the lesson. Tapping into prior knowledge may be part of the lesson assessment to ensure the students are learning new information. Tapping in can avoid teaching students who may already *know* the information. It also assists you in designing lessons to meet the current needs of your students. Tapping in to what students already know can also serve as a check-in toward the middle and near the end of the unit to let a teacher know how closely the lesson objectives are being met.

Directions: Share a lesson plan you recently created to show where you include assessment (formal or informal) and how you tap into students' prior knowledge. Review these questions with your mentee as you share your ideas.

1. Share informal and formal assessments you have integrated into your lesson planning. List your ideas here.

2. Share strategies for assessing students' prior knowledge. List your ideas and review these others.

Here are some ideas to consider.

- Ask students to individually respond to these questions in writing.
  - *What do you already know about this topic/skill?*
  - *What do you think you know or have you heard about this topic/skill?*
  - *What would you like to learn or know?*
- Give a pretest on the topic or content.
- Have students write a paragraph about what they know about the topic.

Companion Website

Product or Process?

Key Question: How do you help your mentee choose assessments for diverse learners?

Directions: How does a teacher see evidence of student achievement? Will a product illustrate the student has met the objects or will a performance be better suited to demonstrating achievement? Explain the difference between *product* and *process* assessment. Remind your mentee that the assessment depends on the lesson's objective. Be sure the achievement measure matches the objective designed in the teacher's lesson plan. Review these examples.

Product (paper/pencil)	Product (visual)	Performance Process (with or without product)
Essays	Posters	Oral reports
Book reports	Banners	Speeches
Biographies	Models	Raps
Journals	Diagrams	Dramatizations
Letters	Displays	Debates
Editorials	Videotapes or audiotapes	Songs
Scripts	Portfolios	Poems
Tests	Exhibits	Demonstrations
Research reports	Paintings	Interviews
Short answers	Photos	Skits
Position papers	Websites	News reports

Companion Website

NOVEMBER

Formative and Summative Assessments

Key Question: How are formative and summative assessments used in effective teaching?

Directions: Review the differences between formative and summative assessments so your novice teacher understands that assessment is ongoing and should not be just done at the end of a unit.

1. Formative Assessment Is Practice: The Rehearsals

   It is authentic, ongoing, sit beside, self-assessing, learn as we go, practice, group work, conversations, checklists, surveys, drill, practice tests. It lets the teacher know how the students are learning before the final tests.

   When should your mentee be using formative assessments?

2. Summative Assessment Is Final: The Opening Night of the Play

   It is the final test, grade given to an individual student, final evaluation, judgment given at the end of the unit or term, report card grade, SAT final product, paper test, project artwork, final performance, Spanish oral exam.

   When should your mentee be using summative assessments?

3. What should students learn?

   Discuss the following questions with your mentee.

   - What should students have a *REAL understanding* of that will last and carry over?

   - What should they be *familiar with* that can be built upon in later years?

   - What should they have an *awareness level* of that will be built upon in later years?

   - What should English language learners be expected to know?

   - How do special education students' plans relate to assessment?

4. What types of rubrics need to be created and used in formative or summative assessments? Share samples and discuss options.

Companion Website

NOVEMBER

Evidence and Documentation of Progress

Key Question: How does an effective teacher document evidence of learning?

Directions: Share the common practices of record keeping and documenting student work. Review the ideas on this page with your mentee and add any of your own. Be sure to explain how evidence relates to assessments and lesson planning.

1. Share your grade book and any digital system your district is using.

2. Review student folders or portfolio systems the school is using this year.

3. Discuss progress charts that can be placed in the room for students to see and those that you keep in your grade book.

4. Discuss multiple ways to record grades in a grade book and review it for . . .

   missing assignments

   failing quizzes or tests

   homework

5. Discuss ways color-coding with highlighters in a hard copy gradebook or online e-grade book can assist a teacher in "seeing" the big picture.

   For example, highlight all the students' assignment grid boxes who have B or better grades in pink.

   Missing assignments in yellow to let the teacher scan easily and remind students.

   Failing tests or quizzes in orange let the teacher be alerted to struggling students.

Companion Website

Communicating With Students

Key Question: How can you encourage your mentee to keep students informed of their progress?

Teachers use a variety of systems to communicate with their students and keep them on track. The most common processes used in schools are the progress slip and the report card. Sharing progress slip information with students before sending it home to parents ensures the student understands what he has earned and why. Progress also includes growth in behavior as well as academics.

Directions: Share the report card and progress slip format your school is using and discuss these other ways to communicate. Help your mentee select one or more ways to implement this year. If one system doesn't work, another can be tried at any time.

Keeping Students Informed

1. *Student mailboxes/teacher mailbox.* Teachers and students can leave notes for one another about assignments, papers due, makeup work, for example.

2. *Student conference.* Teacher establishes a schedule and meets with individual students privately about progress. All students meet with teacher, not just failing students.

3. *Progress chart.* A subject-related progress chart is given to each student that visually documents the number of assignments completed, scores, projects, for example.

4. *Warnings.* When in danger of failing, a student receives a "red" note.

5. *Compliments.* Written or verbal acknowledgment of quality work is given to students.

6. *Checklist.* Placed inside daily or weekly folders—students can see what has been checked by you and approved for credit.

7. *Progress list.* Secondary students may be instructed to maintain their own grades.

8. *Midterm progress reports.* These list completed assignments and suggestions for improvement.

9. *Student-led parent conference.* Students attend and share their progress with the parents.

Students Can Share Their Learning

Key Question: How can you help your novice teacher implement ways for students to give feedback?

Directions: Discuss ways effective teachers encourage their students to check for understanding. Discuss the following ideas and add your own to this list.

1. Hard or Easy?

   - Ask students whether they are finding the work hard or easy. They can put thumbs up or down.

   - Hold up a green card or a red card.

   - Count the responses to get a quick sense of the response. Modify the lesson as needed.

2. What Are You Learning?

   - Take a minute at the end of each class as part of the closing to ask students to write two things they learned in class today.

   - Collect and review the responses to see what students are learning. This exercise can serve two purposes: (1) to see what they recall and (2) to let you know how to plan the next lesson.

   - Write your own prediction of how the lesson went and what they will say before reading the students' responses.

3. More Time?

   - Have students raise hands to tell the teacher whether they need more time

   - Let students reply anonymously on paper or by putting their heads down and raising their hands.

4. Work Habits Self-Assessment

   Create a worksheet that asks students to rate their behavior or understanding.

   For example:

   - I worked hard in groups today. 1–5 (didn't work–worked very hard)

   - I understand the concepts presented. 1–5 (don't understand–really understand)

5. Teacher Assessment

   Create a survey with your mentee to assess her teaching skills. Rate each 1–5.

   For example:

   - My teacher presents information in a way I can understand.

   - My teacher listens to my questions.

   - There is time in class for me to practice the skill.

Classroom and Behavior Management Issues

Key Question: How can you help your mentee learn how to minimize misbehavior?

Directions: Ask your mentee to list the three most common classroom misbehaviors she is dealing with right now and how she is handling them. Categorize the issues by seeing if they relate to routines, student issues, or lack of planning. Discuss how she can minimize these disruptions. A digital version of this form is available on the companion website.

Misbehavior	How it is currently being handled	How to avoid it or minimize it
1.		
2.		
3.		

Looking at Student Work Together

Key Question: How can the novice teacher learn to modify assignments and still have students achieve?

Directions: Review these four ways to differentiate for diverse learners and then review a sample of student work to see if modification would have helped the students achieve.

1. *Find out what students know.*

This is also an opportunity to find out who exceeds standards in the classroom on this topic so more advanced work can be given to enrich students' learning.

2. *Use varied reading levels and audio devices to teach content.*

Vary expectations for beginning learners by limiting vocabulary or adding enrichment words.

3. *Vary the instructional method to meet diverse learning needs.*

Using partners and small groups, or a choice of process or product assignments, graphic organizers, and varied strategies, keep students engaged as well as respond to various learning needs.

4. *Offer a variety of ways to show they have learned the content.*

Quizzes and tests are only one way to demonstrate learning. Success in school may make the difference in students staying in school.

Ask your mentee to bring several samples of ONE student's work to a meeting. You will look at the work and share what you see. What "story" can be told from looking at this student's work? Ask the novice teacher to share his or her perspective about this student. A form for this process is available on the companion website.

What does this work say about this student?	What is the evidence for that statement?	What is the next learning step for this student? How could the work be modified for this student based on the ideas on this page?

Communicating With Parents

Key Question: How can your mentee informally communicate effectively with parents?

You have already discussed formal communication with your mentee, but it is also important to review other ways he can keep parents informed on a consistent basis. Report cards and progress slips are milestones for students, but regular communication will support the progress on these high-stakes reports.

Directions: Discuss the following ideas and which ones may be most relevant for your mentee.

Informal Teacher Communication

1. In Between Formal Progress Reports

Sometimes there is a need to contact parents between the formal cycle. Students who were failing last term may be doing well now, and novice teachers need to let the parents know that their support made a difference. Or parents may want to check in to see if the student is doing better because they may need to continue the monitoring at home. Share the formats you have used to communicate progress. Do you use a note? A checklist? Ask your mentee how she would like to implement this type of system.

2. Students Who Fail a Test or Major Project

If a student fails a test or a major project, it is usually a good idea to tell the parents. Some teachers send the test home and require a signature so the parents can see what was missed. If a meeting is required, then the parents know exactly what the meeting is about and the student could also be present.

3. The Notebook

Many teachers use a notebook with students who have challenges with schoolwork or behavior. It goes from home to school every day or once a week. This communication from parents to teacher keeps an open line of communication.

4. Compliment Cards, E-mails, or Phone Calls

Don't forget that all communication isn't about failure or problems. Creating a system where each student's parent receives a positive message once a term is an important way to stay connected to parents.

November Mentor Reflections

Directions: Complete any of these prompts that stand out for you and add your own prompts to the blank stems. Write your responses here or use your Mentor Planning Guide and Journal on the companion website. Share your reflections with your mentor coordinator or with other mentors at a mentor support meeting.

Something I would like to show my novice teachers in my classroom . . .

A recommendation I have right now is . . .

One way I can be helpful is . . .

I am excited about . . .

Using Mindfulness to Explore Mentoring Dilemmas

Directions: Read the mentoring dilemma and think about how you would respond in this situation. Consider discussing this dilemma at a mentor support meeting or with another mentor. Share your perspectives about how you would proceed and why you think this would be the best way to forward your novice teacher's practice.

Dilemma 4: Cheating

Your mentee has been successfully assessing students' progress using both formal and informal assessments. You have reviewed the pages in the November chapter, and she has a good sense of rubric design and the difference between formative and summative assessments. She knows the district really wants high scores, so she is pushing the students to achieve. When she brings her student papers to you to review prior to a work session you had planned this week, you discover that she has four students with exactly the same answers on their final tests! *What do you say when you meet with her the next day?*

Respond to these prompts in your journal available on the companion website.

1. State the mentor dilemma as clearly as possible in one sentence if you can.

2. What decision do you need to make in regard to this situation?

3. Write about the emotions that come up for you that relate to this situation. If you have two choices, write how the emotions might be different.

4. Stop and reread what you have written. Underline any key words or phrases that stand out for you.

5. Soften your eyes or close them and take three deep breaths. Ask yourself, what am I missing that I have not noticed? Write that down in your journal.

6. What will you say to your mentee? Write your reflection in your journal.

7. If you are truly stuck, bring your dilemma to your lead mentor, a mentor support group meeting, or another experienced mentor. Ask him or her to listen to what you have written and to ask you questions to clarify your dilemma. *Your lead mentor's role is not to tell you what to do! No advice!* Just questions to help you clarify what you want to do.

8. After you have spoken to your mentee, write his reaction and how you feel about this dilemma now. All dilemmas are not resolved! This is a process of clarifying and understanding how you feel and how you could respond.

Directions: Complete all three goal-setting processes and write your responses on this page or in your Mentor Planning Guide and Journal available on the companion website.

1. *Goal for Improving Your Mentee's Teaching Practices*

   - Review the PLAN–CONNECT–ACT–REFLECT pages you completed in this chapter with your mentee. Look ahead to December ACTs to see what you may focus on to continue development.

   - Acknowledge what your mentee is learning. Write a compliment and put it on her desk.

   - Agree on ONE goal to focus on and reinforce for next month.

   - Goal:

2. *Goal to Support the Social and Emotional Well-Being of Your Mentee*

   - Discuss any challenges your mentee may be facing right now. Challenges often bring stress.

   - Don't ignore any signs of stress in your mentee. Pay attention and teach her ways to manage her stress. Using mindfulness practices can help reduce stress.

   - Continue to learn about mindfulness by reading *Educators' Social and Emotional Skills Vital to Learning*, available on the companion website.

   - Goal:

3. *Goal for Enhancing Your Mentoring Skills*

   - Reflect on your own mentoring experience this month. How did you use your strengths and interests to mentor? What will you do differently next month? Write a reflection in your Mentor Planning Guide and Journal.

   - Goal:

A good teacher is someone who listens to you as a
student and always tries to challenge you."

—FIFTH-GRADE STUDENT

NEW TEACHER PHASE: CAN I DO THIS?

"I'm having trouble keeping the students on task,
and I am losing valuable teaching time."

MINDFUL MENTORING AFFIRMATION

I encourage my novice teacher to try a
variety of instructional strategies.

DECEMBER

MAINTAINING BALANCE
Teaching and Keeping the Students Interested

GUIDING QUESTIONS

1. How do you help your novice teacher keep all learners engaged? The **Brain ACTivities** will provide ways to approach this task.

2. What does your mentee need to know about support? The **Support ACTivities** offer you ideas to review and discuss.

3. How will you keep students central to mentoring conversations? Use the **Student ACTivities** as a way to focus on students.

4. What is a parent communication option for this month? Use the **Communication ACTivity** as a way to connect when all is well with the student!

Interstate Teacher Assessment and Support Consortium—InTASC Standards

Review InTASC Standard 8.

- **Standard 8 Instructional Strategies**

The teacher understands and uses a variety of instructional strategies to encourage learners to develop deep understanding of content areas and their connections, and to build skills to apply knowledge in meaningful ways.

Chapter Overview

Students know good teachers. Like the fifth-grade quote on the previous page says, "A good teacher is someone who listens to you as a student and always tries to challenge you." In this high technology world, it is a challenge to keep students' attention. Beginning teachers who don't know what students are capable of doing may give them work that is too easy. Students want to be challenged and want to succeed. Assist your mentee in implementing a variety of strategies that will forward student learning. Remind him to listen to the students to find out what they like and how they learn best. Curriculum can be so overwhelming that many beginning teachers just want to "get it done" and move on, forgetting that students need to be at the center of any curriculum work. When a teacher feels she is losing valuable teaching time, she gets stressed because she will not be on track to meet district goals.

As your mentee questions herself because she is having difficulty and asks, "Can I do this?" you need to be prepared to demonstrate effective strategies and encourage her to continue to try new approaches. Maintaining her balance in December is important because it is a stressful month, and this can be a tipping point for burnout. Explore ways you can provide short breaks for your mentee and encourage her to focus on her health and wellness. Social and emotional learning for adults is just as important as for students. If the adults in a school are not healthy, then it is difficult to teach students who also have their own emotional issues.

VIDEO 2.11

December Chapter Introduction

Your Mindful Mentoring Affirmation this month is, "I encourage my novice teacher to try a variety of instructional strategies." Your encouragement to try new ways to engage her learners will help her to stay focused on teaching and not on the emotional drama students present when they are not on task.

Follow the PLAN, CONNECT, ACT, REFLECT, and SET GOALS sections in this chapter to guide your mentoring conversations and reflections.

Watch and listen to a mentor share her insights in the December Chapter Introduction (Video 2.11), available on the companion website or by scanning the QR code on a mobile device.

Use Questions to Guide Mentoring Conversations

Invite your mentee to write down a short list of questions and bring them to your first December meeting. Use the questions below as a guide for your discussions throughout the month.

Anticipate Beginning Teachers' Possible Questions

1. Can you help me select a variety of strategies that will work for me?

2. I need help incorporating problem-solving into my lessons. What should I do?

3. Critical thinking is important, but I have to cover so much content. How can I incorporate that skill into my lessons?

4. What are the successful strategies you have used that encourage students to think?

5. I am losing track of the other InTASC principles we covered from September to November. There is so much to know. Can you review them with me?

Note the other questions your novice teacher asked you so you will have them for the future.

Questions for Your Novice Teacher

1. What is working for you right now in your classroom?

2. When are your students most interested in learning?

3. What do you most enjoy about teaching, and why do you think that is so?

4. What can I do to assist you right now that would reduce your anxiety?

Meetings and Observations

Plan brief weekly meetings with your mentee. The ACTs in this chapter serve as mentoring conversation starters and can also be used to assess or review what your mentee may already know about a given topic. Use the Appendices to guide you in scheduling short meetings as well as longer conversations.

Plan to meet at times that allow you to have quality time together in a place without interruptions. Knowing when you will meet each week reduces anxiety for both of you. Novice teachers look forward to regularly scheduled meetings even if they are short. Use a calendar to plan your meetings and classroom visits to ensure they will happen! Include watching videos and reading pages in the *Mentoring in Action* book as part of your *PLAN* for mentoring. A digital version of this calendar (December Calendar.pdf) is available on the companion website.

Novice teachers can learn a lot by observing their own teaching! One way to begin that process is using audio recording. Encourage your mentee to begin with audio by using the audio on a phone or tablet. Before he presses record, have him write two or three things he would like to hear about his voice, for example, the tone of his voice, or how he uses students' names, or how he gives directions. He may self-reflect on his own or share the recording with you. Reflect on what he learned by listening to his voice.

December Calendar

MONDAY	TUESDAY	WEDNESDAY	THURSDAY	FRIDAY

Use this calendar to PLAN the month as well as to document meetings and mentor planning.

CONNECT to Additional Resources

CONNECT to School and District Resources

What resources exist in your school and community that could assist novice teachers in December?

CONNECT With Colleagues, Parents, and Families

How can other colleagues in the school support the mentee in learning effective strategies for engaging students?

CONNECT to Student Voices

Watch the Reactions to the Student Survey video (Video 2.7; see page 84) on the companion website with your mentee. Respond to these prompts together. Would you consider conducting a student survey in your classroom? Why or why not? Would you consider sharing your survey results with a novice teacher? Why could this be useful? For more information about student surveys, refer to the Interactive.pdf "Integrating Student Perspectives into Mentoring Conversations" on the companion website.

CONNECT to Education Hot Topics

Homework! Read the latest research on this education matter. What is your school policy on homework? Understand the needs of homeless students in regard to assigning homework and projects. These students are struggling and need emotional support and options for fulfilling these requirements. How can you support homeless students in being successful in school?

CONNECT With the Companion Website

Video links, forms for this chapter, a featured book, and other resources are located at http://resources.corwin.com/mentoringinaction.

Companion
Website

DECEMBER

The First ACT!

Differentiating Mentoring Conversations

Teaching is complex work, and novice teachers can easily become overwhelmed. It is appropriate to customize your mentoring conversations to respond to the varied needs and skills of the mentee.

Directions: Interview your mentee at the beginning of the month to document her areas of strength and needs. Skim the ACTs for this month and decide together which topics are most relevant. Use your state or district teaching standards to focus the mentee's responses to each prompt so you are also teaching her the "common language" of the standards.

Mentee _____ Date _____

Monthly Needs Assessment

1. What is going well in your classroom? (i.e., What is working?) As a teacher, what do you feel you are doing well right now? *Refer to the teaching standards to guide your response.*	3. What would you like to improve or enhance in your practice this month? *Refer to the teaching standards to guide your response.*
2. How do you know your practice is working? (i.e., What is your evidence of success? or Why do you feel confident or competent in an aspect of your teaching?)	4. Review the ACT mentoring conversations for this month with your mentee. Ask which of the ACTs will support you in enhancing your teaching practice? (i.e., What would you like us to focus on this month?)

A digital version of this template (Monthly Needs Assessment Sample With Standards.pdf) is available on the companion website. Keep a copy of this assessment for your files and make a copy for the mentee.

Overview of the ACTs for December Conversations

Directions: Skim the ACTivities listed here and complete the pages that will forward your novice teacher's learning. Your mentee has complementary ACTs in *The First Years Matter* book. Digital copies of any of the reproducible ACTs are available on the companion website.

Key Question Topic	ACTivities	PAGE
Brain	ACT 1 **Problem-Solving and Thinking**	122
Brain	ACT 2 **Focus on Teaching Style**	123
Brain	ACT 3 **Engage the Brain**	124
Support	ACT 4 **Revisiting Behavior Management**	125
Support	ACT5 **Avoiding Common Problems and Keeping Students Interested**	126
Support	ACT 6 **Keeping ALL Students Engaged**	127
Support	ACT 7 **When Is it Time to Seek Additional Support?**	128
Students	ACT 8 **Classroom and Behavior Management Issues**	129
Students	ACT 9 **Looking at Student Work Together**	130
Communicate	ACT 10 **Communicating With Parents**	131

DECEMBER

Problem-Solving and Thinking

Key Question: How can you help your mentee use brain-based strategies to engage learners?

Directions: Discuss the strategies you have used that work in your classroom to enhance students' problem-solving abilities. Review the ideas on this page and note where your mentee is challenged or strong. Sometimes the mentee teaches the mentor some new ideas.

1. Critical thinking allows students to go beyond the basic memorization and to actually engage with the content. Find several examples of critical thinking in your own teaching and share them with the novice teachers. Why is this so important? Refer to Bloom's Taxonomy and encourage your mentee to integrate these action verbs into her lesson plans to promote higher order thinking.

   Review your mentee's lesson plans to note places where critical thinking can be integrated.

2. Performance skills are natural ways for students to share what they know and are able to do. Students enjoy plays, reading poetry, writing original stories, drawing, and dancing. Discuss ways in which these important skills can be integrated into daily lessons and units. Refer to November Product or Process ACT 3 for ideas.

   List examples here:

3. Sports and games use physical activity to get the body and brain moving. Taking a short break helps students refresh and recharge. Eliminating recesses for students who are struggling actually does the opposite for their success. Think about ways you can help your mentee integrate short brain-based physical movement into her lessons. Discuss how these short breaks can minimize misbehavior in students who just can't sit for long periods of time.

Review a lesson plan and point out where a physical break would be helpful to students.

Companion Website

Focus on Teaching Style

Key Question: How can a teacher's style influence student learning?

Directions: Every teacher has a preferred style of presenting information and organizing classroom resources. Answer these questions first and then interview your novice teacher to find out her preferred style. Your style may not match your mentee's preferred style. Use these questions to guide your interview and discussion to relate to how a teacher must vary her preferred style to meet the needs of her students. Being mindful and aware of your teaching style means you can change it when needed. One style is not better than another, and effective teachers know their preference but can use all learning styles. How the students respond to a teacher's style is what is important to their learning. Asking students what their preferred style is important to this process. Refer to ACT 4 in September for some reminders. An effective teacher must teach to ALL students' styles.

1. *Do you like to talk and explain concepts verbally?*

Then as a teacher you may prefer to lecture for most of the class and hold student conferences. Students with an auditory preference will thrive in this type of classroom.

2. *Do you prefer to write and see concepts on paper?*

Then as a teacher you probably use the board or computer to illustrate ideas. You will create written guides and require students to take notes in your classes. Students with a learning style where they prefer to write will thrive.

3. *Do you enjoy creating and showing visual displays of content?*

Then as a teacher you will most likely been seen demonstrating concepts with models or computer displays. You may also use graphic organizers, video, and drawings to show students key ideas. Students who love to draw and use visuals will thrive.

4. *Do you like to see how things work and use your senses?*

Then as a teacher you may design experiments and hands-on lessons using manipulatives. Students with this preference will excel in this type of classroom.

Engage the Brain

Key Question: What are some brain-based strategies your mentee should be using?

Directions: Review any articles or professional development on brain-based teaching with your mentee. Much of what is in this book relates to the cognitive process of engaging learners but isn't specifically called brain-based teaching. Any time your mentee focuses on reasoning, memory, and problem-solving, the brain is involved at a higher level. Even the room temperature and the way it is organized in a comfortable way influences the brain. Paying attention to all of the senses as you think about effective teaching strategies is important. Discuss these key ideas in a mentoring conversation and observe the ways your mentee is engaging the brain to support learning in the classroom.

1. Applying learning through meaningful activities. Where is your mentee using this strategy to help his students "connect" the neural networks from that lecture to an actual real life experience the student can relate to in his life?

2. Purposefully activating prior knowledge from students can make teaching more effective. Help your mentee find easy strategies for getting at prior learning and helping students transfer what they already know to this new learning. How often have we heard students say, "We did this last year!" Teachers cover the same content and aren't able to bring it to a higher or deeper level of understanding when they are not skilled at transferring knowledge.

3. Teaching to notice "insights" and big ideas makes learning exciting for students. Effective teachers know their content but also see the big ideas and the meaning that is often embedded in the content. Helping your mentee step back and see the tree in the forest helps him to gain insight too. Teachable moments are available every day in teaching, and we often miss them because we are too busy trying to finish the lesson or complete the objective.

4. Planning lessons and teaching units that intentionally activate cognitive learning processes are time well spent. Novice teachers often don't want to spend their time writing long lesson plans because they just want to get up and teach. As a mentor, you know that planning is crucial and it is time worth spending.

5. Taking care of ourselves helps the brain function efficiently. You know that there is too much to do and not enough time, but that doesn't mean we stop being healthy. You can't emphasize enough the importance of health and wellness with your mentee. Set goals for social and emotional learning at the end of this chapter.

Companion Website

Revisiting Behavior Management

Key Question: What does your mentee need to review at this time of year?

Directions: Schedule a mentoring conversation that has your mentee review her discipline philosophy. If you have been noticing her talking about students in a disrespectful way or feeling disillusioned with the behavior of her students, this is a good time to address this topic. Get back to the basics in the August and September chapters. The ACTs that didn't seem so important at the time may need to be implemented now or perhaps reviewed and revised. Share your philosophy of managing misbehavior and how teachers handle disruptions differently. Discuss how respect for students is integrated into a teacher's response. Refer to ACT 8 in October as a reminder about disciplining a student.

Incident 1: A student has forgotten his books and homework for the fifth time this year. He is failing the course and now will miss the information again. The novice teacher is frustrated and overwhelmed. What does she do?

Teacher A responds this way:

Teacher B responds this way:

Which response promotes future success in this class for the student?

Discuss positive appropriate ways to deal with recurring misbehavior.

Incident 2: A male student in the mentee's class has been bullying and bothering a girl in another class. She comes to the novice teacher for help because she knows the teacher has this student in class.

Teacher A responds this way:

Teacher B responds this way:

Which response promotes future success for the male student?

Discuss positive appropriate ways to deal with recurring misbehavior.

There is not always a clear cut way to respond to any misbehavior. How will you guide your mentee to be respectful while still carrying out the rules of the school? Sometimes building relationships with the most troubled students can be the most rewarding experience for a novice teacher.

Companion Website

Avoiding Common Problems and Keeping Students Interested

Key Question: How can you help your mentee understand that common problems can be handled with solid classroom routines?

Directions: Review these key areas and ask the appropriate questions that relate to your mentee. Effective teachers that have efficient classroom management in place minimize misbehavior.

1. *Classroom Management.* Have you structured your classroom in an orderly way to avoid potential problems? Traffic flow? Room setup? What could you change to avoid any further issues?

2. *Lesson Planning.* Have you designed lessons that meet the needs of all students so they don't get frustrated and angry when they can't succeed? Are the lessons challenging but doable? Do you have accommodations for grouping that avoid off task behavior? How can you redesign lessons to avoid problems you are experiencing?

3. *Rules, Rewards, and Consequences.* Are the rules clearly posted and understood? Do students "own" them, or are they imposed on them? Are you consistent when you apply the consequences? Do you treat all students fairly? What do you need to do to be sure your rules, rewards, and consequences are working to avoid problems?

In the review of behavior management, make sure you discuss what is working and why. Find out what is working in your mentee's classroom!

Classroom Behavior	What Mentee Is Doing	Why Is It Working?
Class is passing in papers in an orderly way every day with their names on them!	Stopping class 3 minutes before the bell to allow time to pass in papers.	Consistently ask students to check their names and pass in papers.

Companion Website

Keeping ALL Students Engaged

Key Question: How can you support your mentee in including all students?

Directions: Novice teachers need to continually think about ways in which they can modify lessons for the diverse learners in their classrooms. By December, these continual modifications get tiring, and sometimes they just want to keep moving. Take some time to review individual education plans (IEPs) with your mentee to see if any of the students who are struggling have special needs. The strategies for teaching special needs students can be effective for all students. Review the modifications and make sure your mentee understands them.

1. Examples of modifications:

   - Giving a student more time to complete an assignment.
   - Assigning fewer questions or examples to be completed.
   - Allowing students to tape-record their answers instead of writing.
   - Working with a partner who would write the answers the student stated verbally.
   - Accepting printed work instead of cursive.
   - Using the computer to complete work.

2. Discuss these questions:

   - How does a teacher know when to move on when there are some students who still did not learn?
   - How does a teacher pace a lesson so that all or most students complete the task?
   - How does a teacher still have high expectations for learners who work more slowly?

3. Know the students in the classroom:

   - Who needs modifications in your mentee's classroom?
   - Ask her to list the students' names and share it with you.
   - How can parents help?

Companion Website

When Is It Time to Seek Additional Support?

Key Question: How does your mentee learn when to get more support?

Directions: Review the list of criteria on this page and explain that students come to school with issues that are beyond the teacher's skill set. Some students are homeless, others are in need of medical and psychological help. As a mentor, you can be an advocate for getting the help that is needed.

1. How do you know when your mentee needs more support with a student?

   - When the mentee has exhausted all existing solutions within the classroom.

   - When the student continues to exhibit problems beyond the scope of common issues.

   - When the mentor has determined the student needs additional help.

   - When parents have indicated a need for support.

2. What should your mentee do?

   - Maintain accurate records of any disturbing behavior.

   - Write a request for help to the administrator in charge.

   - Document all requests for help and strategies tried in the classroom.

3. Next steps?

   - Follow up with your mentee to ensure the administrator responds.
   - Decide whether the issue requires the students in the classroom be informed.

Companion Website

Classroom and Behavior Management Issues

Key Question: How does a novice teacher learn how to manage degrees of inappropriate behavior?

Directions: Discuss recurring problems teachers may have with an individual student or the whole class. Review the four categories below and assist your mentee in identifying appropriate responses. Add your own ideas to the discussion.

Problems	What You Need to Do
Chronic Work Avoidance Evidenced, for example, by being absent regularly, fooling around in class, not passing in assignments, tardiness.	• Make sure student is capable of work. • Keep accurate records of what is missing. • Talk with mentor teacher. • Let student know how assignments affect grade. • Talk with parents. • Other?
Habitual Rule Breaking Evidenced, for example, by calling out in class, not bringing pencil to class regularly, being talkative, forgetting other materials.	• Use consequences established. • Try behavior modification systems. • Talk with student privately. • Discuss issue with mentor teacher. • Talk with parents. • Other?
Hostile Verbal Outbursts Evidenced, for example, by angry loud yelling, chip-on-the-shoulder attitude, defiance when asked to complete assignments.	• Determine whether the outburst is just momentary. • Don't engage in a power struggle. • Remove the student if anger persists. • Talk with mentor teacher. • Talk with principal. • Talk with guidance counselor. • Talk with parents. • Other?
Fighting, Destruction, Weapons, Alcohol, or Drug Abuse Evidenced, for example, by hallway pushing, violence with peers, threats, glazed look in class.	• Send a student for help. • Disperse crowds that may gather to watch. • Calmly talk; do not shout or scream. • Report the incident immediately. • Other?

Looking at Student Work Together

Key Question: How does using criteria help a novice teacher rate student work effectively?

Directions: Discuss the indicators of success for student work. How does a teacher know students have learned? How does a teacher use data to analyze student work? Designing rubrics and making lists of indicators of success allow teachers to use concrete evidence to demonstrate progress. What indicators or criteria are used in your district? Complete these two processes together.

1. Randomly select a sample of student work from a completed set of papers and discuss why you think each student fits into each category. Use the rubric or criteria from the district.

Below Standard	Meets the Standard	Above Standard
What indicates that it is below standard?	What evidence shows this work meets the standard?	What makes you say it is above the standard?
Be specific in your discussion.	Check the indicators.	Be specific.

2. Complete the entire class and sort the papers into these categories. What did you learn? What is your mentee's next step for this assignment?

Below Standard	Meets the Standard	Above Standard
How many papers here?	How many papers here?	How many papers here?
% of class _____	% of class _____	% of class _____

Companion Website

Communicating With Parents

Key Question: Why is it important to share compliments with parents?

Directions: One sure way to keep students interested in school is to compliment them for what they are doing right! Parents and students love to hear good news. Because the school day is so hectic and the needs of failing students have to be a priority for a novice teacher, there often is not time to compliment the students who are doing well. Share these ideas with your mentee and other novice teachers in your school.

1. *Compliment Phone Calls*

The goal is that every student in the class will receive a compliment within a month. Using a class list, the novice teacher schedules a few phone calls each night after school. She either leaves a message on an answering machine or speaks personally to the parents. Everyone in the class is called once a month. Ask your mentee to keep track of any parent responses. The student actually doesn't know the call is coming. Keep that a surprise. Find out what the student says to your mentee the next day! You may want to try this in your classroom too and compare your responses.

> *The message script might sound something like this: "This is an official Compliment Phone Call from Mr. Jones, Susan's teacher at Sunnyside School. I am calling to compliment your daughter for her outstanding work in class this week. She worked with other students who needed help, she answered questions in class, and she did very well on her project. Please let Susan know that she received this compliment. Have a great day!"*

Remind your mentee that this is not a student conference! It is a compliment phone call. It is a compliment for something very specific. Finding a compliment for each student may be challenging particularly if the student has been difficult. Brainstorm some ideas together and find that good behavior or work! It will make such a difference and may even change that student's attitude in class.

2. *Positive Notes*

This compliment could be given electronically as an e-mail or e-card. The key is to be specific about what is being complimented so the student is clear about what positive behavior or academic performance is. The goal is to identify good specific behavior and reward it by telling the parents.

December Mentor Reflections

Directions: Complete any of these prompts that stand out for you and add your own prompts to the blank stems. Write your responses here or use your Mentor Planning Guide and Journal on the companion website. Share your reflections with your mentor coordinator or with other mentors at a mentor support meeting.

DECEMBER

What I am learning by completing these reflections is . . .

Something I am working on to be a better mentor is . . .

My advice to novice teachers in December is . . .

I am feeling great about . . .

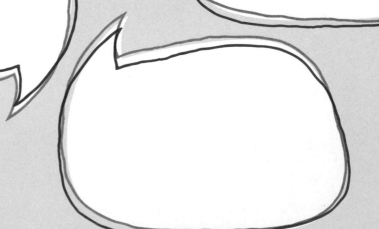

Using Mindfulness to Explore Mentoring Dilemmas

Directions: Read the mentoring dilemma and think about how you would respond in this situation. Consider discussing this dilemma at a mentor support meeting or with another mentor. Share your perspectives about how you would proceed and why you think this would be the best way to forward your novice teacher's practice.

Dilemma 5: Took Your Advice and It Didn't Work

Your mentee came to the district with high marks and graduated top of his class in education classes. He is a career changer who knows a lot about engineering and chose teaching because he wanted to give back and was tired of corporate. He is enthusiastic and wants to be a great teacher, but your observations and mentoring conversations demonstrate his inability to engage students in relevant ways. You gave him some suggestions. So to try to be more engaging, he planned a fantastic lesson with lots of props and role-playing a Roman election. He shared that the students just couldn't stop talking, and he got frustrated and said, "That's it. We are not doing it! Open your books to page 20 and start answering the questions." *What do you say when you meet for your next mentoring conversation?*

Respond to these prompts in your journal available on the companion website.

1. State the mentor dilemma as clearly as possible in one sentence if you can.

2. What decision do you need to make in regard to this situation?

3. Write about the emotions that come up for you that relate to this situation. If you have two choices, write how the emotions might be different.

4. Stop and reread what you have written. Underline any key words or phrases that stand out for you.

5. Soften your eyes or close them and take three deep breaths. Ask yourself, what am I missing that I have not noticed? Write that down in your journal.

6. What will you say to your mentee? Write your reflection in your journal.

7. If you are truly stuck, bring your dilemma to your lead mentor, a mentor support group meeting, or another experienced mentor. Ask him or her to listen to what you have written and to ask you questions to clarify your dilemma. *Your lead mentor's role is not to tell you what to do! No advice!* Just questions to help you clarify what you want to do.

8. After you have spoken to your mentee, write his reaction and how you feel about this dilemma now. All dilemmas are not resolved! This is a process of clarifying and understanding how you feel and how you could respond.

Directions: Complete all three goal-setting processes and write your responses on this page or in your Mentor Planning Guide and Journal available on the companion website.

1. *Goal for Improving Your Mentee's Teaching Practices*

   - Review the PLAN–CONNECT–ACT–REFLECT pages you completed in this chapter with your mentee. Look ahead to January ACTs to see what you may focus on to continue development.

   - Acknowledge what your mentee is learning. Create a short video on your mobile device or leave a phone message sharing what you have observed your mentee doing well.

   - Agree on ONE goal to focus on and reinforce for next month.

   - Goal:

2. *Goal to Support the Social and Emotional Well-Being of Your Mentee*

   - Discuss any challenges your mentee may be facing right now. Challenges often bring stress.

   - Don't ignore any signs of stress in your mentee. Pay attention and teach her ways to manage her stress. Using mindfulness practices can help reduce stress.

   - Watch the video interview with Kristen Lee Costa, available on the companion website, to learn about burnout and how you can help your mentee minimize stress.

   - Goal:

3. *Goal for Enhancing Your Mentoring Skills*

   - Reflect on your own mentoring experience this month. How did you use your strengths and interests to mentor? What will you do differently next month? Write a reflection in your Mentor Planning Guide and Journal.

   - Goal:

DECEMBER

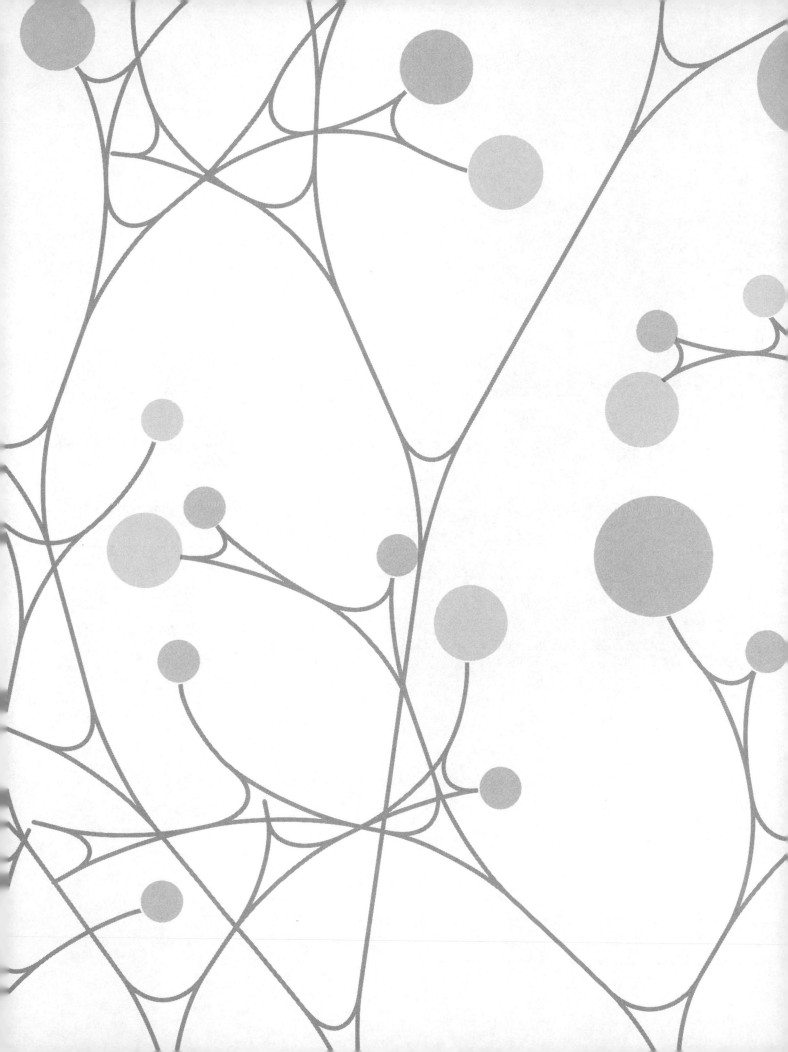

"I think patience makes a good teacher.**"**
—SECOND-GRADE STUDENT

NEW TEACHER PHASE: REFRESHED AND READY

"I want to start the year over again because
I know so much more now."

MINDFUL MENTORING AFFIRMATION

I model a healthy balance in my personal and professional lives.

JANUARY

BEGINNING A NEW CALENDAR YEAR
*Looking Back and
Moving Forward*

GUIDING QUESTIONS

1. How do you help your novice teacher reflect on her teaching practice systematically? The *Reflect ACTivities* offer you options to think about or discuss with your mentee.

2. How do you continue to reinforce the importance of student voices? The *Student ACTivities* offer you ideas to share, try in the classroom, and discuss.

3. How can a formal agenda and meeting with parents help communication? Use the *Communicate ACTivity* as a way to plan a meeting.

Interstate Teacher Assessment and Support Consortium—InTASC Standards

Review InTASC Standard 9.

- **Standard 9 Professional Learning and Ethical Practice**

The teacher engages in ongoing professional learning and uses evidence to continually evaluate his/her practice, particularly the effects of his/her choices and actions on others (learners, families, other professionals, and the community), and adapts practice to meet the needs of each learner.

Chapter Overview

Patience is a virtue, and it does make a good teacher, just like the second-grade student says in the quote on the previous page. Remind your mentee to be patient. He won't learn everything at once. In fact it will take this entire year to go through the stages of effective teaching. Novice teachers are growing and developing with each new experience and interaction with their students. Sometimes they are moving so quickly they don't even see what they are learning.

You also need to be patient with your mentee. You may provide guidance and think you said something, and she just doesn't do it. You wonder why she isn't listening to you. Perhaps she just can't take all this information in. There is so much to learn. If you can help her focus and select a few areas, it will improve her efforts. The beginning of a new calendar year is a perfect opportunity to look back at the progress that has been made and look ahead to what the second half of the year will bring. Be the guide they need to see the light at the end of the year. Be the patience your mentee needs right now.

The holiday vacation may bring your mentee back refreshed and ready to begin. Sometimes a beginner returns more cautious and concerned that he can't do this work. Be with your mentee in whatever phase he finds himself. Don't judge it or try to change it. Use this month to ground him in reflective practice and goal setting. New Year's resolutions are fun to make and easy to break, so be sure to guide your mentee to create doable measurable goals. Review the ACT 7, Where is Your Sense of Humor? To help your mentee see the bigger picture of teaching.

Your Mindful Mentoring Affirmation this month is, "I model a healthy balance in my personal and professional lives." Some novice teachers who are committed to being excellent teachers often go overboard and only focus on work, work, work! They spend their entire vacation correcting papers, stay at school late every night, and work on weekends. This is not healthy, and it actually doesn't help. We all know there is always more work, and it is impossible to catch up. A healthy balance is required in this profession. Let your mentee know it is okay to take a break! Review the SET GOALS for supporting the social and emotional well-being of your mentee at the end of each month. Watch Video 1.4, *Managing Your Stress to Promote Well-Being*, and Video 1.5, *Managing Your Stress: Take a Break* (see page 13), on the companion website. Most of all, be a good role model.

Follow the PLAN, CONNECT, ACT, REFLECT, and SET GOALS sections in this chapter to guide your mentoring conversations and reflections.

Watch and listen to a mentor share her insights in the January Chapter Introduction (Video 2.12), available on the companion website or by scanning the QR code on a mobile device.

VIDEO 2.12

January Chapter Introduction

Use Questions to Guide Mentoring Conversations

Invite your mentee to write down a short list of questions and bring them to your first January meeting. Use the questions below as a guide for your discussions throughout the month.

Anticipate Beginning Teachers' Possible Questions

1. I would like to share ideas and learn from others. How do I connect with other novice teachers?

2. What opportunities are available in the district, through the teachers' union, or from local professional development providers?

3. In your professional opinion, what should I focus on to improve my practice for the rest of the year?

4. Is there a way I could easily connect with the parents and the community that would assist me in my teaching?

5. Do you have any suggestions for assisting me in reflecting more systematically so I don't lose my good ideas?

List the other questions your novice teachers brought to the meeting so you will have them for your next mentoring cycle.

Questions for Your Novice Teachers

1. Do you keep a journal? Why or why not? How do you reflect on your practice?

2. Are you a member of a professional organization?

3. What changes have you already made in what you are doing and why?

4. What can I do to assist you right now that would reduce your anxiety?

Meetings and Observations

Plan brief weekly meetings with your mentee. The ACTs in this chapter serve as mentoring conversation starters and can also be used to assess or review what your mentee may already know about a given topic. Use the Appendices to guide you in scheduling short meetings as well as longer conversations.

Plan to meet at times that allow you to have quality time together in a place without interruptions. Knowing when you will meet each week reduces anxiety for both of you. Novice teachers look forward to regularly scheduled meetings even if they are short. Use a calendar to plan your meetings and classroom visits to ensure they will happen! Include watching videos and reading pages in the *Mentoring in Action* book as part of your *PLAN* for mentoring. A digital version of this calendar (January Calendar.pdf) is available on the companion website.

Your novice can create a video of part of a lesson to share with you. Using technology from the school or a portable device, a short 10–15 minute clip of the teacher in action can provide data for a reflective conversation. If your novice teacher doesn't want to share the clip with you, ask her if she will reflect and share what she learned about her practice by doing this video. Be sure to get permissions from parents. Let the novice observe the recording first alone and then consider watching it together. If it is difficult for you to get time to observe, use this as a formal observation and provide a postconference.

January Calendar

MONDAY	TUESDAY	WEDNESDAY	THURSDAY	FRIDAY

Use this calendar to PLAN the month as well as to document meetings and mentor planning.

CONNECT to Additional Resources

CONNECT to School and District Resources

What resources exist in your school and community that could assist novice teachers in January?

CONNECT With Master Teachers

Who in the professional community or district inspires professional growth and reflection? Encourage your mentee to meet with teachers in your school or district who model excellence in teaching. Set up a time for a meeting and let your colleague know why you are recommending him to meet with your novice. Read "25 Things Excellent Teachers Do Differently" on TeachThought.com and review the advice with your novice.

CONNECT to Student Voices

Student choice is another way to include student voice in the classroom. Refer to the form titled "How Can Student Choice Help Learning?" available on the companion website and share these ideas with your mentee. Creating a sociogram is a powerful tool; if you have never done this before, use the ACT in this chapter. Think about how you use student choice in your classroom and then share with your mentee.

CONNECT to Education Hot Topics

Attendance matters! Students who come to school regularly have a better chance of retaining learning, succeeding in school, and socializing within society. Search for attendance motivators with your novice teacher to encourage him to reward attendance in his classes. It saves a lot of work doing make up if students show up!

CONNECT With the Companion Website

Video links, forms for this chapter, a featured book, and other resources are located at resources.corwin.com/mentoringinaction.

The First ACT!

Differentiating Mentoring Conversations

Teaching is complex work, and novice teachers can easily become overwhelmed. It is appropriate to customize your mentoring conversations to respond to the varied needs and skills of the mentee.

Directions: Interview your mentee at the beginning of the month to document her areas of strength and needs. Skim the ACTs for this month and decide together which topics are most relevant. Use your state or district teaching standards to focus the mentee's responses to each prompt so you are also teaching her the "common language" of the standards.

Mentee _____ Date _____

Monthly Needs Assessment

1. What is going well in your classroom? (i.e., What is working?) As a teacher, what do you feel you are doing well right now? *Refer to the teaching standards to guide your response.*	3. What would you like to improve or enhance in your practice this month? *Refer to the teaching standards to guide your response.*
2. How do you know your practice is working? (i.e., What is your evidence of success? or Why do you feel confident or competent in an aspect of your teaching?)	4. Review the ACT mentoring conversations for this month with your mentee. Ask which of the ACTs will support you in enhancing your teaching practice? (i.e., what would you like us to focus on this month?)

A digital version of this template (Monthly Needs Assessment Sample With Standards.pdf) is available on the companion website. Keep a copy of this assessment for your files and make a copy for the mentee.

Overview of the ACTs for January Conversations

Directions: Skim the ACTivities listed here and complete the pages that will forward your novice teacher's learning. Your mentee has complementary ACTs in *The First Years Matter* book. Digital copies of any of the reproducible ACTs are available on the companion website.

Key Question Topic	ACTivities	PAGE
Reflect	ACT 1 **Looking Back**	144
Reflect	ACT 2 **Moving Forward**	145
Reflect	ACT 3 **What Do I Believe?**	146
Reflect	ACT 4 **Mentee Self Reflection**	147
Students	ACT 5 **Constructing a Sociogram**	148
Students	ACT 6 **Using Drawings to Gain Student Perspective**	149
Students	ACT 7 **Where Is Your Sense of Humor?**	150
Students	ACT 8 **Classroom and Behavior Management Issues**	151
Students	ACT 9 **Looking at Student Work Together**	152
Communicate	ACT 10 **Communicating With Parents**	153

JANUARY

Looking Back

Key Question: How can you support your mentee in reflecting on the first half of the year?

Directions: Discuss the successes and challenges of the first part of the year. Let your mentee share what she feels and just listen. Ask her to select one of the following activities to use for a written reflection that she can share with you at a future meeting.

1. *Self-Reflection*

Write a letter to yourself that highlights areas of growth, new insights about teaching and learning, or successes. Also include one challenge you are facing that you would like to discuss at a future meeting. Also share what you would like to be acknowledged for so far this year. Indicate one goal you have for the second half of the year. Consider handwriting the letter to slow yourself down a bit and allow the reflective process to emerge. Sign and date your letter. Look back at this letter at the end of the year.

Note: If the challenge you list relates to one student in the classroom, consider doing this reflective process as well.

2. *A Student's Perspective*

Write an imaginary essay from the perspective of the most difficult student in your classroom. Yes that one! In this process, pretend you are the student. Your teacher has required you to write a journal entry about your life and success in school.

Begin the journal by writing Dear Diary, Today I am in school and. . . . My teacher thinks. . . . My life at home is. . . . Sign the student's name at the end.

This is a very powerful process and is especially enlightening when you put yourself in one of your student's shoes. It is an imagined response, and you may not have any idea what this student would think or say. The purpose of the exercise is to guess why a student like this would behave in these ways. Just go with the flow on this one. See what emerges from this student.

Debrief with your mentee after she has completed one or both of these reflection activities. Looking back on successes and challenges can be a rewarding activity. After this, you are ready to move forward to ACT 2.

Moving Forward

Key Question: How can you support your mentee in moving forward?

Directions: Novice teachers worry. They have challenges and problems they struggle with sometimes. One way to move forward is to just get those problems out and to notice they are not insurmountable. By teaching your mentee or small group of novice teachers to see "possibilities" in these problems, you help them grow. Use your skills as a mentor to dissect the problem and make it manageable and measurable. It is also important to note that not all problems can be solved easily. There are also some issues that are out of this teacher's control. Assisting your mentee in using strategies for letting go of issues they can't do anything about is important at this time of year. This process works best in a small group, but you can do it with one mentee too.

Problems to Possibilities

1. Ask the novice teachers to write their most challenging problems or worries on *blue* sticky notes (symbolizes what makes the novice teacher "blue"). Then classify the problems into categories (e.g., student misbehavior, managing paperwork, organizing the room, parent issues) and write that on the top of the sticky note. Invite them to share the problems with each other. Adapt categories as needed to make common categories understood by all novice teachers.

2. Place the blue problems on the Worry Wall at the front of the room in categories as defined by the classifications at the top of the sticky notes.

3. Invite the teachers to walk up to the wall and read all the problems and think about the possible solutions to any of them. Using *yellow* sticky notes, the teachers can place possible solutions on any problems. They can provide multiple solutions to as many problems as they want.

4. The novice teachers who originally placed the problems on the wall now go back and pick them up with the solutions attached to them. Let the teachers talk in pairs about what they received for possibilities.

Debrief: Discuss categories and types of solutions with the entire group at the end of the meeting. Your goal as a mentor is to always provide possible solutions to existing issues and to use available resources to do that. Reminding novice teachers that they can't be all things to all students is important. Working together in small groups demonstrates that everyone has problems and challenges, and it often makes the novice teachers feel more confident.

Companion
Website

What Do I Believe?

Key Question: How can you assist your mentee in documenting her beliefs?

At this time of year, it is important for novice teachers to revisit the philosophy statements they may have written in college or for their job applications. Explain why it is important to revisit their beliefs and ideas about teaching and learning periodically. As a mentor, you should do this too! What do you believe about mentoring? What is your mentoring philosophy? Use this exercise to revisit your ideas and share them with other mentors or your mentor coordinator. This activity works best verbally.

Directions: Ask the following questions.

1. List three words that describe you as a teacher.

   The first words that come to mind . . .

2. List three words your students would use to describe you as a teacher.

   The first three that come to mind . . .

   How do these words compare?

   Why are they alike or different?

3. Now think about your beliefs about teaching and learning. Complete this prompt twice.

   I believe . . .

   I also believe . . .

4. Finally, list one way you are demonstrating what you believe in the classroom. What are you doing that shows what you believe in or who you are (as described in your descriptive words)?

5. Set a goal at the end of the activity to reinforce the ways in which your mentee is actually implementing his belief in the classroom. Sometimes teachers believe in ideals, but their behavior doesn't match. Make this connection explicit for your mentee.

Mentee Self-Reflection

Key Question: What can a novice teacher learn by completing reflection on a lesson?

Directions: One powerful activity at this time of year is to have your mentee look at his practice. When a novice systematically takes time to reflect on practice, he may begin to see what is working and how to modify instruction. Invite your mentee to select one lesson to assess in depth. The reflection prompts below will be in your mentee's book, *The First Years Matter.* Schedule a time to review his reflections and assist him in the next steps.

Directions for the novice teacher: Respond to the prompts below after teaching a lesson. Share your reflections with your mentor and discuss ways to enhance your teaching practices.

1. Did the students learn from my lesson? Were they actively engaged? How do I know?

2. How closely did I follow my lesson plan? Did I have to modify during the lesson? Why?

3. What do I think was the most effective part of the lesson?

4. Were the materials/visuals/aids appropriate? Why? Why not?

5. What would I change/keep the same the next time I do this lesson?

6. What do I see as my teaching strengths?

7. What are my next steps?

Constructing a Sociogram

Key Question: How does knowing what students think about each other inform a teacher's practice?

Directions: Explore the types of sociogram options online. A sociogram illustrates the dynamics in a classroom visually so the novice teacher can see who the stars and isolates are in the classroom. By having this information, she can be more aware of tensions or friendships in the classroom. Assist your mentee in actually doing this process. It is amazing what information is gained. Remind her that this is only for a teacher's eyes and students never see the responses.

Sample Sociogram Process

Step 1 Ask students in the classroom to list three students, by first, second, and third choice, whom they would prefer to work with in the classroom. (Make a distinction between work partners and social partners outside of school.) Tell them it is for possible future group projects and that you may use it to try and create teams with at least one person they prefer to work with.

Step 2 Have the students write why they selected each student. This will give you some insight, and themes may repeat themselves.

Step 3 Collect the data and make a grid with students' names across the top and down the left side. Graph paper works well. Place a 1, 2, or 3 under the student's name as indicated to show choices.

Step 4 Tally the choices to indicate most preferred working partners (commonly called *stars*) and least selected working partners (referred to as *isolates*).

	Sue	David	Adam	Kat
Sue	—	1	3	2
David	3	—	1	2
Adam	3	2	—	1
Kat	3	2	1	—

Using Drawings to Gain Student Perspective

Key Question: How can a visual representation of a teacher illustrate what students think?

Directions: One way to capture perspectives is to have the students draw a picture of the classroom or the teacher. Review these prompts and select one with your mentee that would be a good fit. Younger students love to draw their teachers. High school students may find this boring, but some may like the opportunity to express themselves in a different way. Here are some basic prompts. Feel free to create one of your own!

1. Draw a picture of your teacher (leave it very general—see what students do).

2. Draw a picture of your teacher in the classroom (again, leave it general—just in the classroom).

3. Draw of picture of your teacher teaching (keep it general).

4. Draw a picture of the classroom (don't mention the teacher). See if they put the teacher in or not.

5. Draw a picture of yourself (the student) in the classroom (this would give some insight as to what the student thinks).

6. Draw a picture of yourself (the student) learning something in the classroom.

Obviously, the directions for younger students may have to be more explicit. Some teachers might say, if a camera was brought into this room, what would it see? Draw a picture (i.e., a snapshot of the classroom to capture what it looks like) just like the camera would. Explain to the students that this assignment is being given to allow them to express their ideas in a different way instead of giving a written survey.

Debrief: Discuss the completed drawings and look for themes or interesting illustrations. Together you can note how the teacher is portrayed. Is she standing up front saying "sit down" or "stop talking," or is she at her desk reading, or perhaps the teacher isn't even in the room. This is just one unique way to capture perspectives. Ask your mentee what he learned by doing this that he didn't know. Perhaps compare these results to the sociogram.

Where Is Your Sense of Humor?

Key Question: How can you assist our mentee in seeing the funny side of teaching?

Directions: Most of your meetings are probably spent trying to resolve issues, share challenges, and discuss problems. Even though there is a place for acknowledgment, it often gets buried by pressing emotional worries the novice teachers bring to the table. So what is fun about teaching? Sometime the kids say hysterical things or respond to questions in a funny way. As long as respect is part of the process, it is okay to laugh! Sometimes we just take it all so seriously! Where is the joy?

Remind your mentee that talking about students, their parents, or any other school issue is not appropriate at any event. Everyone has had an experience where you have heard gossip and inappropriate information being transferred about students. Professionalism and confidentiality must be a priority for novice teachers. Have fun but not at others' expense. Using humor does not mean "making fun of" someone else.

Review these activities and consider doing one or more with your mentee.

1. Invite your mentee to share how she uses humor in the classroom with students. Students like teachers who laugh and make learning fun.

2. Schedule a social activity for you and your mentee and talk about other things besides school! Try it!

3. Organize a movie night or social activity just for novice teachers and mentors.

4. Hold a teacher appreciation event for beginning teachers and publically acknowledge what the beginning teachers are doing well.

5. Create a social directory for the novice teachers in the district so they can network and socialize!

JANUARY

Classroom and Behavior Management Issues

Key Question: How can you help your mentee brainstorm solutions to her common problems?

Directions: Read the case with your mentee and discuss how each situation could be handled. Expand the details of the case by adding some grade-level context so it is meaningful to your mentee. Brainstorm at least three possible ways a teacher could respond. Ask your mentee, what would you do if this happened in your classroom?

Case 1: The Class Clown

The class clown comes in late and tells jokes every day during class. Everyone loves her and laughs so hard it is difficult to get their attention. Valuable class time is being wasted.

Case 2: The Bully

This girl hits at least one person a day. She walks by people and punches their arms, or she trips anyone who walks by her desk. She is the terror of the playground.

Case 3: The Lie

A very likable student who always completed his homework lied and said he had handed it in one day. The teacher discovered he had not done it at all and just called out YES when she asked students during roll call.

Case 4: A Destructive Student

A very quiet student exhibits aggressive behavior by quietly breaking pencils at his desk while the teacher is giving the directions.

Case 5: Shouting Out

This student is so excited and wants to participate in class discussions. She always shouts out the answers when the novice teacher asks the class general questions. No one else has a chance to even talk.

Case 6: Sleeper

This student slumps over his desk in the back of the room. He is not disturbing anyone, but he is not learning the material either. He is in danger of failing the class.

Case 7: Cheating

A student was caught cheating on a test. The answers were clearly on her hand, and she was copying them onto her paper. She had cheated before, and at that time said she would not do it again.

Case 8: A Fist Fight

Two students hit each other in the hallway outside the teacher's door about a personal issue. No one is hurt, but a group of students is surrounding them.

Looking at Student Work Together

Key Question: How can a novice teacher find common errors students are making?

Directions: Ask your mentee to bring a set of completed and corrected papers to a meeting with you. Sort the papers into these categories or into the categories in the rubric you are using in your district. Discuss the importance of talking to analyze errors to see if a reteach of a lesson could move students to higher learning.

Below Standard	Meets the Standard	Above Standard
How many papers here?	How many papers here?	How many papers here?
% of class _____	% of class _____	% of class _____

1. Look at all the papers in the Below Standard category or the lowest category in your rubric.

    Is there a pattern illustrating common errors students are making?

    What could your mentee do next to move these students to Meets the Standard category?

2. Look at all the papers in the Meets the Standard category.

    Is there a pattern for errors?

    What could your mentee do next to move these students to Above Standard?

Companion Website

Communicating With Parents

Key Question: How can organized parent meetings help students learn?

Directions: Novice teachers are usually revitalized after a break, and this is a good time to encourage them to schedule meetings with the parents of students they are finding particularly challenging. The purpose of the meeting is how the novice teacher and the parents can work together to support this student's learning. Make sure your mentee lets the parents know this is not a "failing" meeting but rather a "support" meeting so the student will not fail.

Sample Meeting Agenda

1. **Opening the Meeting (options to consider)**

   - I am so glad you could join me today in discussing John's progress.
   - The purpose of this meeting is . . .
   - Can you tell me some things that are going on at home or outside of school right now . . .
   - You know your child better than I do, can you give me some insights so I can help him be successful in school?

2. **Sharing the Positive**

   - This is what I see going well for John right now . . .
   - This sample of work shows he can . . .
   - I also know that John is very good at . . .

3. **Standards and Curriculum Goals**

   - These are the learning goals for ___ grade this year.
   - Let's look at the areas where John needs assistance. By the end of the year, John needs to meet _____ standards.
   - My concerns for John are . . .

4. **Working Together to Set Goals**

   - How can we assist John together?
   - One thing you could do at home is . . .
   - When should we meet again to check on John's progress?

5. **Closing the Meeting on a Positive Note**

   - Thanking parents for attending.
   - Praising them for their support.

January Mentor Reflections

Directions: Complete any of these prompts that stand out for you. Write your responses here or use your Mentor Planning Guide and Journal on the companion website. Share your reflections with your mentor coordinator or with other mentors at a mentor support meeting.

Using Mindfulness to Explore Mentoring Dilemmas

Directions: Read the mentoring dilemma and think about how you would respond in this situation. Consider discussing this dilemma at a mentor support meeting or with another mentor. Share your perspectives about how you would proceed and why you think this would be the best way to forward your novice teacher's practice.

Dilemma 6: Doesn't Matter What the Students Think

It is January, and it is time to reflect back over the first months of the year and reflect on your mentee's strengths and where you need to focus. In a recent conversation in the teacher's room, you overheard your mentee say that it's not the students' voices that matter, it is the principal who will do the rehiring. He said, "Students don't know how to teach, and they shouldn't be evaluating me. They need to just be quiet and listen so I can teach them!" You know that your state's evaluation system is moving toward student feedback, and you have always included students' perspectives in your teaching. *What do you say when you meet for your next mentoring conversation?*

Respond to these prompts in your journal available on the companion website.

1. State the mentor dilemma as clearly as possible in one sentence if you can.

2. What decision do you need to make in regard to this situation?

3. Write about the emotions that come up for you that relate to this situation. If you have two choices, write how the emotions might be different.

4. Stop and reread what you have written. Underline any key words or phrases that stand out for you.

5. Soften your eyes or close them and take three deep breaths. Ask yourself, what am I missing that I have not noticed? Write that down in your journal.

6. What will you say to your mentee? Write your reflection in your journal.

7. If you are truly stuck, bring your dilemma to your lead mentor, a mentor support group meeting, or another experienced mentor. Ask him or her to listen to what you have written and to ask you questions to clarify your dilemma. *Your lead mentor's role is not to tell you what to do! No advice!* Just questions to help you clarify what you want to do.

8. After you have spoken to your mentee, write his reaction and how you feel about this dilemma now. All dilemmas are not resolved! This is a process of clarifying and understanding how you feel and how you could respond.

Directions: Complete all three goal-setting processes and write your responses on this page or in your Mentor Planning Guide and Journal available on the companion website.

1. *Goal for Improving Your Mentee's Teaching Practices*

- Review the PLAN–CONNECT–ACT–REFLECT pages you completed in this chapter with your mentee. Look ahead to February ACTs to see what you may focus on to continue development.

- Acknowledge what your mentee is learning. Be specific and consider using *The 5-Minute Meeting: Giving an Authentic Compliment* in the Appendices to guide you.

- Agree on ONE goal to focus on and reinforce for next month.

- Goal:

2. *Goal to Support the Social and Emotional Well-Being of Your Mentee*

- Discuss any challenges your mentee may be facing right now. Challenges often bring stress.

- Don't ignore any signs of stress in your mentee. Pay attention and teach her ways to manage her stress. Using mindfulness practices can help reduce stress.

- Watch Video 1.5, *Managing Your Stress: Take a Break*, (see page 13), on the companion website, to learn how to take a break at school and minimize your stress.

- Goal:

3. *Goal for Enhancing Your Mentoring Skills*

- Reflect on your own mentoring experience this month. How did you use your strengths and interests to mentor? What will you do differently next month? Write a reflection in your Mentor Planning Guide and Journal.

- Goal:

JANUARY

"

What I think makes a good teacher is that they can teach all kinds of things your parents don't know."

—SIXTH-GRADE STUDENT

NEW TEACHER PHASE: STAYING FOCUSED

"There is so much to teach before the end of the school year. How will I do it all?"

MINDFUL MENTORING AFFIRMATION

I provide positive support and a sense of optimism to novice teachers.

FEBRUARY

ENGAGING STUDENTS IN THE CURRICULUM
Focus on Content Through Active Inquiry

GUIDING QUESTIONS

1. How do you help your novice teacher create a community of learners? The *Reflect ACTivities* will provide ways to approach this task.

2. How will you reinforce students' voices? Use the *Student ACTivities* as a way to think about the options for engaging students.

3. Why is it important to tell parents what you are learning in class? Use the *Communicate ACTivity* as a way to focus on how to update parents on classroom content.

Interstate Teacher Assessment and Support Consortium—InTASC Standards

Review InTASC Standards 4 and 5.

- **Standard 4 Content Knowledge**

The teacher understands the central concepts, tools of inquiry, and structures of the discipline(s) he or she teaches and creates learning experiences that make these aspects of the discipline accessible and meaningful for learners to ensure mastery of the content.

- **Standard 5 Application of Content**

The teacher understands how to connect concepts and use differing perspectives to engage learners in critical thinking, creativity, and collaborative problem solving related to authentic local and global issues.

Chapter Overview

At this time of year, it is important to just keep your mentee focused on teaching. As the quote for this chapter says, "What I think makes a good teacher is that they can teach all kinds of things your parents don't know." So help your mentee remember they do know things!

There is so much new information that beginning teachers often get so scattered that they don't know what they know. Then they don't know what to do first. Break the teaching process and curriculum into bite-sized pieces that your mentee can understand and implement. The curriculum is often a challenging part of the first year because a novice is teaching it for the first time. Remember when you taught a new unit for the first time? This is how your mentee feels every day, every period of the day! Then add getting to know the students, their parents, staff at the school, administration, colleagues, and a mentor! It is a wonder a first-year teacher survives at all. You are critical to supporting this novice teacher's development.

This chapter highlights the continued use of varied teaching strategies as well as the opportunity to give students choices in the classroom. When a teacher can give options to students about what they can do for homework, for example, the students engage and commit to participation in the classroom.

Follow the PLAN, CONNECT, ACT, REFLECT, and SET GOALS sections in this chapter to guide your mentoring conversations and reflections.

The Mindful Mentoring Affirmation for this month is, "I provide support and a sense of optimism to novice teachers." By focusing on what is working and what your mentee brings to teaching, you highlight strength. Optimism brings hope and a sense that your mentee CAN teach effectively.

Watch and listen to a mentor share her insights in the February Chapter Introduction (Video 2.13), available on the companion website or by scanning the QR code on a mobile device.

VIDEO 2.13

February Chapter Introduction

FEBRUARY

Use Questions to Guide Mentoring Conversations

Invite your mentee to write down a short list of questions and bring them to your first February meeting. Use the questions below as a guide for your discussions throughout the month.

Anticipate Beginning Teachers' Possible Questions

1. How do I get my students to support each other and work together?

2. Are there easy ways to integrate media and audiovisual aids into my lessons?

3. I want to foster active inquiry in my lessons, but it just gets too complicated. Can you suggest some teachers I could observe who use this technique to engage their students?

4. I feel like I am talking too much. What are some nonverbal ways I could communicate with my students that will create a supportive environment for learning?

Note other questions your novice teacher asked you so you can have them for the future.

Questions for Your Novice Teacher

1. What are your goals for creating a collaborative learning environment?

2. How do you communicate these goals to your students?

3. What would you do if you could do anything in your classroom right now?

4. What can I do to assist you right now that would reduce your anxiety?

FEBRUARY

Meetings and Observations

Plan brief weekly meetings with your mentee. The ACTs in this chapter serve as mentoring conversation starters and can also be used to assess or review what your mentee may already know about a given topic. Use the Appendices to guide you in scheduling short meetings as well as longer conversations.

Plan to meet at times that allow you to have quality time together in a place without interruptions. Knowing when you will meet each week reduces anxiety for both of you. Novice teachers look forward to regularly scheduled meetings even if they are short. Use a calendar to plan your meetings and classroom visits to ensure they will happen! Include watching videos and reading pages in the *Mentoring in Action* book as part of your *PLAN* for mentoring. A digital version of this calendar (February Calendar.pdf) is available on the companion website.

If you have not already done so, schedule a time to observe your novice teacher for an entire class period this month. Ask the novice what she would like you to look for during the class. Focus on one or two areas so she is not overwhelmed with data. Make sure you have a postconference and you understand how she would like to receive feedback from you. Collecting your thoughts first and writing them down is a good plan. Use ACT 4 in the January chapter to guide you.

February Calendar

MONDAY	TUESDAY	WEDNESDAY	THURSDAY	FRIDAY

Use this calendar to PLAN the month as well as to document meetings and mentor planning.

CONNECT to Additional Resources

CONNECT to School and District Resources

What resources exist in your school and community that could assist novice teachers in February?

CONNECT With Colleagues, Parents, and Families

Who in the professional community could assist with ideas for engaging students?

How can parents be used as resources for sharing content?

CONNECT to Student Voices

How a classroom is organized and what it "feels" like to students matters. Review the ideas on the form "How Does Classroom Space Influence Learning" available on the companion website to discuss physical space issues in the classroom.

CONNECT to Education Hot Topics

Engage students with videos and feature films! Discuss the policies for using online clips and feature films in the classroom in your district. Using a study guide so students know what to look for in the film guides the novice to use the video appropriately. It also demonstrates to the principal that this is time on task.

CONNECT With the Companion Website

Video links, forms for this chapter, a featured book, and other resources are located at resources. corwin.com/mentoringinaction.

The First ACT!

Differentiating Mentoring Conversations

Teaching is complex work, and novice teachers can easily become overwhelmed. It is appropriate to customize your mentoring conversations to respond to the varied needs and skills of the mentee.

Directions: Interview your mentee at the beginning of the month to document her areas of strength and needs. Skim the ACTs for this month and decide together which topics are most relevant. Use your state or district teaching standards to focus the mentee's responses to each prompt so you are also teaching her the "common language" of the standards.

Mentee _____ Date _____

Monthly Needs Assessment

1. What is going well in your classroom? (i.e., What is working?) As a teacher, what do you feel you are doing well right now? *Refer to the teaching standards to guide your response.*	3. What would you like to improve or enhance in your practice this month? *Refer to the teaching standards to guide your response.*
2. How do you know your practice is working? (i.e., What is your evidence of success? or Why do you feel confident or competent in an aspect of your teaching?)	4. Review the ACT mentoring conversations for this month with your mentee. Ask which of the ACTs will support you in enhancing your teaching practice? (i.e., What would you like us to focus on this month?)

A digital version of this template (Monthly Needs Assessment Sample With Standards.pdf) is available on the companion website. Keep a copy of this assessment for your files and make a copy for the mentee.

Overview of the ACTs for February Conversations

Directions: Skim the ACTivities listed here and complete the pages that will forward your novice teacher's learning. Your mentee has complementary ACTs in *The First Years Matter* book. Digital copies of any of the reproducible ACTs are available on the companion website.

Key Question Topic	ACTivities	PAGE
Reflect	ACT 1 **Using Varied Teaching Strategies**	166
Reflect	ACT 2 **How Much Time?**	167
Reflect	ACT 3 **Engaging Learners**	168
Students	ACT 4 **Student Choices to Enhance Learning**	169
Students	ACT 5 **Homework: Does It Work?**	170
Students	ACT 6 **Classroom and Behavior Management Issues**	171
Students	ACT 7 **Looking at Student Work Together**	172
Communicate	ACT 8 **Communicating With Parents**	173

FEBRUARY

Using Varied Teaching Strategies

Key Question: How many different teaching strategies is your mentee using?

Directions: Reflect with your mentee to assess how she is meeting the needs of the diverse learners in her classroom. Review her preferred teaching style in December ACT 2 and discuss how she is expanding her style to include the students who may have a different learning style.

1. **Is she using both auditory and visual directions?** Students in the classroom may prefer auditory or visual directions, so to ensure everyone understands what to do, an effective teacher does both. By writing the directions on the board or displaying them on the computer, the teacher makes the assignment visible and available for late-arriving students.

2. **Is she demonstrating key concepts by using visual examples?** After directions are given and the novice teacher feels students understand the directions, specific examples should be given to concretely show what is expected. This does not mean students are supposed to copy the example. It is to provide a visual prop that is used by the teacher to demonstrate what is expected.

3. **Is she allowing for student choice when appropriate?** Example: If the goal is to solve a word problem in math, choices for solving could include paper and pencil, manipulatives, working alone, or working with a partner. The point is that students use their best learning style to complete the assignment. Does your mentee know how to do this?

4. **Is she allowing for different learning paces?** Students think and work at different speeds. The faster thinkers are not necessarily the most accurate or the most creative problem solvers. Don't let your mentee reward students for completing their work quickly. Sometimes students rush just to receive a reward and their work may not be correct. If students do finish early, the teacher has to be prepared to provide additional activities. Discuss the challenges of students who work too quickly and those who work very slowly. Brainstorm possible solutions to each situation.

5. **Is she assisting students who need support?** Some students will need additional support during a lesson because they do not understand the directions or are unable to complete the task. You may not have time to walk around the room and meet with these students individually. One strategy is to let them work with a partner who is able to explain more clearly what is expected. These "partner coaches" can be selected before class begins, and they do not have to have their own work done to assist.

How Much Time?

Key Question: How do you help your mentee learn how to pace a lesson?

Directions: Observe your novice teacher and record the start and end times for each part of a lesson. Share what you learned and discuss adjustments that need to be made to ensure this is enough time for learning.

Sample			
Topic	**Time Starts**	**Time Ends**	**Total**
Introduction to lesson			
Giving directions			
Lecturing			
Answering questions			
Asking questions			
Practice work			
Reprimanding			
Checking for understanding			
Students actively engaged/ demonstrating learning			

Debrief

1. What took up the most time during the lesson?

2. What took up the least time during the lesson?

3. Ask your mentee what stands out for him when he sees the data.

Companion Website

FEBRUARY

Engaging Learners

Key Question: How well is your mentee engaging all learners?

Directions: Review this list of ideas and ask your mentee to select the two that stand out as the most important. Encourage her to think about creative ways to keep all the students interested and motivated.

1. Create a classroom where students ask and answer questions. In most classrooms, the teacher asks a question and the same students raise their hands and get called on. Other students are silent, and the class becomes a boring back and forth with the teacher and a few students. What if the students wrote the questions and other students answered them? How can your mentee create this kind of environment? More engagement, less distracted students.

2. Create opportunities for project-based learning. Let your students create teams and show you what they know by working together on a common task. Help your mentee design an assessment tool that measures work quality as well as effort.

3. Have students correct their own papers. Design a process where students get to assess how sure they are their answers are correct before they pass their work in. For example, if they are 100% sure the answer is correct, they put a C next to their answer. If they are not sure, they put an NS or perhaps as 50%. By looking back at their own work, they can assess how sure they are about their responses. This requires the brain to work in a different way, and the students stay engaged.

4. Create an emotionally safe classroom environment. Discuss the ways this shows up with your mentee such as we don't talk about anyone in this class, and we don't say shut up, or laugh at others. A respectful classroom allows for students to feel safe, and then they can engage in learning. By including compliments from students to students in the day, the novice teacher can ensure students feel good about themselves.

Student Choices to Enhance Learning

Key Question: How can student choice motivate and engage learners?

Directions: Discuss ways your mentee can integrate choice to motivate the unmotivated learner. Students usually know how they learn best, and if you can offer them a variety of ways in which to show you that they know the material, they will feel more successful and will be more invested in the work. Discuss how this can be particularly useful for students whose first language is not English or students with special needs. If you use student choice in your classroom, share what works for you.

1. Examples of ways choice can be incorporated into your mentee's classroom:

   - Choosing a homework assignment from three that are acceptable.
   - Choosing a partner to work with on a project.
   - Choosing an independent reading book.
   - Choosing the type of test (multiple choice, essay, short answer).
   - Creating a test by choosing all the items that would go on the test.

2. Brainstorm some other ways to incorporate choice to promote interest and enthusiasm in the content.

3. Discuss how options for completing a learning task could create more interest in demonstrating learning. For example, students could choose to . . .

   - Use paper and pencil
   - Use manipulatives
   - Draw the answer
   - Work alone
   - Work with a partner
   - Act out the answer
   - Use a mobile device
   - Make a video

Companion Website

FEBRUARY

Homework: Does It Work?

Key Question: What does your mentee need to know about homework?

Directions: Discuss homework policies with your mentee. Review the following questions with her and share you opinion of homework and its value.

1. Do students have to pass in homework? Is it always required?

2. Does homework only relate to the content?

3. Do students get to select homework activities?

4. Is homework extra credit or required?

5. Does homework "count" and get corrected by the teachers in the school?

6. Can homework be "extra credit" for students who are really motivated?

7. Can students create their own homework?

8. Does homework have to be by the book, or can students create their own way to demonstrate what they learned? Draw a floor plan of a dream house using geometry skills, for example.

9. What happens if students don't do their required homework? For example, students are assigned a chapter to read in a book and you designed a lesson around the expectation that they had read it. What do you do about the planned lesson?

10. If homework doesn't really count and it isn't corrected by teachers, why is it assigned?

Classroom and Behavior Management Issues

Key Question: What are appropriate rewards for students?

Directions: Discuss this list and decide how any rewards should be implemented in your school and your mentee's classroom. It is important to find appropriate rewards. Here are some typical rewards for elementary and secondary students. What would you add to the list? What would you never use as a reward? Why?

Elementary Rewards	Secondary Rewards
Free time	Free time
Watch a video	Read a magazine
Do errands for the teacher	Work on computer
Lead the line	See a film/video
Go to the reading center	Food
Pick out a book	Class trip
Play with the pet in class	Play sports during day
Listen to music in class	Listen to music in class
Stickers	Wear a hat in class
Pencils	Use the video camera
Ice cream	Time off from school
A certificate	Be coach's assistant
Pizza party	Make a t-shirt
Magic markers	Teach a class
Free recess	Free homework pass
Sit next to a friend for a day	Read a newspaper

Companion Website

FEBRUARY

Looking at Student Work Together

Key Question: How can identifying one key skill enhance student learning?

Directions: By looking at student work with your mentee, you can help him understand what students need to move to the next level of learning. Ask your mentee to bring four work samples that are below standard. Assist him in finding one skill per student that would be the next thing this student should learn. Taking underperforming learners and moving them step-by-step allows the student and the novice teacher to feel some level of success. It also clearly identifies one skill to focus on. What should the student learn next that is developmentally appropriate? How can that one skill be a tipping point for more learning?

Student	List several skills student is not meeting.	What is the one skill the student could focus on next to improve learning?
1		
2		
3		
4		

Discuss any patterns or trends that emerge in the novice teachers' discussion about what one thing these students need to do next to learn.

Communicating With Parents

Key Question: How could a novice teacher update parents about content?

Directions: Review this process with your mentee and encourage her to try this or another idea.

Monthly Content Updates

Parents need to know what the students are learning so when novice teachers contact them, they understand how they can be helpful at home. Parents can also be valuable partners to teaching if they are familiar with the topic and have experience speaking in classrooms. Use the update as a way to get volunteers, guest speakers, and even some donations! Elementary teachers may use this model, and secondary teachers would focus on their content and list units of study.

Content Update for February Ms. Smith Grade 5		
Content Areas	**What We Are Learning**	**How You Can Help Us Learn . . .**
Math	Fractions	Donate some manipulates we can use. Come to class as a volunteer to tutor students.
Science	Ecology unit (saving our rivers)	Be a guest speaker. Allow us to visit you at your work (i.e., field trip).
Social Studies	World War II	Be a guest speaker (you know about the war or a grandparent may have served in the war).
Language Arts	Writing letters	Sharing your letter writing skills and sample letters you have written. Donating stationery, stamps, pens so the class can write real letters to people in a nursing home.

Add at the end of the memo to: Contact Ms. Smith at 552-XXXX if you can help our class this month. Thank you!

February Mentor Reflections

Directions: Complete any of these prompts that stand out for you and add your own prompts to the blank stems. Write your responses here or use your Mentor Planning Guide and Journal on the companion website. Share your reflections with your mentor coordinator or with other mentors at a mentor support meeting.

Using Mindfulness to Explore Mentoring Dilemmas

Directions: Read the mentoring dilemma and think about how you would respond in this situation. Consider discussing this dilemma at a mentor support meeting or with another mentor. Share your perspectives about how you would proceed and why you think this would be the best way to forward your novice teacher's practice.

Dilemma 7: Is This Content Accurate?

It is February, and it is time for state content tests. The focus on the content this year is very important at your school because the school is underperforming. You observe a lesson and discover the content the teacher is using does not seem to be accurate. When you question her, she says this is what she received from the department chair and was told to teach it this way. You are not a history major, but your interpretation of history seems to differ from what is being presented. You are worried that the students might be confused and give the incorrect answer on the test based on this lesson. *What do you say?*

Respond to these prompts in your journal available on the companion website.

1. State the mentor dilemma as clearly as possible in one sentence if you can.

2. What decision do you need to make in regard to this situation?

3. Write about the emotions that come up for you that relate to this situation. If you have two choices, write how the emotions might be different.

4. Stop and reread what you have written. Underline any key words or phrases that stand out for you.

5. Soften your eyes or close them and take three deep breaths. Ask yourself, what am I missing that I have not noticed? Write that down in your journal.

6. What will you say to your mentee? Write your reflection in your journal.

7. If you are truly stuck, bring your dilemma to your lead mentor, a mentor support group meeting, or another experienced mentor. Ask him or her to listen to what you have written and to ask you questions to clarify your dilemma. *Your lead mentor's role is not to tell you what to do! No advice!* Just questions to help you clarify what you want to do.

8. After you have spoken to your mentee, write his reaction and how you feel about this dilemma now. All dilemmas are not resolved! This is a process of clarifying and understanding how you feel and how you could respond.

Directions: Complete all three goal-setting processes and write your responses on this page or in your Mentor Planning Guide and Journal available on the companion website.

1. *Goal for Improving Your Mentee's Teaching Practices*

- Review the PLAN–CONNECT–ACT–REFLECT pages you completed in this chapter with your mentee. Look ahead to March ACTs to see what you may focus on to continue development.

- Acknowledge what your mentee is learning. Be specific and encouraging especially if your mentee has taken some risks to try to learn new teaching strategies this month.

- Agree on ONE goal to focus on and reinforce for next month.

- Goal:

2. *Goal to Support the Social and Emotional Well-Being of Your Mentee*

- Discuss any challenges your mentee may be facing right now. Challenges often bring stress.

- Don't ignore any signs of stress in your mentee. Pay attention and teach her ways to manage her stress. Using mindfulness practices can help reduce stress.

- Explore mindfulness books for teachers online. Review this one to see if it may be helpful to you and your novice teacher, *Mindfulness for Teachers: Simple Skills for Peace and Productivity in the Classroom* by Patricia Jennings.

- Goal:

3. *Goal for Enhancing Your Mentoring Skills*

- Reflect on your own mentoring experience this month. How did you use your strengths and interests to mentor? What will you do differently next month? Write a reflection in your Mentor Planning Guide and Journal.

- Goal:

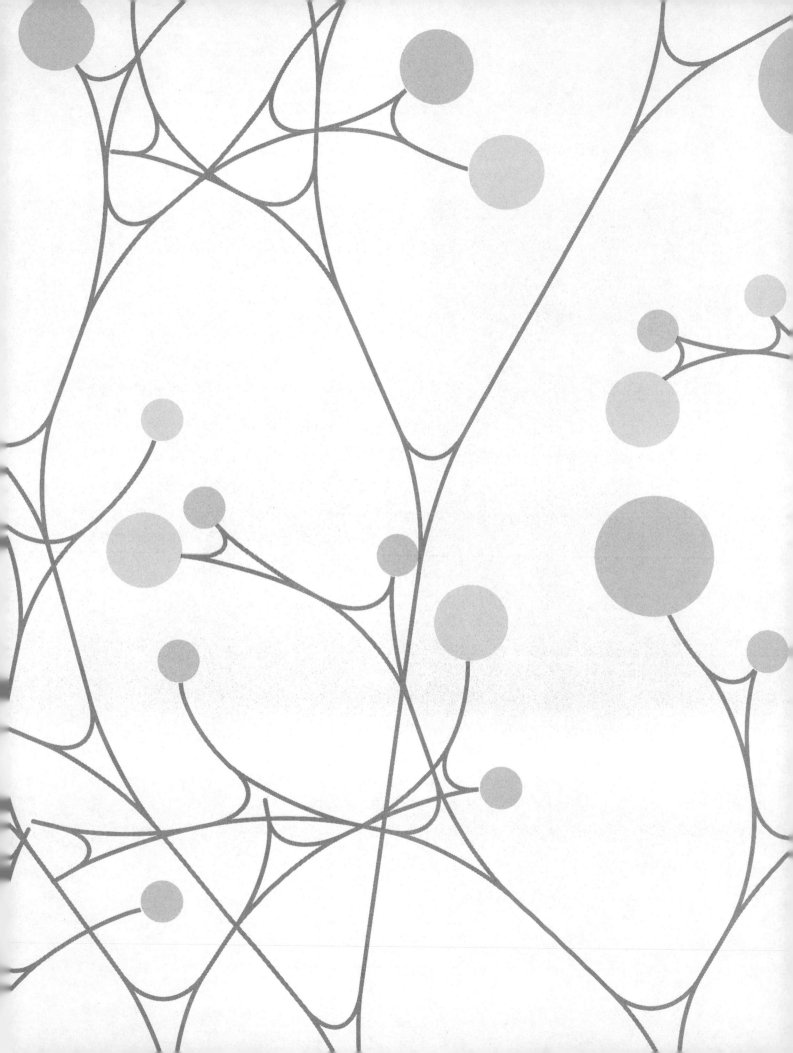

"

In my opinion, a good teacher is someone who teaches you
what you need to know for everyday life and has fun doing it."
—EIGHTH-GRADE STUDENT

NEW TEACHER PHASE: COLLEGIALITY

"I want to improve my practice.
Can you help me?"

MINDFUL MENTORING AFFIRMATION

I collaborate and empower novice teachers
to solve daily challenges.

MARCH

COLLABORATING WITH NOVICE TEACHERS

Observing and Building a Trusting Relationship

GUIDING QUESTIONS

1. How do you help your novice teacher reflect and improve his teaching practices? The **Collaborate ACTivities** will provide you with options to discuss with your mentee.

2. How will you help your novice teacher stay connected to professional groups? The **Network ACTivities** offer you ideas to discuss.

3. How will you keep students central to your mentoring conversations? Use the **Student ACTivities** to revisit these topics.

4. Why is it important to reach out to the community and business partners? Use the **Communicate ACTivity** as a way to introduce this topic.

Interstate Teacher Assessment and Support Consortium—InTASC Standards

Review InTASC Standard 10.

- **Standard 10 Leadership and Collaboration**

The teacher seeks appropriate leadership roles and opportunities to take responsibility for student learning, to collaborate with learners, families, colleagues, other school professionals, and community members to ensure learner growth, and to advance the profession.

Chapter Overview

Collaboration can be fun. Teaching has often been called an isolating profession, and many people think it is still that way. Today there are more opportunities to co-teach, create curriculum together, work across disciplines, and create teacher study groups. Collaboration can be challenging work. It means meetings, discussions, and decisions based on input from more than one person. Some teachers think it just isn't worth it. Others have made it enjoyable and a refreshing departure from a day spent mostly with students. Discuss collegiality and professionalism with your mentee. What does collegiality mean to her?

The quote from the student illustrates that students notice when teachers are having fun when they teaching. Students know when teachers love their content too. As a mentor, share what you love about teaching and what is fun for you with your mentee.

InTASC Principle 10 Leadership and Collaboration highlights the importance of leadership roles in the school. Novice teachers can be leaders to. You can help this emerging leadership by encouraging your mentee to host a novice teacher meeting or colead a seminar for other teachers in the school with you. Watch Video 1.1, *Sharing Best Practices: Emerging Teacher Leaders* (see page 5), to see how a mentor and a novice teacher collaborate to build a support group for beginning teachers.

The Mindful Mentoring Affirmation for this month is, "I collaborate and empower novice teachers to solve daily challenges." Collaboration is key to development. Mentors at this time of the year should be less directive and more collaborative. As you empower your novice, she will emerge with more confidence and be willing to take on leadership roles within the school. Your role becomes more behind the scenes as you create the space for her success. Like the butterfly metaphor in the beginning of Part II of this book, the mentee will slowly open her wings as she breaks through the chrysalis. You are the assisting in this transformation.

Follow the PLAN, CONNECT, ACT, REFLECT, and SET GOALS sections in this chapter to guide your mentoring conversations and reflections.

Watch and listen to a mentor share her insights in the March Chapter Introduction (Video 2.14), available on the companion website or by scanning the QR code on a mobile device.

VIDEO 2.14

March Chapter Introduction

MARCH

Use Questions to Guide Mentoring Conversations

Invite your mentee to write down a short list of questions and bring them to your first March meeting. Use the questions below as a guide for your discussions throughout the month.

Anticipate Beginning Teachers' Possible Questions

1. How can I get to know the other teachers in this school?

2. What are some of the local agencies I should be aware of that can assist me with students or that offer resources for teachers?

3. I would like to sponsor some kind of parent event in my classroom. Can you help me navigate school politics to do that?

4. What else do I need to know about relationships in this school that will assist me with my students?

List the other questions your novice teachers brought to the meeting so you will have them for your next mentoring cycle.

Note the other questions your novice teacher has asked you so you will have them for the future.

Questions for Your Novice Teacher

1. How can I help you connect with other novice teachers in the school or district?

2. How are you getting along with other teachers right now?

3. What is your next step to connecting with parents?

4. What can I do to assist you right now that would reduce your anxiety?

Meetings and Observations

Plan brief weekly meetings with your mentee. The ACTs in this chapter serve as mentoring conversation starters and can also be used to assess or review what your mentee may already know about a given topic. Use the Appendices to guide you in scheduling short meetings as well as longer conversations.

Plan to meet at times that allow you to have quality time together in a place without interruptions. Knowing when you will meet each week reduces anxiety for both of you. Novice teachers look forward to regularly scheduled meetings even if they are short. Use a calendar to plan your meetings and classroom visits to ensure they will happen! Include watching videos and reading pages in the *Mentoring in Action* book as part of your *PLAN* for mentoring. A digital version of this calendar (March Calendar.pdf) is available on the companion website.

Encourage your mentee to assess her lessons regularly and "self-assess" how effective she is in the classroom. Have her review the InTASC or district evaluation standards to see if she would assess herself as proficient.

March Calendar

MONDAY	TUESDAY	WEDNESDAY	THURSDAY	FRIDAY

Use this calendar to PLAN the month as well as to document meetings and mentor planning.

CONNECT to Additional Resources

CONNECT to School and District Resources

What resources exist in your school and community that could assist novice teachers in March?

CONNECT With Colleagues, Parents, and Families

How can you promote collaboration among the school community with your mentee?

How are parents and families part of collaboration in your school?

CONNECT to Student Voices

One way to create a positive community is to encourage student compliments. Their voices will model respect and demonstrate verbally how they show respect. Discuss with your mentee how compliments can be integrated into the daily routine. The teacher can model this process by saying, "I would like to compliment John for helping Sarah with her homework yesterday." Compliments should always relate to learning or respectful behavior for the classroom.

CONNECT to Education Hot Topics

Interact with colleagues! Collaboration is often listed as an important teacher skill. Check out "Five Ways to Get More Out of Teacher to Teacher Collaboration" posted on the We Are Teachers website. Sometimes collaboration is difficult. Discuss with your mentee what to do when you have to engage in a hard conversation and check out the featured book *Having Hard Conversations* by Jennifer Abrams.

CONNECT With the Companion Website

Video links, forms for this chapter, a featured book, and other resources are located at resources. corwin.com/mentoringinaction.

The First ACT!

Differentiating Mentoring Conversations

Teaching is complex work, and novice teachers can easily become overwhelmed. It is appropriate to customize your mentoring conversations to respond to the varied needs and skills of the mentee.

Directions: Interview your mentee at the beginning of the month to document her areas of strength and needs. Skim the ACTs for this month and decide together which topics are most relevant. Use your state or district teaching standards to focus the mentee's responses to each prompt so you are also teaching her the "common language" of the standards.

Mentee _____ Date _____

Monthly Needs Assessment

1. What is going well in your classroom? (i.e., What is working?) As a teacher, what do you feel you are doing well right now? *Refer to the teaching standards to guide your response.*	3. What would you like to improve or enhance in your practice this month? *Refer to the teaching standards to guide your response.*
2. How do you know your practice is working? (i.e., What is your evidence of success? or Why do you feel confident or competent in an aspect of your teaching?)	4. Review the ACT mentoring conversations for this month with your mentee. Ask which of the ACTs will support you in enhancing your teaching practice? (i.e., What would you like us to focus on this month?)

A digital version of this template (Monthly Needs Assessment Sample With Standards.pdf) is available on the companion website. Keep a copy of this assessment for your files and make a copy for the mentee.

Overview of the ACTs for March Conversations

Directions: Skim the ACTivities listed here and complete the pages that will forward your novice teacher's learning. Your mentee has complementary ACTs in *The First Years Matter* book. Digital copies of any of the reproducible ACTs are available on the companion website.

Key Question Topic	ACTivities	PAGE
Collaborate	ACT 1 **Ways to Provide Feedback**	186
Collaborate	ACT 2 **Observation Options**	187
Collaborate	ACT 3 **Preconference Is a Must**	188
Collaborate	ACT 4 **Observation Feedback Form**	189
Collaborate	ACT 5 **Preparing a Novice Teacher for a Principal Observation**	190
Students	ACT 6 **Classroom and Behavior Management Issues**	191
Students	ACT 7 **Looking at Student Work Together**	192
Communicate	ACT 8 **Communicating With Parents**	193

Ways to Provide Feedback

Key Question: How does a mentor provide nonjudgmental feedback to a novice teacher?

Directions: Novice teachers want feedback so they know how to improve. They like praise, but need specific direction to continue practices that actually have an impact on student learning. Sometimes they don't know what they are doing right because they spend so much time seeing what is wrong. Respectful feedback that relates to standards will allow your mentee to grow. This feedback should be data driven and not simply advice.

Before giving feedback to your mentee, reflect on your own experiences and remember what you liked about getting feedback. How did feedback make you feel? What types of feedback were useful to you? Do you like written feedback so you can think about it later? Do you prefer to have an informal conversation or a formal sit down meeting? Your reflections will provide a lens through which to understand how your mentee may feel. The key is to *ask* how your mentee would prefer to receive feedback. Then provide the feedback the way she can hear it and implement it.

	Verbal	**Written**
Informal Unplanned	• Talking after a lesson • Seeing each other in the hallway • A 5-minute compliment meeting (see Appendix)	• A written note put into the teacher's mailbox
Informal Planned	• Any meetings from Appendix for 10, 15, 20, 30 minutes • Audiotaping a lesson and listening together	• A dialogue journal that you and the novice teacher keep
Formal Planned	• A mentoring conversation • A formal observation • Videotaping a lesson and discussing	• Data collected at formal observations

Companion Website

Observation Options

Key Question: What are the options for observing a mentee?

Directions: Decide together which strategy you will use to gather data. Use any of the techniques on this page or create a process of your own. If you are new to observing, watch Videos 1.7 and 1.8, *Observation and Feedback Tools Part 1 and Part 2* (see page 20), on the companion website.

1. *Scripting.* Writing what the novice teacher says and how she moves during the lesson. This is a profile of the lesson in narrative form.

2. *Verbal Feedback.* Listening to your novice teacher's tone and voice. Noting speaking as it relates to asking questions, giving praise, talking time, reprimanding, or calling on students.

3. *Movement.* Recording how the teacher moves around the room or how students interact with the teacher.

4. *Timing.* Recording the time it takes for introducing, giving directions, answering questions, doing assignments, and cleaning up.

5. *Audiotaping.* Providing equipment and taping you for voice, articulation, directions, or any specific aspect of speech.

6. *Videotaping.* Recording a lesson and observing the lesson together with nonjudgmental questions prepared by the mentor.

Preconference Is a Must

Key Question: Why is a preconference important?

Directions: An observation cycle consists of (1) a preconference, at which the process is discussed; (2) the observation, when the data are collected; and (3) a postconference for discussion and feedback about the lesson. Before formally observing your mentee, schedule a preconference with your mentee.

1. Share observation techniques and mutually agree on one that you will use to observe the lesson. If this is your first time observing a novice teacher, you may get some advice from your mentor coordinator or another experienced mentor.

2. Review the standards and ask your mentee what she would like you to focus on. Discuss the specific purpose of the observation so she understands what type of data you are collecting. The more focused you are the easier it will be to observe. The two of you can decide which technique may be suited to the lesson and what particular skill the novice teacher is interested in learning more about.

3. Request a formal lesson plan and review it at the preconference so you know what you will be seeing in this class.

4. After the data is collected, sit together and discuss one specific thing that would improve the novice teacher's practice and his or her students' learning. Acknowledge what is going well and set a date to check in on the goal's progress.

5. Reflect on the experience of observing. What went well? What will you do differently next time?

Observation Feedback Form

Key question: How can you share your observations in writing?

Directions: Use this form as a summary of key ideas to be shared at the postconference. This form is available on the companion website.

Date: _____ Subject/Grade: _____

Time of lesson: _____ Title: _____

1. Clarity of lesson plan:

2. Student learning objective:

3. Engagement of students during the lesson:

4. Modifications for varying abilities:

5. Standards addressed in the lesson:

6. Assessment:

7. Pacing of the lesson:

8. Other observations:

9. Recommendation:

10. Commendation:

Companion Website

Preparing a Novice Teacher for a Principal Observation

Key Question: How can a mentor prepare a novice for an evaluation observation?

Directions: Novice teachers get nervous when they are observed by an evaluator. Review the ideas on this page to prepare your mentee. You can also do a practice observation and use the same forms the principal will be using. Share the following.

Before the Observation . . .

- Remind your mentee that the purpose of the principal's observation is to assess, not to criticize. The principal can learn a lot about a teacher by observing.

- Tell your mentee to write the objective of the lesson on the board and how it relates to the school standards. What will the students be learning in this lesson, and why are they learning this?

- Encourage your mentee to talk to other teachers who have been observed to find out what the format of the observation will be.

- Meet with the administrator in advance to share the lesson plan and find out what will be expected during the observation.

- Plan the lesson completely and be sure that all materials and supplies are in place.

- Organize and clean the classroom so the principal can walk around student desks.

During the Observation . . .

- Be yourself and forget that the principal is in the room (if you can!).

- Remember you are not perfect, and you are willing to learn from feedback during the postconference.

After the Observation . . .

- Write down your thoughts about how the lesson went and what you think could be better.

- Attend the postconference meeting with the principal.

- Listen to the feedback and share your perspective.

- Don't defend your actions; rather, be open to suggestions and new learning.

- After the meeting, write in your journal what you learned about yourself in this process.

- Meet with your mentor and share what you learned.

Classroom and Behavior Management Issues

Key Question: How can you help your mentee document student meetings?

Directions: Review this conference report format with your mentee and discuss other ways to document meetings.

Individual Student Conference Reports

If novice teachers are having difficulty with one student, encourage them to meet with the student privately to discuss the issue. Use a conference report like the one on this page to document the conversation and to let the student know that this is a formal meeting. A digital version of the Conference Report is provided on the companion website. The conference report system provides documentation if further action is required by the teacher.

Conference Report

Student's Name: _____ Date: _____

Reason for Conference:

Summary of Conference:

Next Steps:

Signature of Teacher _____

Signature of Student _____

Companion
Website

Looking at Student Work Together

Key Question: How can a novice teacher assess growth over time with one student?

Directions: Ask the novice to select a student in the class who is struggling and bring four work samples (from different assignments) to a meeting with you. Take turns looking at each assignment using your school rubric and assess which skills the student is not meeting for each assignment. Notice if there is a pattern or trend in this student's errors.

Then decide what is one thing the novice teacher could do to help this student improve. Is the student making the same error on each assignment? Specifically what does the teacher have to teach this student to move her to the next level?

Assignment Topic	List several skills student is not meeting.	What is ONE skill to focus on that would improve the quality of this assignment?	What does the novice teacher need to do to move the student to the next level of learning?
1.			
2.			
3.			
4.			

Communicating With Parents

Key Question: How can you support novice teachers in collaborating with parents and the community?

Directions: There are a variety of ways in which novice teachers can collaborate with parents and other adults in the community. If the school or district has a formal program for community collaboration, share this information with your mentee. Discuss the ideas below with your mentee and consider collaborating to organize one of these events.

1. *Parent Workshop or Lecture Night*

Invite a parent or community member to speak at an evening event held at the school. Select a topic that relates to the content that is being taught this month. The purpose of the event is for the parents to learn the content so they can either help their children at home or just have a better understanding of what their children are learning in school. Students come to the event with their parents and participate in the workshop or listen to the lecture together. An example of an elementary or middle school workshop could be a hands-on math night where the teacher uses manipulatives to teach fractions. A secondary lecture on a historic event related to a history course or a science lecture related to the science curriculum could be fun for both parents and students. Perhaps the students could be part of the workshop or lecture where they introduce the guest speaker or share some of the work they have done on the topic.

2. *Business Partnerships*

Mentors from local business may be interested in tutoring or reading to students. By using adult human resources, novice teachers get to know who is who in the community while also getting some help for their classroom. The partnerships could also provide guest speakers for in-school talks or lecture nights. There is also the possibility of donations of older computers and file cabinets that businesses often toss when they are updating and redesigning. Do you have any connections for your mentee?

3. *Alumni Mentoring Program*

Graduates of local high schools and colleges often like to come back to mentor students at risk. Students who have successfully completed a college program often want to give back and pay it forward with students at their school. These young role models show the students that there is a reason to stay in school and get good grades. Graduating from high school is important today, and the dropout rate is growing because of failure on high-stakes tests. Mentoring may help, and it can begin early. How could this idea support your mentee?

March Mentor Reflections

Directions: Complete any of these prompts that stand out for you and add your own prompts to the blank stems. Write your responses here or use your Mentor Planning Guide and Journal on the companion website. Share your reflections with your mentor coordinator or with other mentors at a mentor support meeting.

I would like to have my novice teacher(s) observe me teach . . .

A professional conference or meeting I would like to share with my novice teacher(s) . . .

I would like to connect my novice teacher(s) with the following educator adults . . .

I am surprised by . . .

Using Mindfulness to Explore Mentoring Dilemmas

Directions: Read the mentoring dilemma and think about how you would respond in this situation. Consider discussing this dilemma at a mentor support meeting or with another mentor. Share your perspectives about how you would proceed and why you think this would be the best way to forward your novice teacher's practice.

Dilemma 8: A Mentor's Role

March's topic is about collaboration and observing the novice teacher. You have built a wonderful trusting relationship with your mentee, and she willingly invites you to her classroom. At this time of year, the principal is also coming to observe and provide feedback. Since the principal is new to your school, she has asked if you would provide her with some information about your mentee before she goes to observe. She wants to make sure she sees the strengths and areas for growth before she makes her recommendation to the superintendent for rehiring. She knows you are an experienced mentor and keen observer. *What do you say to the new principal?*

Respond to these prompts in your journal available on the companion website.

1. State the mentor dilemma as clearly as possible in one sentence if you can.

2. What decision do you need to make in regard to this situation?

3. Write about the emotions that come up for you that relate to this situation. If you have two choices, write how the emotions might be different.

4. Stop and reread what you have written. Underline any key words or phrases that stand out for you.

5. Soften your eyes or close them and take three deep breaths. Ask yourself, what am I missing that I have not noticed? Write that down in your journal.

6. What will you say to your mentee? Write your reflection in your journal.

7. If you are truly stuck, bring your dilemma to your lead mentor, a mentor support group meeting, or another experienced mentor. Ask him or her to listen to what you have written and to ask you questions to clarify your dilemma. *Your lead mentor's role is not to tell you what to do! No advice!* Just questions to help you clarify what you want to do.

8. After you have spoken to your mentee, write his reaction and how you feel about this dilemma now. All dilemmas are not resolved! This is a process of clarifying and understanding how you feel and how you could respond.

Directions: Complete all three goal-setting processes and write your responses on this page or in your Mentor Planning Guide and Journal available on the companion website.

1. *Goal for Improving Your Mentee's Teaching Practices*

   - Review the PLAN–CONNECT–ACT–REFLECT pages you completed in this chapter with your mentee. Look ahead to April ACTs to see what you may focus on to continue development.

   - Acknowledge what your mentee is learning. Use the Observation Feedback Form ACT 4 to provide some specific details in writing.

   - Agree on ONE goal to focus on and reinforce for next month.

   - Goal:

2. *Goal to Support the Social and Emotional Well-Being of Your Mentee*

   - Discuss any challenges your mentee may be facing right now. Challenges often bring stress.

   - Don't ignore any signs of stress in your mentee. Pay attention and teach her ways to manage her stress. Using mindfulness practices can help reduce stress.

   - Explore mindfulness and Jon Kabut-Zinn's work. Select any one of his YouTube videos to learn more ways to reduce stress and promote wellness.

   - Goal:

3. *Goal for Enhancing Your Mentoring Skills*

   - Reflect on your own mentoring experience this month. How did you use your strengths and interests to mentor? What will you do differently next month? Write a reflection in your Mentor Planning Guide and Journal.

   - Goal:

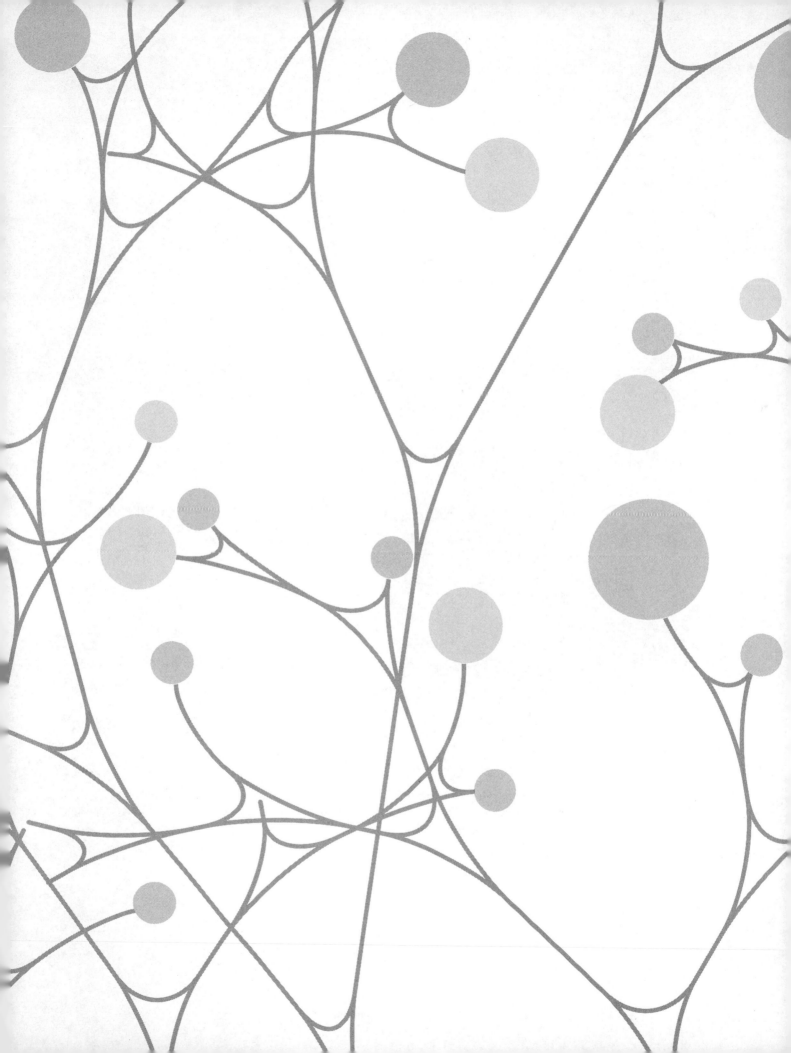

"

A good teacher goes to teacher school."
—FIRST-GRADE STUDENT

NEW TEACHER PHASE: CONFUSION

"How can I teach what is important and also meet the district standards for high-stakes tests?"

MINDFUL MENTORING AFFIRMATION

I am a mindful mentor who focuses mentoring conversations on learning.

APRIL

STANDARDS
Creating Meaningful Standards-Based Learning Experiences for Students

GUIDING QUESTIONS

1. How do you help your novice teacher set realistic goals to improve his practice? The **Goals ACTivities** will provide ways to approach this task.

2. How can you introduce student observation as a way to improve practice? Use the **Student ACTivities** as a guide.

3. How can you share the importance of good study skills with parents? Use the **Communicate ACTivity** as a discussion starter with your mentee.

Interstate Teacher Assessment and Support Consortium—InTASC Standards

Revisit InTASC Standards 1, 2, and 3.

- **Standard 1 Learner Development**

The teacher understands how learners grow and develop, recognizing that patterns of learning and development vary individually within and across the cognitive, linguistic, social, emotional, and physical areas, and designs and implements developmentally appropriate and challenging learning experiences.

- **Standard 2 Learning Differences**

The teacher uses understanding of individual differences and diverse cultures and communities to ensure inclusive learning environments that enable each learner to meet high standards.

- **Standard 3 Learning Environments**

The teacher works with others to create environments that support individual and collaborative learning, and that encourage positive social interaction, active engagement in learning, and self motivation.

Chapter Overview

The first-grade student who said, "A good teacher goes to teacher school" recognized the importance of professional development. Teaching is a lifelong learning profession. There is so much to learn and it all can't be front-loaded at the beginning of the teacher preparation program. Your mentee may have been prepared in a college of education, or perhaps he took an alternative route to teaching as a career changer. In either case, whatever he learned will change and expand. Differentiated mentoring is needed to be able to accommodate a fully prepared teacher, and one who was on a fast track may be missing some courses. Because the knowledge base for entering teachers varies based on their preparation, you may recommend summer courses if they are needed to support your mentee's content or pedagogy.

This chapter focuses on standards because they relate to the high-stakes standardized tests that are used to measure student progress. Effective teaching is tied to tests because student success is measured on tests. The dilemma for novice teachers is how can they teach the content in their classrooms at the appropriate pace so that students will have the knowledge to pass these tests. Do they have to teach to the test to meet the passing rates? Many schools and districts are wrestling with this dilemma. Are students supposed to miss art, music, and physical exercise to prepare for these tests? Is there any room in the day for the teacher to teach content that is not on the tests? Where IS the fun in teaching? Some novice teachers are finding there is a disconnect between the models of learning they were taught in teacher preparation programs and the test-taking focus when they get to their first teaching assignment. Discuss this dilemma with your mentee.

The Mindful Mentoring Affirmation for this month is, "I am a mindful mentor who focuses mentoring conversations on learning." By paying attention to the purpose of each interaction and conversation you have with your mentee, you bring focus and direction to her needs. Learning how to teach means you need to talk about the learning process for teachers and students.

Follow the PLAN, CONNECT, ACT, REFLECT, and SET GOALS sections in this chapter to guide your mentoring conversations and reflections.

Watch and listen to a mentor share her insights in the April Chapter Introductions (Videos 2.15 and 2.16), available on the companion website or by scanning the QR codes on a mobile device.

VIDEO 2.15

April Chapter
Introduction, Part 1

VIDEO 2.16

April Chapter
Introduction, Part 2

APRIL

Use Questions to Guide Mentoring Conversations

Invite your mentee to write down a short list of questions and bring them to your first April meeting. Use the questions below as a guide for your discussions throughout the month.

Anticipate Beginning Teachers' Possible Questions

1. Can you review with me how to make content meaningful?

2. My students seem to be changing at this time of year. I need help remembering my adolescent and child psychology. Is this supposed to be happening, or are my students different?

3. The diversity in my room is overwhelming. I have so many learning styles. What can I do?

4. Instructional strategies for diverse learners are important, but I find myself teaching the whole class the same way. Do you have any suggestions?

5. The behavior in my room is really challenging. I need a refresher. Are there any support systems for me right now?

6. I am trying to communicate in different ways with my students. Can you review them with me to make sure I am on track?

7. I don't have time to plan the way I did in the fall. I know that when I do, the day goes much better, but I just can't fit everything in. Can you help me get organized?

Note the other questions your novice teacher asked you so you will have them for the future.

Questions for Your Novice Teacher

1. What can I do to assist you right now that would reduce your anxiety?

2. What do you already know about teaching diverse learners?

APRIL

Meetings and Observations

Plan brief weekly meetings with your mentee. The ACTs in this chapter serve as mentoring conversation starters and can also be used to assess or review what your mentee may already know about a given topic. Use the Appendices to guide you in scheduling short meetings as well as longer conversations.

Plan to meet at times that allow you to have quality time together in a place without interruptions. Knowing when you will meet each week reduces anxiety for both of you. Novice teachers look forward to regularly scheduled meetings even if they are short. Use a calendar to plan your meetings and classroom visits to ensure they will happen! Include watching videos and reading pages in the *Mentoring in Action* book as part of your *PLAN* for mentoring. A digital version of this calendar (April Calendar.pdf) is available on the companion website.

In April, many districts have to make decisions about rehiring. If your mentee has not been observed formally by the department chair or principal, he may be observed this month. Practice this observation cycle together and role play a postconference with a principal. Review the evaluation standards and any pages in this book that can support your mentee in demonstrating proficiency.

April Calendar

MONDAY	TUESDAY	WEDNESDAY	THURSDAY	FRIDAY

Use this calendar to PLAN the month as well as to document meetings and mentor planning.

CONNECT to Additional Resources

CONNECT to School and District Resources

What resources exist in your school and community that could assist novice teachers in April?

CONNECT With Colleagues, Parents, and Families

Who can help our mentee understand standards-based learning in your school?

How can parents be helpful in supporting a teacher with testing?

CONNECT to Student Voices

Encourage your mentee to personally interview students who are showing recurring misbehavior in the classroom. The mentee needs to come from a place of respect and tell the student that these behaviors are not acceptable, but also share that he wants to change the behavior. These personal conferences allow the teacher to look into the student's eyes. Questions to consider are (1) Why are you behaving this way in the classroom? and (2) How can I help you? By taking the time to meet alone, the student's voice can be heard.

CONNECT to Education Hot Topics

Exercise, sleep, and diet. Your mentee may find herself exhausted at this point in the year. Encourage your mentee to "move" and stand up and stretch or take a walk around the building when she feels stressed or tired. Have a "walk and talk" mentor conversation instead of sitting. Encourage her to go home and sleep for at least 8 hours! Drop a healthy snack on her desk with a compliment note.

CONNECT With the Companion Website

Video links, forms for this chapter, a featured book, and other resources are located at http://resources.corwin.com/mentoringinaction.

The First ACT!

Differentiating Mentoring Conversations

Teaching is complex work, and novice teachers can easily become overwhelmed. It is appropriate to customize your mentoring conversations to respond to the varied needs and skills of the mentee.

Directions: Interview your mentee at the beginning of the month to document her areas of strength and needs. Skim the ACTs for this month and decide together which topics are most relevant. Use your state or district teaching standards to focus the mentee's responses to each prompt so you are also teaching her the "common language" of the standards.

Mentee _____ Date _____

Monthly Needs Assessment

1. What is going well in your classroom? (i.e., What is working?) As a teacher, what do you feel you are doing well right now? *Refer to the teaching standards to guide your response.*	3. What would you like to improve or enhance in your practice this month? *Refer to the teaching standards to guide your response.*
2. How do you know your practice is working? (i.e., What is your evidence of success? or Why do you feel confident or competent in an aspect of your teaching?)	4. Review the ACT mentoring conversations for this month with your mentee. Ask which of the ACTs will support you in enhancing your teaching practice? (i.e., What would you like us to focus on this month?)

A digital version of this template (Monthly Needs Assessment Sample With Standards.pdf) is available on the companion website. Keep a copy of this assessment for your files and make a copy for the mentee.

Overview of the ACTs for April Conversations

Directions: Skim the ACTivities listed here and complete the pages that will forward your novice teacher's learning. Your mentee has complementary ACTs in *The First Years Matter* book. Digital copies of any of the reproducible ACTs are available on the companion website.

Key Question Topic	ACTivities	PAGE
Goals	ACT 1 **Novice Teacher Goals**	206
Goals	ACT 2 **Classroom and District Learning Standards**	207
Goals	ACT 3 **Reducing Teacher Talking Time (TTT)**	208
Goals	ACT 4 **Designing Relevant Lessons**	209
Students	ACT 5 **Observing a Student or Small Group**	210
Students	ACT 6 **Classroom and Behavior Management Issues**	211
Students	ACT 7 **Looking at Student Work Together**	212
Communicate	ACT 8 **Communicating With Parents**	213

APRIL

Novice Teacher Goals

Key Question: How do you review novice teacher goals and needs and assess growth?

Directions: Review your notes, the First ACT pages, and your reflections and observations to assess your mentee's growth over time. We know that teaching is a developmental process, and the novice teacher learns as she is teaching. Take some time to reflect and decide where you need to focus your mentoring conversations for this final part of the year.

1. What were your mentee's goals this year? Have you seen progress toward these goals?

2. What are your mentee's three strengths?

3. What two areas should you focus on for the rest of the year that will provide the most support?

4. Do you need additional support with this mentee? (i.e., Do you need to talk with your mentor coordinator about better ways to support her?)

5. Write a goal together that will focus the mentee and use her strengths to move her forward. Select a goal that encompasses an area that would improve her overall teaching.

Sample goals:

- Have motivating introductions for each lesson to settle students and gain attention.
- Culminate a lesson in an orderly way that includes a summary and a short informal assessment.
- Move around the classroom more to engage learners.
- Pronounce words correctly and names of students clearly.
- Create efficient routines for collecting papers, passing out materials, collecting homework, etc.

Companion Website

Classroom and District Learning Standards

Key Question: How does a novice teacher relate district standards to classroom teaching?

Directions: Review the standards and make sure your novice teacher understands what the students will be required to demonstrate for school or district tests. Lesson plans and curriculum needs to stay on track at the end of the year so students have the content required. Remind your mentee that standards are not activities. Many novice teaches get excited about "doing activities" with their students but then have difficulty relating what they are doing to a standard. You can help make that connection.

Review a lesson plan with your novice teacher using these guiding questions.

1. What is the purpose of this lesson?

2. Why are you teaching this?

3. Why are you teaching it now?

4. Is it part of a larger unit of study?

5. Which standards relate to this lesson?

6. Why did you select them?

7. How do you think students will respond to this lesson?

8. Will all learners be engaged? How will you know?

9. Is there any aspect of your lesson you anticipate may be challenging? Why?

10. What is the most valuable part of this lesson that relates to learning?

Reducing Teacher Talking Time (TTT)

Key Question: How can you support your mentee in letting students talk more?

Directions: An excellent soccer coach once said that you create good players by giving them as many "touches on the ball" as possible during every practice session. Teachers who talk the whole lesson and never let the students talk or engage in the curriculum are like coaches who tell the players how to do it, but never let them practice.

Ask your novice teacher to notice how much time she is talking during any lesson and how much time she allows the students to talk to each other. Review the ideas on this page with your mentee and encourage her to integrate more student talking time.

How can your mentee increase appropriate Student Talking Time (STT)?

- Integrate paired sharing into lessons.

- Allow time for discussion in lessons.

- Begin each class with time for students to share what they already know about a topic.

- End a class with time to share what they learned today.

- Partner English language learners with native speakers.

- Include read-aloud activities in lessons.

- Add your ideas!

Emphasize that the talking needs to relate to learning objectives that relate to the standards. Novice teachers need to be mindful at all times of what they are teaching and why. Allowing student learners to talk in class is one way to keep them alert and engaged. Just like in soccer, players who are on the field have to be engaged. The students won't be bored and are less likely to misbehave if they are "playing" in the game.

Designing Relevant Lessons

Key Question: How can your mentee connect the standards to real life activities?

Directions: Service learning engages students and makes the curriculum come alive for all learners. Service projects are offered to the community as a way for students to contribute and learn how to be good citizens. These projects can be part of the existing curriculum or offered as enrichment, extra credit, and homework for those students who are committed to make a difference. Your mentee can connect to the community and make the standards come alive for his students. Assist him in finding ways his unmotivated students can participate in "service learning" in the community. Review the ideas below and discuss what the students would have to demonstrate as a result of doing this service.

Add the standard that is met by participating in this service activity.

History, middle/high	Interview and audiotape World War II veterans and then have them come to the classroom as guest speakers. Provide a service to the local veteran's association as part of this activity. Standard:
Science, middle/high	Connect with a recycling center on a project that relates to the science chapter on recycling. Standard:
Elementary	Write to elderly and visit them on holidays; use as language arts standard. Standard:
Elementary, middle, high	Volunteer at a shelter or soup kitchen and write about the experience. Standards:
Elementary	Invite local businesses into the classroom while learning about professions and select one that needs a special project completed. Standard:

Companion Website

Observing a Student or Small Group

Key Question: How can you support your mentee in observing in his classroom?

Directions: At this time of year, there is often a student that is still challenging your mentee. This process allows her to step back and observe how the student is interacting. If there is not one challenging student, then encourage your mentee to observe a small group to notice the dynamics when students interact.

Teach a lesson for your mentee. This way your mentee can really observe this student or group without being distracted by teaching. Have your mentee observe her most challenging student or a small group—whichever option she decides to do. Encourage her to be more clinical and less personal in her observation. Encourage her to use her observation skills, without judgment, and to think like an ethnographer. The exercise may bring new perspective that may assist her in working with this student differently for the rest of the year.

1. First Name of Student: _____

   Date of Observation: _____

   - What do you notice about this student (physical appearance, cultural background, language, social interaction, skills and abilities, motivation, attitude, self-concept, etc.)?

   - How is the student responding to the teacher's lesson?

   - Is the student interacting with any other students? Describe.

   - What is the quality of the student's work?

   - Name something positive the student did during the lesson.

   - What other things did you observe that you didn't know about the student?

2. Small Group Members: _____

   Date of Observation: _____

   Novice teachers are encouraged to group their students to enhance learning, but often grouping students creates behavior problems. So what is a teacher to do? Not grouping leaves students bored and teachers doing all the talking, yet grouping may be too challenging. Encourage your mentee to observe a small group in action and see what works and what doesn't. All group work should relate to a curriculum standard and not just be busy work.

   - Why is this small group working together?

   - Who is the leader of the group? Self-appointed or teacher-appointed?

   - How effective is the leader?

   - Is the group completing the assigned task? How do you know?

   - Are all members of the group participating?

   - What are the differences in the individual members' contributions to the group? Give an example.

   - What is your overall impression of this group activity?

Classroom and Behavior Management Issues

Key Question: How can your mentee document changes in student behavior?

Directions: At this time of the year, students will be testing the patience and skills of novice teachers. Sometimes it helps to have the student state in writing how he or she will change the behavior that has been so disruptive. Here is a model. The key here is having the students write how their success will be measured. How will the novice teacher know the student has changed? Also the reward is important, and the teacher should add by when _____ (date) or else the reward expires! Share this process with your mentee to create a system for improving behavior.

Student Contract

I state that I will (*change a certain behavior*)

_____

_____

_____

I will measure my success by (*how the behavior will be noted as being done*)

_____

_____

_____

For successful demonstration (*I will receive a reward*)

_____

_____

_____

Signed (teacher)_____ Date _____

Signed (student) _____ Date _____

The contract can also be designed for groups by changing *I* to *we*.

Companion Website

Looking at Student Work Together

Key Question: How can you focus your mentee on seeing one good thing in student work?

Directions: What are the students doing right even if they are below standard? Ask your mentee to bring a variety of work samples of to a meeting. After the samples have been sorted into one of the three standards categories (or your own categories), select one sample from each pile. Look for one thing that this student can be complimented for on this paper. Discuss why complimenting students is important to improving progress.

Below Standard	Meets the Standard	Above Standard
How many papers here?	How many papers here?	How many papers here?
% of class _____	% of class _____	% of class _____
Select ONE paper:	Select ONE paper:	Select ONE paper:
What can this student be complimented for?	What can this student be complimented for?	What can this student be complimented for?

Companion Website

APRIL

Communicating With Parents

Key Question: How can you help your mentee educate parents to help with study skills?

Directions: Parents know schoolwork, homework, and tests are important, but they often don't know how to help their children learn. Discuss ways you and your mentee can educate parents in ways to help their children.

1. Offer a parent study skill information night.

2. Create a parent "study guide" to help your children.

3. List the effective skills you would discuss and note the behaviors the parent would see if their child were effectively "studying" at home.

Effective Study Skill	Elementary Students	Secondary Students
What is it? Describe the skill.	What behavior would parent see?	What behavior would parent see?
Homework paper		
Studying for a test		
Reading a chapter and taking notes		

APRIL

April Mentor Reflections

Directions: Complete any of these prompts that stand out for you and add your own prompts to the blank stems. Write your responses here or use your Mentor Planning Guide and Journal on the companion website. Share your reflections with your mentor coordinator or with other mentors at a mentor support meeting.

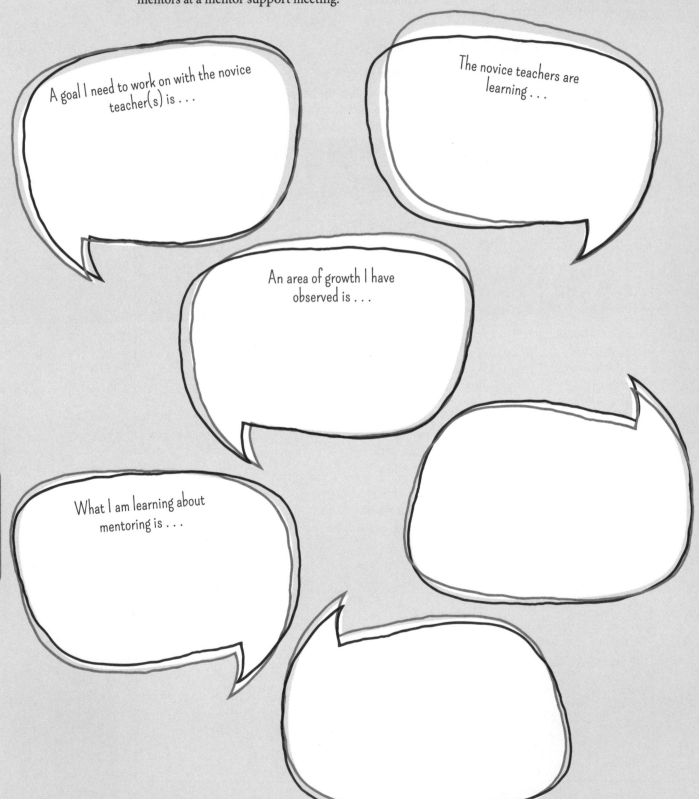

A goal I need to work on with the novice teacher(s) is . . .

The novice teachers are learning . . .

An area of growth I have observed is . . .

What I am learning about mentoring is . . .

Using Mindfulness to Explore Mentoring Dilemmas

Directions: Read the mentoring dilemma and think about how you would respond in this situation. Consider discussing this dilemma at a mentor support meeting or with another mentor. Share your perspectives about how you would proceed and why you think this would be the best way to forward your novice teacher's practice.

Dilemma 9: Teaching to the Test

Your district needs higher scores to keep their funding. Your experience is that most novice teachers find it difficult to cover the content quickly enough to ensure it is discussed before the test is given. You know your mentee is struggling with doing enough content because she wants to engage the learners and her activities take so much time. You know she is doing all the right things; it is just that it takes her longer. You are worried that all the content won't be covered before the test date. *What do you say?*

Respond to these prompts in your journal available on the companion website.

1. State the mentor dilemma as clearly as possible in one sentence if you can.

2. What decision do you need to make in regard to this situation?

3. Write about the emotions that come up for you that relate to this situation. If you have two choices, write how the emotions might be different.

4. Stop and reread what you have written. Underline any key words or phrases that stand out for you.

5. Soften your eyes or close them and take three deep breaths. Ask yourself, what am I missing that I have not noticed? Write that down in your journal.

6. What will you say to your mentee? Write your reflection in your journal.

7. If you are truly stuck, bring your dilemma to your lead mentor, a mentor support group meeting, or another experienced mentor. Ask him or her to listen to what you have written and to ask you questions to clarify your dilemma. *Your lead mentor's role is not to tell you what to do! No advice!* Just questions to help you clarify what you want to do.

8. After you have spoken to your mentee, write his reaction and how you feel about this dilemma now. All dilemmas are not resolved! This is a process of clarifying and understanding how you feel and how you could respond.

APRIL

Directions: Complete all three goal-setting processes and write your responses on this page or in your Mentor Planning Guide and Journal available on the companion website.

1. *Goal for Improving Your Mentee's Teaching Practices*

   - Review the PLAN–CONNECT–ACT–REFLECT pages you completed in this chapter with your mentee. Look ahead to May ACTs to see what you may focus on to continue development.

   - Acknowledge what your mentee is learning. List three things that you noticed that are going well and share them with your mentee.

   - Agree on ONE goal to focus on and reinforce for next month.

   - Goal:

2. *Goal to Support the Social and Emotional Well-Being of Your Mentee*

   - Discuss any challenges your mentee may be facing right now. Challenges often bring stress.

   - Don't ignore any signs of stress in your mentee. Pay attention and teach her ways to manage her stress. Using mindfulness practices can help reduce stress.

   - Explore the *CARE for Teachers* website and the *RESET* book to learn ways to support teachers.

   - Goal:

3. *Goal for Enhancing Your Mentoring Skills*

   - Reflect on your own mentoring experience this month. How did you use your strengths and interests to mentor? What will you do differently next month? Write a reflection in your Mentor Planning Guide and Journal.

   - Goal:

"

Good teachers listen to their students and care
how their students are doing academically."
—HIGH SCHOOL STUDENT

NEW TEACHER PHASE: HOPE

"It looks like my students are passing tests and learning.
Maybe I can do this."

MINDFUL MENTORING AFFIRMATION

I use my strengths to lead by example.

ASSESSING STUDENTS' PROGRESS

High-Stakes Tests and Teacher Assessment

GUIDING QUESTIONS

1. How do you help your novice teacher review her teaching practices? The *Reflect ACTivities* will provide ways to discuss and reflect.

2. How will you help your novice teacher review assessments required by the district? The *Assess ACTivities* offer you ideas to discuss.

3. How will you continue to include students' perspectives? Use the *Student ACTivities* to focus.

4. Why is it important to encourage your mentee to reach out to parents? Use the *Communicate ACTivity* as a way to focus on ways to connect with parents and families.

Interstate Teacher Assessment and Support Consortium—InTASC Standards

Revisit InTASC Standard 6.

-   **Standard 6 Assessment**

The teacher understands and uses multiple methods of assessment to engage learners in their own growth, to monitor learner progress, and to guide the teacher's and learner's decision making.

Chapter Overview

Good teachers care about how their students are doing academically, says the high school student on the opening page of this chapter. CARE is an important word. Helping your mentee understand how to express caring to his students is one way to engage learners. Teachers who are trying to help students learn, as opposed to just giving tests and recording scores, build relationships with students. How is your mentee doing in the "caring" department? Does your mentee care about his students and want them to succeed in school and life? Does he carry a sense of respect into the classroom?

The end of the year can be very stressful for some novice teachers, but others are seeing signs of hope. The year is almost over, and maybe they did actually teach something! The novice teacher phase for this month is hope. When students demonstrate their learning, many novices see that they *can* teach after all. Novice teacher phases go up and down all year. It is important to notice if your mentee is in an upward phase at this point in the year. By having a sense of hope, this teacher is demonstrating success and a willingness to return to the classroom next year. If your mentee is still disillusioned and feeling discouraged with teaching, you may need to talk about whether teaching is the right career choice.

The InTASC Principle 6 (Assessment) focuses on both formal and informal assessments. High-stakes tests are not the only measure of success. Learning is developmental, and all students do not learn the identified curriculum the year it is listed in the scope and sequence for the school. Discuss the options for students who do not learn at the expected rate with your mentee.

The Mindful Mentoring Affirmation this month is, "I use my strengths to lead by example." As a mentor, you are a role model. You are a teacher leader in your school who stepped up to mentor a beginner. You have a lot of power in your role, and your strengths will serve to demonstrate to your mentee how you approach teaching, students, and families. Use your strengths to guide your mentee.

VIDEO 2.17

May Chapter Introduction

Teachers, both beginning and experienced, hope for the best with their students. They hope what they're teaching is making a difference to their students. You hope you are mentoring effectively. Hope is a positive feeling that allows teachers to sustain their energy and move forward. Keep hope alive for your mentee this month.

Follow the PLAN, CONNECT, ACT, REFLECT, and SET GOALS sections in this chapter to guide your mentoring conversations and reflections.

Watch and listen to a mentor share her insights in the May Chapter Introduction (Video 2.17), available on the companion website or by scanning the QR code on a mobile device.

MAY

Use Questions to Guide Mentoring Conversations

Invite your mentee to write down a short list of questions and bring them to your first May meeting. Use the questions below as a guide for your discussions throughout the month.

Anticipate Novice Teachers' Possible Questions

1. How do I grade these students at the end of the year?

2. High-stakes tests are taking so much time. How do I fit in my teaching?

3. What end-of-the-year assessments do I need to know?

4. How do you think I am doing?

Note the other questions your novice teacher asked you so you will have them for the future.

Questions for Your Novice Teacher

1. What do you need to do right now?

2. What paperwork do you need to discuss?

3. What can I do to assist you right now that would reduce your anxiety?

Meetings and Observations

Plan brief weekly meetings with your mentee. The ACTs in this chapter serve as mentoring conversation starters and can also be used to assess or review what your mentee may already know about a given topic. Use the Appendices to guide you in scheduling short meetings as well as longer conversations.

Plan to meet at times that allow you to have quality time together in a place without interruptions. Knowing when you will meet each week reduces anxiety for both of you. Novice teachers look forward to regularly scheduled meetings even if they are short. Use a calendar to plan your meetings and classroom visits to ensure they will happen! Include watching videos and reading pages in the *Mentoring in Action* book as part of your *PLAN* for mentoring. A digital version of this calendar (May Calendar.pdf) is available on the companion website.

Review any feedback from formal observations from the administrators in the district. Make sure your mentee understands what is being asked of her and that she can meet these expectations in the classroom. Observe her in action and discuss what she would like to focus on. Select ACT topics this month that might relate to her performance in the classroom.

May Calendar

MONDAY	TUESDAY	WEDNESDAY	THURSDAY	FRIDAY

Use this calendar to PLAN the month as well as to document meetings and mentor planning.

CONNECT to Additional Resources

CONNECT to School and District Resources

What resources exist in your school and community that could assist novice teachers in May?

CONNECT With Colleagues, Parents, and Families

What district departments relate to assessing student progress and referrals for next year?

How are parents included in end-of-the-year student assessments?

CONNECT to Student Voices

Encourage your mentee to include informal student self-assessment into lessons and units. Ask the students to respond to a question during class such as, "Is this work hard or easy?" By putting thumbs up or down, the mentee knows if the class is understanding what she is saying. Or ask your mentee to do a ticket to leave at the end of the class where she asks students to tell her one thing they learned today. Another idea is to use colored cards on the students' desks to indicate green (I am done) and red (I need more time). Ask students to use the appropriate card in response to the question, do you need more time?

CONNECT to Education Hot Topics

Dress code! What is the policy at your school? Is your mentee dressing for success, or is she looking like one of the students? Professional dress is always appropriate, and it creates a visual boundary between student and teacher. Review the dress code if you need to at this time.

CONNECT on the Companion Website

Video links, forms for this chapter, a featured book, and other resources are located at http://resources.corwin.com/mentoringinaction.

The First ACT!

Differentiating Mentoring Conversations

Teaching is complex work, and novice teachers can easily become overwhelmed. It is appropriate to customize your mentoring conversations to respond to the varied needs and skills of the mentee.

Directions: Interview your mentee at the beginning of the month to document her areas of strength and needs. Skim the ACTs for this month and decide together which topics are most relevant. Use your state or district teaching standards to focus the mentee's responses to each prompt so you are also teaching her the "common language" of the standards.

Mentee _____ Date _____

Monthly Needs Assessment

1. What is going well in your classroom? (i.e., What is working?) As a teacher, what do you feel you are doing well right now? *Refer to the teaching standards to guide your response.*	3. What would you like to improve or enhance in your practice this month? *Refer to the teaching standards to guide your response.*
2. How do you know your practice is working? (i.e., What is your evidence of success? or Why do you feel confident or competent in an aspect of your teaching?)	4. Review the ACT mentoring conversations for this month with your mentee. Ask which of the ACTs will support you in enhancing your teaching practice? (i.e., What would you like us to focus on this month?)

A digital version of this template (Monthly Needs Assessment Sample With Standards.pdf) is available on the companion website. Keep a copy of this assessment for your files and make a copy for the mentee.

Overview of the ACTs for May Conversations

Directions: Skim the ACTivities listed here and complete the pages that will forward your novice teacher's learning. Your mentee has complementary ACTs in *The First Years Matter* book. Digital copies of any of the reproducible ACTs are available on the companion website.

Key Question Topic	ACTivities	PAGE
Reflect	ACT 1 **Assessing Your Mentee's Progress**	226
Reflect	ACT 2 **Mentee Portfolio Assessment**	227
Assess	ACT 3 **Measuring Student Progress**	228
Assess	ACT 4 **Student Self-Assessment**	229
Assess	ACT 5 **Assessing the Whole Student**	230
Students	ACT 6 **Classroom and Behavior Management Issues**	231
Students	ACT 7 **Looking at Student Work Together**	232
Communicate	ACT 8 **Communicating With Parents**	233

MAY

Assessing Your Mentee's Progress

Key Question: How is your mentee progressing toward the goal of becoming an effective teacher?

Directions: Reflect on your mentee's progress from August until now and rate her performance using a district rubric or this one. Be clear about the evidence and criteria for success. This does not have to be shared with your mentee. It is for your own reflection to guide you where to focus for these last months. If you color-coded this book to the teacher evaluation standards, review the pages you completed and see if you are missing any target areas.

Example of Novice Teacher Rubric for Instructional Practice					
	Excellent Progress	**Good Progress**	**Needs More Development**	**Needs Assistance**	**Unsatisfactory**
Demonstrates creativity and thought in planning					
Uses a variety of teaching strategies and methods to engage learners					
Develops both long-form and short-form lesson plans					
Demonstrates principles and theories of instruction for students in the classroom					
Demonstrates proper sequencing and pacing of lessons					
Develops and modifies curriculum to meet student needs					
Manages the classroom					
Handles difficult situations through problem-solving approaches					
Maintains an organized classroom for student learning					
Disciplines fairly					

Companion Website

Mentee Portfolio Assessment

Key Question: How can your mentee demonstrate effectiveness using a portfolio?

Directions: A portfolio is a collection of carefully selected artifacts that illustrate the standards that have been completed this year. If your mentee is interested in sharing his skills through this method, guide him to select artifacts that align to teacher evaluation standards. Reflecting is a key component to a portfolio. Ask him to explain why he or she is selecting each artifact. Share this steps with your mentee.

Step 1	Review all materials from this year (i.e., lesson plans, units, etc.). What stands out as interesting, colorful, and meaningful to share with your evaluator and others?
Step 2	Select key items, photos, samples of student work, notes from parents, for example, that illustrate something the novice teacher wants to share. It could be a standard for teaching, a competency, a skill, or an interest. It could also be related to the InTASC standards listed on the cover sheet of each month in this book. Less is more!
Step 3	Write a short description or caption for each item selected. Describe what it is and why it is in the portfolio.
Step 4	Write a short reflection for each item and place it below the description or caption. The reflection explains what you learned from teaching this, what you would do differently, or something that is an insight for you that relates to this photo or lesson.
Step 5	Lay the artifact, description, and reflection on a page under a TITLE that clearly identifies the message to the reader. If the novice teacher is organizing the portfolio by InTASC standards, perhaps the standard is part of the title.
Step 6	Put all the pages together. Place the Philosophy Statement up front and write a Final Statement for the last page. This Final Statement could include what I learned this year as a first-year teacher, my goals for year 2, and my future aspirations as an educator.

MAY

Companion
Website

Measuring Student Progress

Key Question: What are the types of assessments your mentee should know?

Directions: Review the three types of assessments: Diagnostic, Formative, and Summative. Share models of each type of test so your mentee understands the difference. At this time of year, high-stakes tests that measure student progress or graduation standards are also being given. Your mentee needs to know how the classroom instruction impacts all these assessment results.

1. Diagnostic Assessments
    - Used before instruction begins
    - Captures prior knowledge and skills
    - Tests for readiness

2. Formative Assessments
    - Used daily to measure understanding
    - Gauge progress on a skill or lesson activity
    - Weekly quizzes or tickets to leave

3. Summative Assessments
    - Tests at the end of units
    - Used to measure growth
    - Report card grades

4. High-stakes tests
    - Benchmarks for district growth
    - Graduation requirements for state
    - Merit pay for teachers

Companion
Website

Student Self-Assessment

Key Question: How can you assist your mentee in creating a student self-assessment survey?

Directions: Create a student self-assessment survey with your mentee to capture the key questions he wants to know from his students. Use these ideas as a guide for your mentoring conversation. The survey assessment can be general, or if the mentee wants to get specific on his own skills, you can design it that way. Prepare your mentee for some answers that might be discouraging. Decide whether these should be anonymous or the students should put their names on the papers. Discuss the benefits of either choice.

1. List something you learned in this class.

2. How would you rate your effort in this class? 1–10

3. What do you like most about this class?

4. What is your goal after high school?

5. How can teachers help you learn better?

6. Did you do your homework regularly? Why or why not?

7. What do you like most about school?

8. How could you be a better student?

9. How did I do in this course?

10. Does my grade match my effort and work?

Companion Website

Assessing the Whole Student

Key Question: How can you support your mentee in seeing the whole child's progress?

Directions: Discuss all the ways in which your mentee can assess a student's progress in school. Encourage her to look at multiple measures of growth and not just the summative and high-stakes tests. Help your mentee to observe each student as a whole person, not just the score on a test. Students may have some level of success and learning this year and just don't score well on a test. Broaden your mentee's view of learning and success. Ask him to look at each student these lenses.

1. *Student Personal Strengths*
   - Ability to speak languages
   - Musical ability
   - Hobbies
   - Technology skills
   - Athletic ability
   - Artistic skills
   - Reading
   - Theatre
   - Sports
   - Sense of humor

2. *Interpersonal and Social Interactions*
   - With other students in the classroom
   - In the school helping others
   - Leadership in community groups

3. *Academic Achievement in Classes*
   - On units of study based on teacher-made tests and quizzes (paper and pencil)
   - Project or performance based
   - Performance portfolios

4. *High-Stakes Testing Results*

5. *Other indicators of success*

Classroom and Behavior Management Issues

Key Question: What does your mentee need to know about students at the end of the year?

Directions: As the year comes to a close, sometimes student misbehavior escalates. Everyone is tired, and the novice teachers may have exhausted their good ideas. Your mentee may have tried these strategies earlier, but it is a good time to review them.

1. Focus on positive behavior when it happens.
    - Give verbal praise for specific behavior.
    - Send notes home with students.
    - Make complimentary phone calls to parents about their child.

2. Don't threaten or bribe students to behave.
    - Students may respond for a short term.
    - Bribes show a sign of weakness in the teacher.
    - The teacher loses respect.

3. Take charge of the classroom in a firm but pleasant manner.
    - Use your sense of humor to keep students in line.
    - Communicate your needs honestly to students.
    - Listen to your students' requests and complaints.

4. Give "I"-messages to students instead of "You"-messages.
    - "I am unhappy with the behavior I am seeing," not "You are misbehaving again."

5. Use body language and signals to prevent disruptive behavior.
    - Make eye contact with the misbehaving student.
    - Use frown or facial expression.
    - Walk near the student and lightly tap his or her shoulder.
    - Use your sense of humor.
    - Use a cue to have the students look at you (e.g., lights off, raise hands).

6. Don't use sarcasm, cruel remarks, or words to embarrass students.
    - No ridicule or intimidation allowed!
    - Never touch a student in an abusive way.
    - Confrontation in front of a whole class is not recommended.
    - If the situation becomes confrontational, remove the student and discuss the problem later.

Companion
Website

Looking at Student Work Together

Key Question: What are your mentee's beliefs about modifying and differentiating instruction?

Directions: Some teachers embrace this concept; others are not sure what it means. Some teachers don't believe there should be any differentiation from the standard and that all learners should be treated the same in a same age-level classroom. What you believe as a mentor will impact your mentee. Philosophies are personal, but district standards and approaches for student learning are public. How can you discuss the intersection of a teacher's personal belief system and the mandate from the district that *all* students must learn? We all know that if novice teachers don't believe some students need modified assignments, it will be a challenge to integrate these ideas into practice. This is a complex topic, and meeting the needs of diverse learners in a classroom is not easy.

Ask your mentee this question:

What do you believe about modifying student work assignments and differentiating instruction?

Look at one sample of student work and differentiate the assignment for this student.

Student	Standard level	What student needs to learn next	How the teacher could differentiate to assist the student in learning

Companion Website

Communicating With Parents

Key Question: How can you assist your mentee in communicating information about tests?

Directions: High-stakes tests are here to stay. In many districts, they mean graduation from high school or not. Teacher-made tests are also part of academic progress, and they serve as the grading system for report cards and moving to the next grade. Both tests are critical to students. So how can parents help? Novice teachers need to assist parents in understanding the difference between high-stakes and teacher tests and how they both impact their children.

Discuss the ways the district lets parents know about high-stakes tests. Help your mentee clarify the differences in the tests and how they are used to measure student progress.

High-Stakes Tests (state or district)	Teacher-Made Tests (measure of content learned in the classroom)
For each type of test, list how it is used and how students benefit from this test.	For each type of test, list how it is used and how students benefit from this test.

MAY

May Mentor Reflections

Directions: Complete any of these prompts that stand out for you and add your own prompts to the blank stems. Write your responses here or use your Mentor Planning Guide on the companion website. Share your reflections with your mentor coordinator or with other mentors at a mentor support meeting.

I can help the novice teacher(s) by . . .

One assumption I made this year is . . .

I see _____ differently now because . . .

An idea I would like to share before the end of the year is . . .

Using Mindfulness to Explore Mentoring Dilemmas

Directions: Read the mentoring dilemma and think about how you would respond in this situation. Consider discussing this dilemma at a mentor support meeting or with another mentor. Share your perspectives about how you would proceed and why you think this would be the best way to forward your novice teacher's practice.

Dilemma 10: Becoming an Effective Teacher

Your novice teacher has demonstrated growth in all of the teaching standards, however she continues to struggle with the unique demographics of the school population. You can't put your finger on it, but you notice that instead of trying to solve a problem she assigns blame to others. She blames parents for not coming to parent conferences and says that is the reason the students are not doing well. She also blames the community for the limited resources she has in the classroom and says, "I never knew it would be like this!" You are now noticing if something goes wrong she even blames her colleagues for not helping or not giving the correct information to her. You have heard other teachers say these same things in the teachers' room, and she is adopting this disposition. All of her teaching skills are stellar, and you do want her to stay at the school because she does have many strong qualities. *What do you say?*

Respond to these prompts in your journal available on the companion website.

1. State the mentor dilemma as clearly as possible in one sentence if you can.

2. What decision do you need to make in regard to this situation?

3. Write about the emotions that come up for you that relate to this situation. If you have two choices, write how the emotions might be different.

4. Stop and reread what you have written. Underline any key words or phrases that stand out for you.

5. Soften your eyes or close them and take three deep breaths. Ask yourself, what am I missing that I have not noticed? Write that down in your journal.

6. What will you say to your mentee? Write your reflection in your journal.

7. If you are truly stuck, bring your dilemma to your lead mentor, a mentor support group meeting, or another experienced mentor. Ask him or her to listen to what you have written and to ask you questions to clarify your dilemma. *Your lead mentor's role is not to tell you what to do! No advice!* Just questions to help you clarify what you want to do.

8. After you have spoken to your mentee, write his reaction and how you feel about this dilemma now. All dilemmas are not resolved! This is a process of clarifying and understanding how you feel and how you could respond.

Directions: Complete all three goal-setting processes and write your responses on this page or in your Mentor Planning Guide and Journal available on the companion website.

1. *Goal for Improving Your Mentee's Teaching Practices*

   - Review the PLAN–CONNECT–ACT–REFLECT pages you completed in this chapter with your mentee. Look ahead to June ACTs to see what you may focus on to continue development.

   - Acknowledge what your mentee is learning. It's getting toward the end of the year, and it is time for praise! Find anything to praise and be specific about what your mentee is doing well!

   - Agree on ONE goal to focus on and reinforce for next month.

   - Goal:

2. *Goal to Support the Social and Emotional Well-Being of Your Mentee*

   - Discuss any challenges your mentee may be facing right now. Challenges often bring stress.

   - Don't ignore any signs of stress in your mentee. Pay attention and teach her ways to manage her stress. Using mindfulness practices can help reduce stress.

   - Explore the CASEL website (casel.org) to learn more ways to promote mindful teaching.

   - Goal:

3. *Goal for Enhancing Your Mentoring Skills*

   - Reflect on your own mentoring experience this month. How did you use your strengths and interests to mentor? What will you do differently next month? Write a reflection in your Mentor Planning Guide and Journal.

   - Goal:

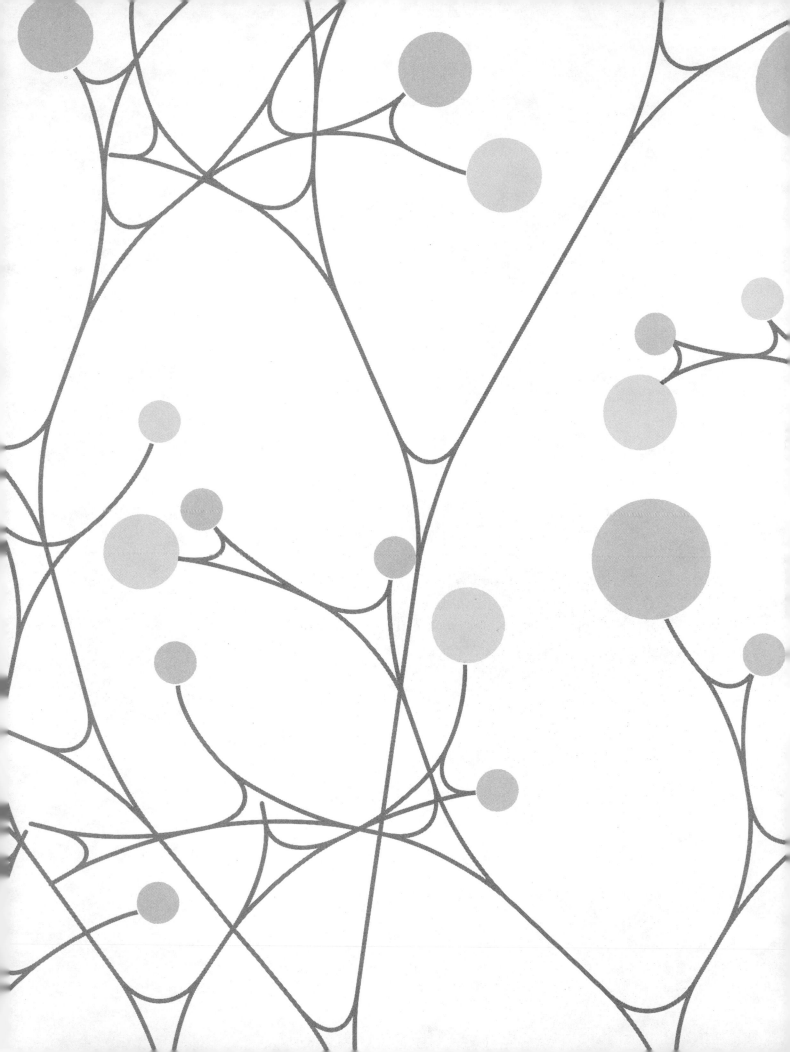

"
A good teacher adds some humor to teaching."
—SEVENTH-GRADE STUDENT

NEW TEACHER PHASE: CELEBRATE, CULMINATE, AND REFLECT

"I felt like I was racing to get everything done for
the last day, and the next day everyone was gone!
No students, no directives from the central office, just me
feeling exhausted and exhilarated. I did it! I finished!
Now I know what I will do differently next year!"

MINDFUL MENTORING AFFIRMATION

I am grateful for the opportunity to mentor a novice teacher.

JUNE

COMPLETING THE YEAR
Paperwork, Relationships, and Closing a Room

GUIDING QUESTIONS

1. How do you help your novice teacher to reflect on the entire year? The *Reflect ACTivities* will share some options.

2. How will you help your novice teacher implement school closing routines? The *Closing ACTivities* offer you ideas to discuss.

3. How will you keep students in mind at the end of the year? Use the *Student ACTivities* as a way to focus on students.

4. Why is it important to communicate to all parents at the end of the year? Use the *Communicate ACTivity* as a way to think about a final communication.

~~~~~~

Interstate Teacher Assessment and Support Consortium—InTASC Standards

Revisit InTASC Standard 9.

- **Standard 9 Professional Learning and Ethical Practice**

The teacher engages in ongoing professional learning and uses evidence to continually evaluate his/her practice, particularly the effects of his/her choices and actions on others (learners, families, other professionals, and the community), and adapts practice to meet the needs of each learner.

~~~~~~

Chapter Overview

VIDEO 2.18

June Chapter
Introduction, Part 1

This is the time to celebrate, culminate the year, and reflect on what your mentee has achieved in 1 year. It may have felt like a whirlwind so far, and it is not over yet! Don't stop mentoring! The cleanup and closing down of a classroom take lots of time and energy and many novice teachers have felt alone doing this task. Watch the June Chapter Introductions, Parts 1 and 2 (Videos 2.18 and 2.19), available on the companion website or by scanning the QR codes on a mobile device.

You have learned so much too. As a mentor, you have guided, shared, and reflected with your novice teacher, and this has helped you understand your role. There were probably times when you just had to laugh. Humor is an underused emotion in teaching. Take some time to reflect on some of the situations you faced this year and use your humor lens. Yes it is okay to laugh and be a teacher. Schedule a meeting with your mentee to just discuss the funny things that happened this year. It may take a few minutes, so make an effort to smile, shake your head, and document the crazy things that happen in school with students. Perhaps you may want to create a closing-the-year survival kit with funny cards and snacks?

VIDEO 2.19

June Chapter
Introduction, Part 2

This chapter focuses on nuts and bolts like cleanup and also the more serious side of looking at what actually happened this year. Just like the orientation in August, the ending of the year brings so many little details. Where do these books get stored? Who gets the report cards? How do I lock up and clean up my room? You have done this so many times it is second nature, but it is the first time for your mentee. Consider taking a video or photos of the classroom for your mentee to document what it looked like before she takes everything down! It will be a great reminder in August when she has to set up the room again.

Use the activities in this chapter to summarize the year and culminate the feelings and emotions with your mentee. Make time for a few short meetings even though the schedules seem packed with other duties. This is the time to celebrate what your mentee has learned. It is also a time to discuss what she will change for next year.

Your Mindful Mentoring Affirmation for this month is, "I am grateful for the opportunity to mentor a novice teacher." If this is your first time mentoring, you may also have experienced a learning curve this year. Hopefully this book provided you with support and ideas to keep you focused.

Your year as a mentor is coming to a close. Review your August reflections and your mentor journal and reflect on your personal development. Acknowledge yourself for doing this work and celebrate your successes this year as you supported your mentee.

July is about reflection and renewing your energy. As you have learned, mentoring takes time and commitment. This new chapter will guide you as you think about ways to enhance the mentoring program in your school and district. Being grateful for this experience is one way to acknowledge all you have learned.

Watch and listen to these mentors share their insights in the June Chapter Introduction (Videos 2.18 and 2.19) available on the companion website or by scanning the QR code on a mobile device.

Use Questions to Guide Mentoring Conversations

Invite your mentee to write down a short list of questions and bring them to your first June meeting. Use the questions below as a guide for your discussions throughout the month.

Anticipate Beginning Teachers' Possible Questions

1. I need help in closing up my room. What should I do first?

2. How should I reflect on my year? Will you meet with me?

3. Should I seek feedback from others (students, parents, colleagues, etc.) to gain insights into my year?

4. Do you have any final words of advice as I complete my first year?

List the other questions your novice teachers brought to the meeting so you will have them for your next mentoring cycle.

Note the other questions your novice teacher asked you so you will have them for the future.

Questions for Your Novice Teacher

1. What did you learn about yourself as a teacher this year?

2. What did you learn about your students and their families this year?

3. How can I help you complete the year and do your June closing work?

4. What can I do to assist you right now that would reduce your anxiety?

Meetings and Observations

Plan brief weekly meetings with your mentee. The ACTs in this chapter serve as mentoring conversation starters and can also be used to assess or review what your mentee may already know about a given topic. Use the Appendices to guide you in scheduling short meetings as well as longer conversations.

Plan to meet at times that allow you to have quality time together in a place without interruptions. Knowing when you will meet each week reduces anxiety for both of you. Novice teachers look forward to regularly scheduled meetings even if they are short. Use a calendar to plan your meetings and classroom visits to ensure they will happen! Include watching videos, reading pages in the *Mentoring in Action* book as part of your *PLAN* for mentoring. A digital version of this calendar (June Calendar.pdf) is available on the companion website.

Reflect on all the observations you completed with your mentee. Ask him which ones were most effective? Did he like the short drop in visits, or did he prefer you saw an entire lesson from start to finish. Use this conversation to improve your observation practices next year. Did you use the strategies from the videos offered with this book, or did you create your own observation practices?

June Calendar

MONDAY	TUESDAY	WEDNESDAY	THURSDAY	FRIDAY

Use this calendar to PLAN the month as well as to document meetings and mentor planning.

JUNE

CONNECT to Additional Resources

CONNECT to School and District Resources

What resources exist in your school and community that could assist novice teachers in May?

CONNECT With Colleagues, Parents, and Families

Who in the school building may be able to help the mentee with June needs?

How can parents be helpful in assisting the novice in reflecting on her first year?

CONNECT to Student Voices

What better way is there to know how well your mentee has succeeded this year than to ask the students? Help your mentee create an end-of-the-year anonymous survey for all the students. You may present it to the students to ensure the answers are honest. Some possible questions could be (1) Which lesson or unit did you most enjoy this year? (2) How could I improve my teaching? (3) Was I fair to all students? Why do you say that? and (4) What advice do you have for me as I prepare for next year?

CONNECT to Education Hot Topics

Play in school! Some research is showing that free play helps the brain and motivates the learner to be more creative. Most schools are limiting recess and any playtime, but after tests are done at the end of the year, some teachers are finding that play time is fun and it is engaging their students. Discuss ways your novice teacher can integrate free play to continue to promote learning in June.

CONNECT With the Companion Website

Video links, forms for this chapter, a featured book, and other resources are located at resources. corwin.com/mentoringinaction.

The First ACT!

Differentiating Mentoring Conversations

Teaching is complex work, and novice teachers can easily become overwhelmed. It is appropriate to customize your mentoring conversations to respond to the varied needs and skills of the mentee.

Directions: Interview your mentee at the beginning of the month to document her areas of strength and needs. Skim the ACTs for this month and decide together which topics are most relevant. Use your state or district teaching standards to focus the mentee's responses to each prompt so you are also teaching her the "common language" of the standards.

Mentee _____ Date _____

Monthly Needs Assessment

1. What is going well in your classroom? (i.e., What is working?) As a teacher, what do you feel you are doing well right now?	3. What would you like to improve or enhance in your practice this month?
2. How do you know your practice is working? (i.e., What is your evidence of success? or Why do you feel confident or competent in an aspect of your teaching?)	4. Review the ACT mentoring conversations for this month with your mentee. Ask which of the ACTs will support you in enhancing your teaching practice? (i.e., What would you like us to focus on this month?)

A digital version of this template (Monthly Needs Assessment Sample With Standards.pdf) is available on the companion website. Keep a copy of this assessment for your files and make a copy for the mentee.

Overview of the ACTs for June Conversations

Directions: Skim the ACTivities listed here and complete the pages that will forward your novice teacher's learning. Your mentee has complementary ACTs in *The First Years Matter* book. Digital copies of any of the reproducible ACTs are available on the companion website.

Key Question Topic	ACTivities	PAGE
Reflect	ACT 1 **Letter to Your Mentee**	246
Reflect	ACT 2 **Novice Teacher Letter to Mentor**	247
Reflect	ACT 3 **A Letter to Future First-Year Teachers**	248
Closing	ACT 4 **Closing Procedures for a Classroom**	249
Closing	ACT 5 **Novice Teacher Letter to Students**	250
Students	ACT 6 **Classroom and Behavior Management Issues**	251
Communicate	ACT 7 **Communicating With Parents**	252
Communicate	ACT 8 **Sharing the Professional Portfolio**	253

Letter to Your Mentee

Key Question: How do you culminate your mentoring experience with your mentee?

Directions: Write a letter to your mentee highlighting her growth and acknowledging her work with you this year. What did you observe? Use the InTASC standards, the teacher evaluation categories, and the topics below as a guide for your letter.

- Personal growth
- Professional growth
- Teaching ability
- Interaction with colleagues
- Acknowledge her expertise in the areas
- If you are mentoring more than one novice teacher, make notes on this page.

	What you will specifically highlight in your letter? You want the letter to be personal to each teacher's strengths and areas of growth. Be sure to share what you learned from each of them too!
Paragraph 1	
Paragraph 2	
Paragraph 3	

Companion Website

JUNE

Novice Teacher Letter to Mentor

Key Question: How can your novice teacher culminate the experience with you?

Directions: Invite your mentee to write his reflections of this year in a letter to you. This is an opportunity for you to receive feedback from your mentee. It is an important way to close the year and wind down the formal relationship you have had all year. Add your own questions to the assignment so you will get the feedback you need to grow as a mentor. Share the stems on this page to guide his letter and encourage him to share his thoughts about the mentoring experience. If he was using the *First Years Matter* book, ask him to share how it was useful.

Sample Letter Stems

Dear Mentor,

This has been a year full of surprises and challenges. Some of them have been . . .

I have learned . . .

I feel good about . . . Personally I appreciate the way I was able to . . .

I see myself . . . next year. I really enjoyed . . .

I am confident that . . . The best thing about being a first-year teacher was . . .

I appreciated . . .

You helped me . . .

I am looking forward to next year because . . .

Sincerely,
Your Mentee

A Letter to Future First-Year Teachers

Key Question: How can your novice teacher share with other teachers to improve their experience?

Directions: Encourage your mentee to write an open letter to future teachers who will be hired to teach at this school next year. If she is willing to talk to prospective student teachers, suggest she leave her e-mail or phone number at the bottom of the letter.

Copy the letter and place it in a Welcome to Our School binder next year. Novice teachers next year will appreciate the advice from another beginner!

Date: _____

Dear First-Year Teacher,

I have just completed my first year, and I have some advice and suggestions for you as you begin preparing yourself for your first class.

Use these stems or create your own.

Some advice I have for you about planning is . . .

What I learned this year is . . .

I can help you with . . .

Ways you can expect your mentor to support you include . . .

What I most enjoyed this year is . . .

Sincerely,
Grade Level

Companion
Website

Closing Procedures for a Classroom

Key Question: How do you help your mentee with closing out her classroom?

Directions: Discuss in detail how your mentee should close the classroom and what must be handed in to the office the last day of school. Very often teacher induction programs do a great job of orienting novice teachers to the school but forget how to end the year. There are cultural norms in schools for doing certain things certain ways. This doesn't mean novice teachers shouldn't question things and try to make them better, it just means you as a mentor need to tell them what the school culture is and why it is that way.

Novice teachers could use students to assist them in some of these closing procedures if they know what is required in advance. Often what happens is that novices don't know what is expected, and they are left doing everything alone the last day of school or after the students are dismissed. Make sure your mentee knows what is expected weeks ahead of time to avoid the stress of closing a classroom.

1. **Possible paperwork might include:**

    - Grades for students by a certain date

    - Promotion cards

    - Paperwork for retaining students

    - Report cards for principal review a week before students get them

    - Special needs student reports and IEPs

    - Other . . .

2. **Closing the room may involve:**

    - Covering all the shelves with paper

    - Removing all the books

    - Putting materials in storage

    - Washing and cleaning desks

    - Putting away technology

    - Other . . .

Novice Teacher Letter to Students

Key Question: How can your mentee culminate the year with his students?

Directions: One way to close out the year is to write a class letter to the students. It provides closure to the year for the novice teacher and it lets the students know the teacher cares about them. Assist your mentee in designing a letter and proofread it for her. It does not have to be long, but it should contain specific highlights from the year and be authentic. Use this sample to guide your conversation.

Sample Letter to Students

Dear Class,

It has been a great year. I would like to highlight some key memories for me as your teacher.

List some specific memories of positive days in class.

I am grateful for . . .

You have been an outstanding class . . .

Thank you for . . .

You taught me a lot about teaching . . . like . . .

I learned from you too . . . for example . . .

I look forward to seeing you . . .

Sincerely,
Your Teacher

Classroom and Behavior Management Issues

Key Question: How do you support your novice teacher in closing the year successfully?

Directions: The year is coming to a close. One last month, and it could be the most difficult. Novice teachers don't know what to expect, and students are anxious to get out of school.

This is the time when some disruptive behavior can emerge. When high-stakes tests are done, students tend to think the year is over. This is the time to review all the ACTs at the end of the months that relate to classroom and behavior management. Point out any ideas that could be useful at this time of year.

Which ACTs do you need to revisit with your mentee at this time?

Month	ACT	Key Question
September	ACT 8	How do routines minimize disruption and promote a positive learning environment?
October	ACT 8	What does your mentee need to think about before disciplining a student?
November	ACT 8	How can you help your mentee learn how to minimize misbehavior?
December	ACT 8	How does a novice teacher learn how to manage degrees of inappropriate behavior?
January	ACT 8	How can you help your mentee brainstorm solutions to her common problems?
February	ACT 6	What are appropriate rewards for students?
March	ACT 6	How can you help your mentee document student meetings?
April	ACT 6	How can your mentee document changes in student behavior?
May	ACT 6	What does your mentee need to know at the end of the year?

Companion Website

Communicating With Parents

Key Question: What does your mentee need to communicate to parents at the end of the year?

Directions: Help your mentee write a letter or year-end report to all parents of the students in his class. The purpose is to thank them for supporting their children to be successful and let them know what the teacher thought about this group. If your mentee wrote a letter in the fall as an introduction, this letter can refer to that one. If you have a sample letter and have done this before, share yours.

The end of the year is a hectic and incredibly exhausting time for any teacher. The novice teachers are especially overwhelmed because they have never closed a year before. They may have to hold a student back or give a report card that is less than satisfactory. Parents may or may not have been as cooperative as the teacher may have liked, and as a mentor, you can assist the teacher in sorting this out in a productive way. In spite of any challenges, this is a time to celebrate the completion of a year and acknowledge what has been done successfully.

The final report cards will focus on the academic work, which is very important. However, there is an opportunity for your mentee to use this final communication to stay connected to the parents. There may be siblings coming through the system, and it is nice for your mentee to know the family ahead of time. Just as in the beginning of the year the teacher wrote a letter of introduction, it is important at the end of the year to write some kind of closing note to parents. This is the novice teacher's first year of teaching, and it is important to take the time to reflect on what went well and to share that with parents and students. You may consider combining the student letter in ACT 5 and the parent letter.

Brainstorm ways your mentee could make this a doable and enjoyable task. You may also recommend the novice create a website or send an e-mail with class photos and direct the parents there. The goal is to end on a positive note with parents.

List any ideas you would like to share with your mentee:

Sharing the Professional Portfolio

Key Question: How does your mentee culminate the year sharing her successes?

Directions: If your mentee created a portfolio (see Part I Figure 11 and ACT 2 May), this is the time to share it! Host a portfolio sharing party and feature your mentee. If there are other novice teachers in the school who created a portfolio, invite them. Get together with other mentors and plan a social event that brings everyone together.

Bring food, play music, and place the portfolios on a table where guests can flip though and sign the register. The guest register page will allow attendees to sign in and make a brief comment that will be shared with the novice teacher.

If time allows, videotape each novice teacher with his or her portfolio. Let each person show just one page and have each one share one thing he or she learned by completing this portfolio. Encourage the novice teachers to share the portfolio next year with the incoming first-year teachers in August.

Invite:

- colleagues
- principal or department chair
- school committee
- parents
- community business partners

Let your mentee share the portfolio with you first as a practice. Enjoy what you have done as a mentor. Your energy has rippled out to this beginning teacher. Celebrate!

June Mentor Reflections

Directions: Complete any of these prompts that stand out for you. Write your responses here or use your Mentor Planning Guide and Journal on the companion website. Share your reflections with your mentor coordinator or with other mentors at a mentor support meeting.

This year as a mentor I have learned . . .

One thing I would change about the mentoring program is . . .

Compliments I would like to give to my novice teachers . . .

An idea I have to improve the program is . . .

I benefited most from . . .

Other thoughts I have about this experience . . .

Using Mindfulness to Explore Mentoring Dilemmas

Directions: Read the mentoring dilemma and think about how you would respond in this situation. Consider discussing this dilemma at a mentor support meeting or with another mentor. Share your perspectives about how you would proceed and why you think this would be the best way to forward your novice teacher's practice.

Dilemma 11: Do You Mentor Again?

You have mentored many teachers in the past and really enjoyed it. However, this year you had a needy mentee and you also had some health issues. You are now feeling better, and the lead mentor for your district has asked if you would mentor again next year. The district is writing a comprehensive plan to support mentors and would like you to take a leadership role. You are tired. It is the end of the year, and you just can't wait for summer break. It has been a wonderful year in many ways because you have watched this novice teacher emerge (finally!) at the end of the year. All of the mentoring conversations have paid off. The time and energy you spent supporting and guiding really mattered. You feel you have influenced this teacher's students too! All is well. *What do you say to the lead mentor?*

Respond to these prompts in your Mentor Planning Guide and Journal available on the companion website.

1. State the mentor dilemma as clearly as possible in one sentence if you can.

2. What decision do you need to make in regard to this situation?

3. Write about the emotions that come up for you that relate to this situation. If you have two choices, write how the emotions might be different.

4. Stop and reread what you have written. Underline any key words or phrases that stand out for you.

5. Soften your eyes or close them and take three deep breaths. Ask yourself, what am I missing that I have not noticed? Write that down in your journal.

6. What will you say to your mentee? Write your reflection in your journal.

7. If you are truly stuck, bring your dilemma to your lead mentor, a mentor support group meeting, or another experienced mentor. Ask him or her to listen to what you have written and to ask you questions to clarify your dilemma. *Your lead mentor's role is not to tell you what to do! No advice!* Just questions to help you clarify what you want to do.

8. After you have spoken to your mentee, write his reaction and how you feel about this dilemma now. All dilemmas are not resolved! This is a process of clarifying and understanding how you feel and how you could respond.

Directions: Complete all three goal-setting processes and write your responses on this page or in your Mentor Planning Guide and Journal available on the companion website.

1. *Goal for Improving Your Mentee's Teaching Practices*

   • Review the PLAN–CONNECT–ACT–REFLECT pages you completed all year.

   • Acknowledge all your mentee has done.

   • Agree on ONE goal to focus on for the second year of teaching!

   • Goal:

2. *Goal to Support the Social and Emotional Well-Being of Your Mentee*

   • Discuss any challenges your mentee may be facing right now. Challenges often bring stress.

   • Don't ignore any signs of stress in your mentee. Pay attention and teach her ways to manage her stress. Using mindfulness practices can help reduce stress.

   • Search for books, articles, videos, and music that you enjoy and bring you a feeling of restful mindfulness. Include the activities that feel "right" to you in your daily life.

   • Goal:

3. *Goal for Enhancing Your Mentoring Skills*

   • Reflect on your own mentoring experience this month. Write a reflection in your Mentor Planning Guide and Journal.

   • Read the July chapter to complete your final reflection for the year and learn how to refresh and renew yourself. You will set your goals in that chapter.

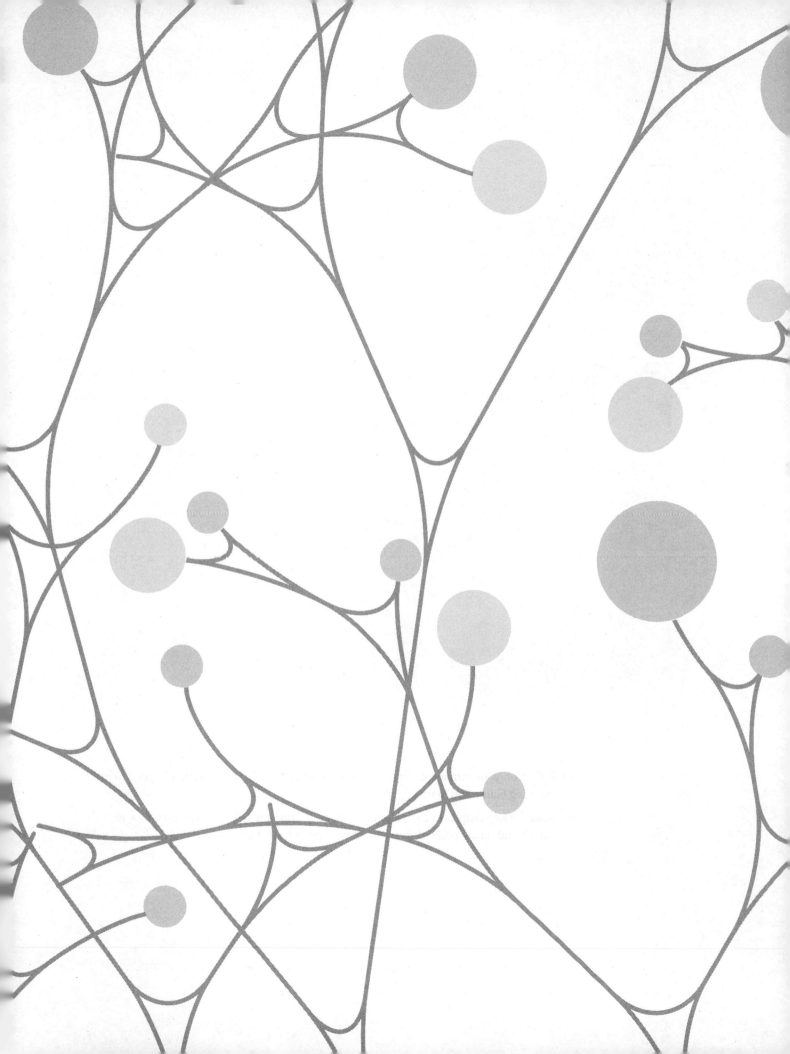

"

My mentor helped me to become an effective teacher. I could not have navigated my first year without her."

—FIRST-YEAR TEACHER

MENTOR PHASE: SUCCESS!

"As a first-time mentor, I was committed to helping my mentee learn how to teach. My short weekly meetings made a difference to her, and I can see the results of all of those mentoring conversations."

MINDFUL MENTORING AFFIRMATION

I will reflect on my experience and acknowledge what I did well.

JULY

FINAL REFLECTION AND PLANNING FOR NEXT YEAR

Retreat, Reflect, Renew

GUIDING QUESTIONS

1. What have I learned that will improve my mentoring practices in the future?

2. How will I share my mentoring ideas with other mentors and district administrators?

3. What are the leadership opportunities available to me related to mentoring?

Interstate Teacher Assessment and Support Consortium—InTASC Standards

Review InTASC Standard 10.

- **Standard 10 Leadership and Collaboration**

The teacher seeks appropriate leadership roles and opportunities to take responsibility for student learning, to collaborate with learners, families, colleagues, other school professionals, and community members to ensure learner growth, and to advance the profession.

Chapter Overview

The year has ended. Your mentee has successfully completed her first year of teaching. Use the activities in this chapter to look back and to also explore next steps. This month is all about YOU. This is your time to think about what you learned, what you would do differently, and how you can engage your district in more focused professional development for mentors. It is also a time to think of leadership roles you may create in the district to keep mentoring central to induction programs.

As you read through the pages in this final chapter, think about what you gained from this experience. Mentors often tell me that they became more effective teachers by using this mentoring curriculum because as they reviewed the content in this book they were reminded of good teaching practices they may have stopped using.

A video of a retreat in ACT 2 will show you how mentors can rejuvenate in the summer and prepare for meeting their next group of mentees. Think about organizing a retreat in your district and use this sample agenda to guide you.

Use this final chapter as a way to culminate your mentoring experience this year. This final reflection will guide you to sustaining your mentoring skills as well as developing a solid mentoring program in your district. Your leadership makes a difference!

Professional Development and a District Action Plan

How can you help your district sustain a mentoring program for novice teachers? Consider designing a formal program with your district to ensure all you mentors are using a common language for mentoring novice teachers. By designing a plan, you will ensure that the district stays committed to mentoring and supports the mentors in being effective.

1. **Professional Development for Mentors**

   - Do you need to learn more about how to mentor effectively?

   - Does your district offer mentor professional development?

   - Would you like to become a lead mentor? Someone who trains other mentors? Consider using the Mentoring in Action curriculum in your training.

   - Monthly mentor meetings provide a place to ask questions, share ideas, and reflect on best mentoring practices. Use this book as a guide, and the final reflection pages each month can be shared at a meeting like this.

2. **A District Action Plan**

   If your district does not have a plan for mentoring, consider designing a district action plan.

   - Go to the MentoringinAction.com website to view the PDF titled *Interactive District Action Plan.*

   - Review plans from other districts.

   - Watch the videos that highlight key components of the plans.

   - Select the school plan that meets your needs and modify it.

Companion Website

CONNECT to Additional Resources

CONNECT to School and District Resources

What resources did you use this year? Do you need more resources to provide support for mentors?

CONNECT With Other Mentors, District Administrators, and Lead Mentors

By having monthly meetings and a summer retreat, mentors can stay connected and support each other. District administrators need to develop a district plan with mentors, and lead mentors can step up to implement the plan and provide support to the mentors. Lead mentors are experienced mentors who make a commitment to prepare and support their colleagues.

CONNECT to Student Voices

Student voices and perspectives are integrated throughout this book because without student engagement a teacher cannot be effective. Review all the ideas that relate to student voices and highlight the ones that you found most useful. The PDF titled *An Interactive Guide to Using Student Perspectives* on the companion website has all of the videos and surveys in one place for easy access. Using this document at a mentor meeting can provide focus and keep students at the heart of teaching. Watching videos at meetings are engaging and bring a fresh perspective to the discussion.

CONNECT to Education Hot Topics

Review the Hot Topics and consider using them in professional development workshops with mentors. They make great conversation starters, and what would you do if . . . stems to develop mentor skills.

CONNECT With the Companion Website

Review all of the resources you have available to you and use them in your district professional development programs. First-time mentors will appreciate the information, and experienced mentors can refresh their skills. A video library with many of the videos mentioned in this book is available on MentoringinAction.com. Each video in the library has a description and a reflective prompt so it can easily be used in professional development meetings with mentors or novice teachers.

Companion
Website

What Have You Learned?

Ask yourself . . .

- Would I mentor again? Why or why not?

- How will I use this Mentoring in Action curriculum next time?

- What is the most significant thing I learned this year?

- What am I most grateful for in this process?

- How will I share what I have learned with the district administrators and induction coordinators?

- What were the "plusses" of participating in this program?

Companion
Website

JULY

Retreat With Other Mentors

VIDEO 2.20

Mindful Mentoring Retreat

Ask your district to sponsor a full day retreat in July or August where you can reflect and share ideas. Watch Video 2.20, *Mindful Mentoring Retreat*, to hear how these mentors took a day and valued their time together. In this video, the mentors are called effective educator coaches.

Sample Agenda

1. Welcome and Overview—District Leaders

2. Creating a District Action Plan—Update

3. Supporting Effective Mentors—Professional Development Opportunities

4. Solving Mentoring Challenges Together—Small Group Sharing

5. Mindful Mentoring—Promoting Health and Wellness in Mentors and Novice Teachers

6. Sharing Effective Mentoring Practices Using Positive Postcards

7. Journey Into Leadership Maps—A Creative Process (see teachers share in Video 2.20)

8. Closing—Circle of Trust (see Video 2.20)

JULY

July Mentor Reflections

- Review all of your journal entries and end-of-month chapter reflections. Look for themes and patterns in your writing.
- Respond to these prompts in your Mentor Planning Guide and Journal to summarize your thoughts. Add two of your own prompts.

Two things that stood out for me . . .

I noticed . . .

An area I wrote a lot about was . . .

By reading these again, I . . .

Directions: Complete all three goal-setting processes and write your responses on this page or in your Mentor Planning Guide and Journal available on the companion website.

1. *Goal for Improving your Mentoring Practices*

    *   Review the PLAN–CONNECT-ACT–REFLECT pages you completed all year with your mentee. Acknowledge what you learned by using a curriculum.
    *   Create ONE goal to focus on when you use this curriculum in the future.
    *   Goal:

2. *Goal to Support Your Social and Emotional Well-Being*

    *   Continue to explore mindfulness and consider taking a retreat day for yourself. Use your senses to relax and renew. What makes you feel relaxed? How can you find the time and space to enjoy nature and the beauty around you? How can you create a space for yourself that allows you to renew?
    *   Goal:

3. *Goal for Enhancing Your Mentoring Skills*

    *   Reflect on your own mentoring experience this year. How did you use your strengths and interests to mentor? What will you do differently next year? Would you like to become a lead mentor in your district and work with administration to design a district action plan?
    *   Write your final reflection in your Mentor Planning Guide and Journal.
    *   Goal:

APPENDICES

The agendas offer you many options for mindful mentoring conversations.

Mentoring Conversations

Directions: Most mentoring happens in a verbal conversation. This entire book is an opportunity for conversation starters. These templates will have you thinking about conversations in time frames. Most mentors and teachers are generally busy, busy, busy! So having a purpose to a meeting ensures the time will be well spent. Shorter meetings are useful because they don't take up a lot of your time and they can have a purpose!

Sometimes you will see your novice teacher in passing. It might be in the hallway, the lunchroom, or before or after school. What can you do or say when you only have 5, 10, or 15 minutes that are unplanned and in a public place? Use these templates to guide your focus. Even though it may not look like a typical meeting, you know you had this plan in your mind.

1: The 5-Minute Meeting: *Giving an Authentic Compliment*

2: The 10-Minute Meeting: *Sharing an Idea or Resource*

3: The 15-Minute Meeting: *Problem to Possibilities*

Sometimes you will find yourself sharing a preparation period together that was not scheduled on your PLAN calendar. You can use this extended time together in a productive way. These options focus your discussion during this typically unscheduled time. You may also want to use these templates as part of a scheduled meeting you plan each month.

4: The 20-Minute Meeting: *What's Working? How Do You Know?*

5: The 30-Minute Meeting: *Looking at Student Work Together*

6: The 60-Minute Meeting: *A Novice Observing the Mentor*

Here are other options you can think about if you have a professional day or planning time to meet:

7: The Integrated Meeting: *Focus on Student Learning*

8: Inquiry Into Practice: *Finding a Question and Finding the Answers*

The purpose of these templates is to provide a structure for you so that the meetings are intentional and useful to the mentee.

The 5-Minute Meeting
Giving an Authentic Compliment

Directions: You are rushing to class, and you see your mentee standing by his door. You know you only have 5 minutes. What can you say? Try giving a compliment! Think about what you have been talking about in your other meetings. What have you noticed about the novice teacher? If you have visited his classroom, what have you seen that stands out to you as positive practice? What are you noticing right now?

As with your own students, you know that unsubstantiated praise does not work. Just saying "I think you are doing a great job" sometimes confuses students and novice teachers. Because novice teachers want to "do it right," they do want some praise or feedback. If you give nonspecific praise, your mentees may be asking themselves, "What am I actually doing that deserves this praise?" Mostly because they want to replicate it to get more praise! If they don't know what "it" is, they may not be able to repeat the behavior.

The key to compliments is to be specific and authentic. Don't just give a compliment because you think you have to say something.

Below are some sample compliments:

> *I noticed the way you were talking to that student. You made eye contact, you lowered your voice, you kept a professional stance, and it looks like you got the results you wanted. Good job!*

> *The bulletin boards in your room are really engaging. I like the way you made them interactive so students who finish their work can go up and complete an activity. Good idea!*

> *The lesson plan you shared at our last meeting was very thoughtful and clearly written. I especially liked the way you tied the district goals to the learning activity. Nicely done!*

Compliments can also be integrated into all of your meetings. Everyone likes a compliment. Remember to give a few to yourself. Mentors need compliments, too!

Try these Mindful Mentoring Affirmations:

> *I like the way I am focusing my time with my mentee.*

> *By planning what I am going to talk about I seem to get more done and it is fitting into my day.*

> *I have time to mentor!*

The 10-Minute Meeting
Sharing an Idea or Resource

Directions: You meet your novice teacher in line at the copy machine during the morning break. Rather than making small talk, use this time productively to share an idea that has been working in your room. If your mentee is not in your subject area or grade level, adapt the idea on the spot to show how many ideas can be used across grade levels and content area.

Sample ideas for sharing:

> *I just tried this history lesson in my classroom. I had the students taking notes during my lecture, and I gave them a worksheet that had some of the notes printed. They had to listen to me and fill in the blanks as they went. It really made them pay attention, and it also helped some of my students who are having difficulty copying everything. How do you think this might fit into your secondary English class?*

> *I just got these manipulatives out of the library. It looks like they are new. I used them, and the kids really stayed engaged. I know you are third grade, but I think your students would like them, too. How do you think they would fit into your elementary curriculum?*

Be sure that your sharing ideas ends with a question so the novice teacher has to think about how to use the resource. Have it be okay for the novice teacher to say "no" to your suggestion. Every idea is not a good or useful one for all teachers. The key is the sharing part and that you are open to consistently throwing ideas the novice teacher's way.

You can also share the names of people, places, and other CONNECTions as they come up. Novice teachers want and need to be networked. Think purposefully and systematically about how you are sharing practical ideas.

The 15-Minute Meeting
Problem to Possibilities

Directions: You see the novice teacher in the library, and you discover that you have 15 minutes to talk. The teacher tells you she is still having trouble with one student who is unmotivated in her classroom.

On the spot, try this activity:

1. Identify the problem: What is the student actually doing? Saying? Not doing? Not saying?

2. What has she already tried? Talking to the students? The parents? The administration? The school counselor?

3. Brainstorm several possible solutions to this problem together.

    Possibility A:

    Possibility B:

    Possibility C:

4. Ask her to summarize the meeting verbally and state what her next steps will be.

5. The next time you talk, check it to see if any possibilities worked. If not, create three more possible solutions.

Let her know that every problem cannot be solved quickly, and you may need to do this problem-solving more than once. Avoid telling the novice how you would solve the problem. One possible option could be yours, but be sure the teacher feels empowered to implement the option of her choice. She may have to try all three! She could bring this problem to the group mentoring meeting and let other novice teachers share their ideas with her. See The Group Mentoring Agenda Figure 9 in Part I of this book.

The 20-Minute Meeting
What's Working? How Do You Know?

Directions: Ask your mentee to list five things that are working for him. Discuss how he knows they are working. The purpose of this discussion is to actually encourage the mentee (with you) to look at the "evidence" that demonstrates what is going smoothly.

You could also do this process in reverse. What is NOT working? How do you know? Then you could complete a Problem to Possibilities process to brainstorm options for making the situation work.

Examples of what might be working:

What's Working?	How Do You Know?
1. My students are on time for class.	I take attendance and they are here.
2. I taught a great science lesson today.	The students were engaged, I had no discipline problems, and they passed the quiz at the end of the class.
3. My students were well behaved in music.	The music teacher gave them a compliment.
4. I integrated my new student who doesn't speak English into the classroom successfully.	I gave her a partner, and they played together and worked together all day.
5. I made time for myself last night at home.	I didn't bring any schoolwork home; instead, I did some exercise and read a personal book. I feel great today.

Complete this table with your mentee. You could also use this process with a group of novice teachers as part of one of a group mentoring meeting agenda. A digital copy of this form is available on the companion website.

What's Working?	How Do You Know?

Companion Website

The 30-Minute Meeting
Looking at Student Work Together

Directions: You have a preparation period scheduled with your mentee. Ask her to select samples of student work that you can look at together. If your district has a rubric, use that to analyze the student work. Design a rubric if there is not one available.

1. Skim through a set of papers:

   Select one paper of a student who achieved the goal of the lesson.

   Select one paper that *may* have met the goal.

   Select one that looks like the student *did not achieve* the goal.

2. Read the papers together and decide where they fit on the rubric. You may each do it separately and compare your ratings.

   Were you similar in your rubric rating?

3. Take it a step further. Take one paper and together analyze it for the following:

   What can we compliment this student for in this paper?

   What is the next learning step for this student?

   What *one* thing should I focus on with this student?

4. Do this for the other two papers you selected.

   What did you learn from doing this process?

   Talk about the process of looking at student work and how it informs the teacher's practice.

   Discuss ways to differentiate curriculum to meet the needs of diverse learners.

Schedule a follow-up meeting to see how your mentee is continuing to learn how to analyze student work samples. Remind her that there is a page at the end of each month's chapter that focuses on this topic. Assessment is an important teacher skill, and it must be developed in a systematic way.

The 60-Minute Meeting
Observing a Mentor

Directions: Your mentee can learn a lot by watching you teach. Demonstration lessons on one particular topic or in a content area can provide a focus for your mentoring conversations. A successful demonstration lesson should be scheduled when you have time before and after the lesson to talk. If you are comfortable being observed, you may consider inviting two novices at the same time. This allows them to talk about what they have seen in your classroom and how they can try these strategies in their own classrooms.

Preparing for the Observation: Before you invite any novice teachers to your classroom, you will want to prepare yourself. Ask yourself the following questions:

1. What do I want the novice teachers to gain by this observation? (i.e., What is your intention?)

2. Should I talk during the class and point out what I am doing—like an instructional demonstration—or should I just teach and let them watch? What are the benefits of either approach?

3. Which lesson should I demonstrate and why?

Before the novice teachers come to class, share the lesson plan and the purpose of this demonstration lesson. Why are you doing this? How will it help the novice teachers? Be explicit in sharing these outcomes. Decide what the mentee should be focusing on during the lesson and how she will record what she observes. If you have more than one novice observing, you may assign different focus areas to them. At the post observation they can share and compare.

The Observation: Possible focus areas for observing could include how you manage the classroom, what instructional strategies you used, how the classroom environment is organized, how the lesson is implemented, modifications for diverse learners, how English language learners were handled, how the lesson is part of a larger curriculum, how the lesson was assessed, and homework or enrichment that was discussed. Encourage the mentee to draw a floor plan of the classroom and note the placement of furniture and teacher's desk. Have the mentee list any visible learning evidence that is on the walls in the room. Use the form on the next page to guide the observation process.

Post Observation With Novice Teacher(s): When will you schedule the post observation discussion? The same day is best for processing. This is the key to learning for the novice teachers. This is an opportunity for them to ask you questions about what you did and why you did it that way. This lab school type activity offers the novice teachers a safe place to analyze their own practice. They are not being observed—you are! This allows them to make connections and model effective practice in their own rooms. Now they may have an idea about what they should be doing.

Refection: Write in your Mentor Planning Guide and Journal what you learned about yourself by demonstrating a lesson for novice teacher(s).

Novice Teacher Observation Form

What to Look for When Observing an Experienced Teacher

Directions: It is important to have your mentee observers collect data while observing you teach. Use the possible focus areas listed on the previous page to create your own observation form or use this one. If there is more than one teacher observing, they can compare and share what they noticed. Some teachers may see one thing and others won't. That is why it is valuable to have a postconference after the lesson to clarify and extend the learning. This form is available in the *First Years Matter* book, or you can download a digital version of this form is available on the companion website.

1. How the teacher manages the classroom. Note the following: Physical layout, traffic flow, routines and procedures, etc. Draw a map of the classroom.

2. Lesson plan. Note the following: Objectives, why do you think she is teaching this lesson? What is the motivator to engage students and the closer at the end of the class to wrap of the learning? Is the lesson part of a unit of study or is it a one-time lesson?

3. How engaged are the students? Note: Who is paying attention? Is anyone off task? How does the teacher bring them back to task? How are disruptions handled? How is praise used? Does the mentor use the students' names?

4. Instructional strategies for learning. Note: Is technology being used? How? What is the teacher using to promote student learning? How does she know the students are learning? Where is the assessment in this lesson?

5. Other things you noticed. What do you want to know more about? List your questions for the postconference.

The Integrated Meeting
Focus on Student Learning

Directions: When you have a longer time during the school year to meet with your mentee, you may take ideas from other templates and combine them into one 60-minute meeting. Create your own meeting agenda! Here is a sample to guide your thinking.

Agenda	
5 minutes	Compliment from mentor for novice teachers. If more than one teacher is present, let them compliment each other, too.
10 minutes	Share an idea or resource—let the mentee share what is working for her.
15 minutes	Problem to possibilities—invite your mentee to share a pressing problem and take some time to brainstorm possible solutions. Discuss how this problem relates to student learning (or not learning).
20 minutes	Look at student work together. Randomly divide the class papers in half. You and your mentee will sort the papers into three piles: below the standard, meets the standard, and exceeds the standard. Share and discuss how you decided where to place each of the students' papers.
10 minutes	Close the meeting with acknowledgment of the mentee's progress so far. Be specific about what you have noticed. Review your schedules to note when you have your next meeting.

Inquiry Into Practice
Finding a Question and Finding the Answers

Directions: Novice teachers often learn how to conduct teacher research during their practicum experiences. They can continue to look at their teaching in a systematic way by looking at the challenges that arise in their classroom. By focusing on one area of challenge, they can see how to change their practice to improve. By inquiring into their practice, they can discover answers to their own questions. If you are interested in sharing this inquiry process with your novice teachers, review the current resources on teacher research.

Reflecting on Practice: Encourage your novice teachers to keep a journal where they can record their thoughts, challenges, assumptions, biases, insights, and new ideas. It is often difficult to maintain a daily journal, but many beginning teachers can do a weekly entry. You may include journaling as part of a monthly meeting.

Finding a Question: When novice teachers write in a journal, often the same topic or situation comes up over and over. These dilemmas or issues deserve more attention and thought. Inquiry is a process of formulating a question and systematically collecting data to reveal some answers. A sample question is, "What is the impact of guided reading on my two English language learners?" Data may be in the form of interviews, student work, observations, surveys, audio, video, and tests to show how the students are responding to this guided reading program. Other research questions may relate to one student, "What can I do to help David learn to read?"

Collecting Data: How the novice collects data can vary. Interviews with student, observations, and surveys are some ways of collecting data. The goal is to try different methods in the classroom related to the question to discover the answer. For example, if a teacher is trying to find out how guided reading is working, she would collect evidence of success by listening to the students read over time and perhaps maintain a journal noting their progress. Comparing her results to another reading method may also be an option. If the question relates to how she can help David learn to read, her methods may be trying several strategies to see which ones help David.

Finding the Answers: After the data is collected, the novice teacher needs to analyze it and see how it provides some answers to the original question. This mini-research study does not have to be complicated. If the results show it is not working and the students are not learning, then the novice teacher needs to make a case for changing the method and finding a reading program that does work.

You may consider conducting inquiry-based research in your own classroom and sharing your results with your mentee. You may consider using the same research question.

INDEX

A SAGE Publishing Company

CORWIN HAS ONE MISSION: to enhance education through intentional professional learning.

We build long-term relationships with our authors, educators, clients, and associations who partner with us to develop and continuously improve the best evidence-based practices that establish and support lifelong learning.

Solutions you want. Experts you trust. Results you need.

AUTHOR CONSULTING

Author Consulting

On-site professional learning with sustainable results! Let us help you design a professional learning plan to meet the unique needs of your school or district. www.corwin.com/pd

INSTITUTES

Institutes

Corwin Institutes provide collaborative learning experiences that equip your team with tools and action plans ready for immediate implementation. www.corwin.com/institutes

ECOURSES

eCourses

Practical, flexible online professional learning designed to let you go at your own pace. www.corwin.com/ecourses

READ2EARN

Read2Earn

Did you know you can earn graduate credit for reading this book? Find out how: www.corwin.com/read2earn

Contact an account manager at (800) 831-6640 or visit
www.corwin.com for more information.